.12   5   12/10

D0053533

ROSENFELD'S LIVES

ROSENFELD'S LIVES

Fame, Oblivion, and the
Furies of Writing

Steven J. Zipperstein

Yale University Press   New Haven & London

Copyright © 2009 by Steven J. Zipperstein.
All rights reserved.
This book may not be reproduced, in whole or in part, including illustrations, in any form (beyond that copying permitted by Sections 107 and 108 of the U.S. Copyright Law and except by reviewers for the public press), without written permission from the publishers.

Designed by James Johnson and set in Fairfield Med. Roman types by The Composing Room of Michigan, Inc.
Printed in the United States of America.

Library of Congress Cataloging-in-Publication Data

Zipperstein, Steven J., 1950–
   Rosenfeld's lives : fame, oblivion, and the furies of writing / Steven J. Zipperstein.
      p. cm.
   Includes bibliographical references and index.
   ISBN 978-0-300-12649-5 (cloth : alk. paper)
   1. Rosenfeld, Isaac, 1918–1956. 2. Rosenfeld, Isaac, 1918–1956—Political and social views. 3. Rosenfeld, Isaac, 1918–1956—Friends and associates. 4. Jews—Illinois—Chicago—Intellectual life—20th century. 5. Chicago (Ill.)—Biography. I. Title.
   PS3535.07138Z98 2009
   818'.5409—dc22
   [B]   2008045797

A catalogue record for this book is available from the British Library.

This paper meets the requirements of ANSI/NISO Z39.48–1992 (Permanence of Paper). It contains 30 percent postconsumer waste (PCW) and is certified by the Forest Stewardship Council (FSC).

10 9 8 7 6 5 4 3 2 1

For Susan

You have captured my heart,
My own, my bride,
You have captured my heart.

—Song of Songs 4:9

To know, to know, to know . . . knowledge and love combined into one ecstasy, the highest good of mind and body.

—Isaac Rosenfeld, journal entry

Once [Marco Polo] was back in Venice, they called him Il Milione, the guy who told a million fibs. But he never budged. His famous line is, "I have not told half of what I saw." He said that on his deathbed.

—Joan Silber, *Ideas of Heaven*

I am my own historian.

—Isaac Rosenfeld, letter to Oscar Tarcov, October 7, 1937

Contents

Acknowledgments

Biography is born of intrusion. No biographer, even the most stalwart or self-possessed, can be unaware of how odd it is to sift through the shavings of someone else's life. Whatever knowledge is gleaned from such labor is the byproduct of digging and prodding, of cajoling bits and pieces of life from archives, from informants, from hidden drawers. Not infrequently, these were packed away in the dark for good reason.

I thank those who permitted me to rummage through their memories and papers so that this book might be written. It is a privilege to be permitted to enter into someone else's past and share the intimate, basic stuff of that life. I managed to speak, sometimes at length, with many of Isaac Rosenfeld's relatives and friends, a number of whom are now deceased. Some of them tolerated frequent phone calls and fact-checking, and were gracious enough to send me letters with their impressions of essays of mine on Rosenfeld that appeared while I was working on the book. I'm grateful for their help, their advice, as well as their warnings and criticisms. The milieu I write on was rarely reticent about criticism, and much of this study is devoted to how its members criticized one another, frequently in unsettling, even ferocious ways. The men and women I encountered while writing this work, many of them in their late seventies and eighties, had lost little of their ability to emphatically challenge anything with which they disagreed. I learned a great deal of information from them, and also managed a glimpse at what it was like to come of age in their contentious, ideologically charged times.

The book took a long time to finish. It occupied my time and thoughts on and off for some ten years. I put it aside for several years, uncertain how to proceed. Working on it in two major spurts in the late 1990s and again more recently, I accumulated many debts.

Rosenfeld's Lives would have been altogether different—probably impossible to write—without access to the material given to me by Nathan Tarcov (a University of Chicago political scientist of singular generosity), Philip Seigelman (always helpful as critic and friend), David Lutzker (Sheila Stern's widower), and Freda (Davis) Segel. I much regret that Freda, a lovely, insightful woman devoted to Rosenfeld's memory, isn't alive to read these pages. Claire Sarant offered me access to her collection of Rosenfeld papers, which I greatly appreciate; these were copies of material her late husband, Rosenfeld's son, George Sarant, had given to Special Collections of the Regenstein Library, University of Chicago. Daniel and Margaret Rosenfeld shared family impressions and documents, and Daniel accompanied me to his cousin Isaac's grave site. Gregory Bellow pushed me often, pressing me to ask tough questions. I benefited from his intimate knowledge and well-honed grasp of life's vicissitudes as a family therapist. Saul Bellow opened his home to me several times, spoke with me for many hours about Rosenfeld, permitted me access to his unpublished papers and letters, and offered me comments, praise, and criticism. I also thank Janis Bellow for her patience, especially one frantic morning as I selected photographs at her home that had to be forwarded immediately to meet my publisher's deadline. Neal Kozodoy, former editor of *Commentary,* provided me with access to the magazine's papers relating to Rosenfeld. My friendship with Monroe and Brenda Engel deepened, over the course of several conversations in Cambridge, as they spoke about their friendship years ago with Rosenfeld. My cousins, Raymond and Inez Saunders, set aside a room for me in their Chicago home during my frequent research trips to the city, and their support proved invaluable during writing and rewriting. I benefited from the assistance of other biographers and literary scholars who have worked on Rosenfeld and Bellow and been generous with their time and expertise: the recently deceased Ted (Theodore) Solotaroff, Mark Shechner, James Atlas, and Zachary Leader.

A recurrent theme of this book is friendship: neither the lives of Rosenfeld and Bellow nor their written work can be understood without reference to it. My friendship with the political theorist Mitchell Cohen has sustained me for more than three decades, and has made me think seriously about the intersections between life and work. Mitchell has assisted in the shaping and reshaping of this work in more ways than I can enumerate: he has read and commented on it, and he has prodded me to think about aspects of it that I might otherwise have avoided.

I spent many hours speaking with Rosenfeld's relatives and friends, and others who knew them and their children. I thank Lionel Abel, Theresa Aiello Gerber, Jim Anthony, Erica Aronson, David Bazelon, Daniel Bell, Pearl Bell, Anne Bernays, Ann Birstein, William Butler, Jules Chametzsky, Zita Cogan, Ruth Denney, John Ellis, Arthur Geffen, Nathan Glazer, Albert Glotzer, Herbert Gold, Victor Gourevitch, Annette Hoffman, George Hudes, Debby Ishihara, Joanne Joseph, Justin Kaplan, Alfred Kazin, Mark Krupnick, Edith Kurzweil, Rudolph Lapp, Marilyn Mann, Wallace Markfield,

Herbert and Mitzi McCloskey, Rolf Meyersohn, Gary Oakes, Cora Passin, Herbert Passin, Ruth Passin, Sidney Passin, David Peltz, William Phillips, Norman Podhoretz, David Ray, Terrence Rogers, Eleni Rosenfeld, Lester Seligman, Evelyn Shefner, Hyman Slate, Harry Smith, June Tanoue, Ernst van den Haag, David Britt White, Vasiliki (Sarant) White, and Karen Yanagisako.

I thank the staff at Special Collections of the Regenstein Library, University of Chicago; the American Jewish Historical Society at the Center for Jewish History, New York; and *Commentary* magazine for access to archival material. I'm appreciative to Lindsay Harris for copies of *The Beacon,* the early publishing venture of her father, Sidney Harris. Alan Goodfried, the journalism teacher at Roberto Clemente High School (the former Tuley High), gave me access to what is probably the only full run of the school newspaper.

I learned much from responses to presentations of this work at the University of Chicago; University of Oregon, Eugene; University of Illinois, Champaign; Northwestern; Stanford; Wesleyan; Smith; Harvard; and Oxford. A reading in May 2006, soon before I left Stanford for an extended academic leave at Harvard, was especially moving, and I thank my friend Arnold Eisen, now chancellor of the Jewish Theological Seminary, and others for their comments. I did much of the final work on the book as the Gerald Weinstock Visiting Professor of Jewish History at Harvard University. I thank the Department of Near Eastern Studies and the Center for Jewish Studies for this honor, and I'm especially grateful to my colleague and friend Ruth Wisse for support and friendship during my time in Cambridge. While there, I was treated with great warmth—and provided with office space, research assistance, and collegiality—by Harvard's Davis Center for

Russian and Eurasian Studies. My thanks go to the Davis Center director Timothy Colton, associate director Lis Tarlow, and all their colleagues. The manuscript was completed —finally—during spring term 2008, in Oxford, when I taught a seminar on biography and history for Stanford's Overseas Program and enjoyed senior common room membership at Brasenose College. My work in Oxford was eased considerably by the careful labor of Milena Hadryznska. Research funds for this book were provided by the Taube Center for Jewish Studies and the office of the Dean of Humanities and Sciences at Stanford University. I acknowledge the support of the Stanford Humanities Center and its former director Keith Baker. Early versions of this work appeared in *Partisan Review, Jewish Social Studies*, and the English and Yiddish editions of *Forward* newspaper.

Many friends and colleagues commented on drafts. Andrew Ramer was a wise reader and is a wonderful friend. Aron Rodrigue, my closest colleague at Stanford, showed characteristic forbearance and offered much sage advice. My teacher and friend Jonathan Frankel, now deceased, read parts of the manuscript and offered—as he did for others over the course of many years—incomparable, gentle wisdom. I benefited from advice from Robert Alter, Arnold Band, David Biale, Joseph Frank, Mitch Hart, Eli Lederhendler, Marcus Moseley, Anita Norich, Arnold Rampersad, Claire Rogger, Richard and Roni Schotter, and Peter Stansky. Joel Beinin, Morris Dickstein, and Alan Wald shared with me their great fund of knowledge about politics and culture in the twentieth century. I thank my research assistants—Amy Brouillette, Jess Olson, Lisa Rampton, and Abraham Socher—whose fact-checking and bibliographical work was invaluable. I remain grateful, as I have since my first years in graduate school, to Zachary Baker, Reinhard Curator of Judaica at the Stanford University Libraries, for prompt, learned answers to numerous queries.

Charlotte Sheedy has been an ideal literary agent— smart, loyal, and, when necessary, pointedly direct. The astute scrutiny and persistence of my Yale University Press editor, Ileene Smith, and copyeditor Kim Hastings can be felt on every page. The care and guidance of Alex Larson and Margaret Otzel helped make my relationship with Yale University Press a pleasurable one from start to finish. I thank the skilled indexer Barbara Roos, whom it has been my pleasure to know since her work on my first book in the mid-1980s.

And then, as always, there are my children, Max and Sam, and now my stepchildren, Noa and Josh, Yossi, and Tzvia. All have taught me much about life's complexities, especially its joys. My wife, Susan Berrin, came into my life while I was still at odds with Rosenfeld, wrestling with how to deal with him. She is at the center of my life now that he is finally imprinted on these pages, no longer the phantom he long was. I'm grateful for her patience, astonished still by her love, and I trust that having thought long and hard about Rosenfeld I'm all the better prepared to live, deeply, with her.

Introduction

"TAKING A GOOD LOOK" IS HOW HE DESCRIBED READ-
ing.[1] Isaac Rosenfeld chewed at ideas, clawing at them with
commodious learning and childlike wonder. He admitted, often desperately, that the world around him was chaotic and
dark, but also found it more mysterious, more splendid, than
the cooler heads around him believed it to be. As a writer he
was loving and fierce, thoroughly committed to the indispensability of books and distrustful of the mind itself. He knew
how excruciating it was to get things right on the page, and
despite mostly joyless detours that led him elsewhere, he remained convinced that nothing was more crucial.

The only recording I have of his voice sounds clipped,
formal, like the sound of someone reared too meticulously.
Rosenfeld was cultivated to be a cloistered, bookish boy. He
grew into an edgy, infectiously charming man, an erudite,
ambitious intellectual who wrote novels, essays, poetry, hundreds of book reviews, and started (soon before his death)
books on the Russian classics and on his hometown, Chicago.
Time and again, Rosenfeld wrote with insight and candor
about what it was that made reading and writing essential,
and the cost of being caught in their grip. He wrote brilliantly
about the capacity of books to deepen and diminish life, to en-
rich it but also to render it abstract, fleshless. His only pub-

lished novel, *Passage from Home*, was about just this wager. Beginning in his early teens, he wrote and rewrote more or less the same story. He never quite mastered it, but he came close. This book examines his pained, insistent quest.

Born in Chicago on March 10, 1918, dead on Bastille Day 1956, he published *Passage from Home* in 1946. By then, he was a contributor to *The Nation, Partisan Review, Commentary, The New Republic,* and *The New Leader;* the latter two he also served as an editor. He taught at New York University, Black Mountain College, the University of Minnesota, and, at the time of his death, at a humanities program of the University of Chicago, where he had finished his BA and received his master's degree in philosophy. He wrote poetry (some eulogies listed him first as a poet), as well as fiction and essays. A collection of his stories, *Alpha and Omega,* and his essays, *An Age of Enormity,* were published posthumously. "He swayed his friends with an unknown power," wrote Saul Bellow in his obituary in *Partisan Review.* "We called it 'charm,' 'wisdom,' 'genius.' In the end, with a variety of intonations, we could find nothing to call it but 'Isaac.'" Spoken of at the time of his death as one of his generation's most promising writers, still in 1966 *Commentary* described *An Age of Enormity* as "one of the finest American books of the last twenty years." A close friend of Bellow's recalls that the first thing Bellow said to him after hearing he had won the Nobel Prize was, "It should have been Isaac."[2]

To be sure, in his lifetime he exasperated many that knew him. Rosenfeld's literary history is an episodic one, filled with gaps, holes, the leaden disappointments of unfinished manuscripts. Half a century after his death, he tends to be recalled, if at all, as a writer of great promise who faltered, as someone of astonishing potential who once seemed still more promising than his closest friend, his lifelong rival, Bellow, and who then fell, as both were aware, far behind. Often the two childhood friends from Chicago are placed side by side, one with the biggest prize of all, the other buried young and little known, a ready, all too obvious metaphor for the cruelties and unpredictability of a writer's life.

The early excitement surrounding his work (he was anointed by discerning critics—Diana Trilling, Irving Howe, Delmore Schwartz—in his early twenties, as a "golden boy") morphed into a gray, dour reputation, with Rosenfeld as the quintessence of writer's block.[3] His one published novel, released by the still small Dial Press, was dwarfed by the proximity, the drumbeat, of Bellow's achievements. Bellow often injected Rosenfeld as a lightly fictionalized character in his work, and he wrote the most widely cited obituary for Rosenfeld. This, too, seemed to highlight Rosenfeld's own imperfect and sparse output.

Rosenfeld has survived, on the whole, in the memoirs of friends—Alfred Kazin, Irving Howe, Norman Podhoretz, and others. They lived far longer, wrote far more, and described him as a man of unrivaled warmth, immense erudition, and talent gone astray. In these works—the mainstay of the huge body of literature that has grown around the New York intellectuals of the 1940s and 1950s—he is depicted, with rare exception, as an exceedingly bookish, boyish man gone bohemian but unable to enjoy the abandon of an unfettered life. He is described as an unlikely ideologue of hopeless causes (above all, the mechanistic, spooky teachings of Wilhelm Reich); a writer of fierce ambition and barely sequestered jealousies (especially of Bellow); and a genius who couldn't manage to sit long enough with any one book to make it great. Particularly as he died young—suddenly, of a heart attack at thirty-eight—his life was reduced to a cautionary tale: all the promise, the sincere expectation engulfing him (all the more striking in a circle known for anything but selflessness), tended to be pushed aside. What remained was a story of waste.

Time and again, it has been related in much the same terms: directionless charm, genius unachieved. "Charm and Death" is what Bellow titled his unpublished novel about Rosenfeld. "Wunderkind grown into tubby sage . . . he died of lonely sloth," wrote Howe. Some spoke of him with uncommon cruelty: "As even the [Greenwich] Village desperados noticed, Isaac was a 'failure.' Precocious in everything, and understandably worn out, he died at thirty-eight. Even his dying would be a kind of failure," stated Kazin. In a novel about the day of Rosenfeld's funeral, *To an Early Grave* (the movie *Bye, Bye Braverman* was based on it), Wallace Markfield described him: "He had a habit of helping himself to whatever was in [his wife's] purse. He begrudged her an old razor blade to shave her legs. No library would issue him books, so he took cards out in her name and in the name of her Bessarabian grandmother. He peed in sinks. He would go to movies in the afternoon. He would demand all kinds of crazy dishes. He sat in the toilet for three hours at a time. He held on to no jobs. He farted away golden opportunities. He met no deadlines. He could be your best friend and, overnight, disappear like Job's boils."[4]

These were among Rosenfeld's closest friends, and a good many of them had praised his work when it first appeared. Irving Howe insisted that it was reading *Passage from Home* that persuaded him to become a writer. "A son to Sholem Aleichem, Franz Kafka's brother," enthused Eliezer Greenberg, an influential Yiddish poet. Diana Trilling, a fiercely acerbic judge of fiction (she hated Bellow's first novel), likened the author of *Passage from Home* to Henry James.[5]

Literary biography is designed characteristically to provide signposts to achievement: on the whole, it begins and ends best with the texts it seeks to open up, expand, deepen, or at least better understand with the help of life experiences the biographer comes to know more about than the literary critic. While there is literature essentially impervious to such efforts, other work feels less resistant to the presumption that one can learn something new from the intersections between experience and interiority. Failure, of course, is an almost unavoidable fellow traveler of most accounts of a life lived with literature. Literary biography is replete with tales of bleak, relentless struggle, reputations made and unmade and, sometimes, remade. The life and work of Herman Melville (Rosenfeld claimed that reading *Moby-Dick* persuaded him to abandon philosophy for fiction) stands as the totemic mountain of such tales, a grim but stunningly hopeful beacon with its interplay of initial promise, eventual oblivion, and posthumous redemption in the form of something far more than mere fame. Still, with Melville no less than with others, the best biographical work begins and ends with the writer's work and with interest in him tied, always, to an interest in *Redburn* or Ahab.[6]

This book seeks to open up Rosenfeld's work, to explore how he sought to produce a luminescent fiction that melded philosophy with the most concrete, fleshly stirrings of life. It leads the reader back to no forgotten *Moby-Dick* but so much of what is most familiar in a life spent with literature— and so much, arguably, that is the hardest to capture—is precisely the uneasy recognition, often despite considerable effort, that aspiration cannot match achievement. Few have examined quite how this feels, day after day, with the depth or candor mustered by Rosenfeld.

This book has been a struggle to write. It has taken too

long, it has been interrupted by too much else, but once I sat down to finish, its basic contour was clear. I started it, and wrote several hundred pages as a rather more standard biography—more densely detailed and structured in a more strictly chronological way than it now is. But I came to see that it was more an extended reflection on a writer's sense of what it meant to be immersed in, and also deeply suspicious of, a life given over to books. That Rosenfeld never resolved this tension is, no doubt, of far less significance than that he faced it, head-on, that he wrote about it with the willingness to be ridiculed, yet with grace, and beauty, and genius.

This struggle of his, at the core of his life as a writer, is at the center of this book. There seems no better way to write about Rosenfeld. He was remarkably alert, self-aware; his reflections on life and work are astute. My study is built around his examination of what it felt like to write or, as was often true, to be unable to do so. Few have written with Rosenfeld's acuity about what life spent at a writing desk gives and takes away.

My work began in much the same way that an interest in a writer's life often starts: I read him and felt startled, jolted by his prose. I found him difficult to put aside, his mind impossible to categorize. Still, after having spent so long thinking about him, I remain unconvinced that such categorization is possible: was he a secular or a religious writer, a political writer, a deeply Jewish one? Why the apparent inability to write a persuasive prose about everyday life when he was such a vivid storyteller, a brilliant gossip? Why the obsessive need (mostly unhelpful, as he knew it to be) to imitate others like Kafka, Melville; why not imitate writers better suited to his tastes or gifts such as Isaac Babel?

Coincidences, odd, jarring, and intriguing, kept stalking me as I circled around Rosenfeld and his work. Above all, there was the way in which I discovered the first of his unpublished manuscripts: Bellow had once insisted that Rosenfeld found in the "squalid stink of toilets and coal bins," in a "disorder [that] ended by becoming a discipline," an "ascetic significance." "I have an idea," Bellow wrote, "that he found good, middle-class order devitalizing—a sign of meanness, stinginess, malice, and anality."[7] And I stumbled on his manuscripts and many other piles of unpublished work in a gray, grim apartment, a place given to dissipation, to the sort of bookless, day-to-day existence that Rosenfeld admired more lavishly than he ought to have.

I went there soon after I learned, through an article by James Atlas, then at work on his biography of Bellow, about Rosenfeld manuscripts in the possession of his son, George Sarant. (Sarant was a shortened version of Rosenfeld's widow's name, Sarantakis; she had dropped the use of Rosenfeld shortly after his death because of a break with his family.) I called Sarant's listing in the Bronx and a woman answered. She told me that George had died about a year earlier but I could come over and look at his papers.

The apartment was in Throg's Neck, wedged at a corner of the Bronx, a shadowy maze of bridges and highways with its streets darkened by concrete overhead, a neighborhood of small, nondescript houses, modest storefronts, bars small and ill-lit and well off the main road. Manhattan was only a few miles away but seemed distant, perilously so. A friend told me this was a neighborhood favored by low-level mafia types—perhaps this was one of the rich welter of urban legends that keeps New York feeling mysterious. Still, the information felt accurate, especially once, while sitting amid George Sarant's papers later that evening, I heard sharp, intermittent sounds that seemed like gunfire. I mentioned this to his widow, and she said it might well be. But she may have been teasing.

Claire Sarant is slight, a woman with brown hair who dresses plainly and has a modest, quiet way of handling herself. She is a person who tells you, very soon after she meets you, all about her life, and she did so that evening as she handed me manuscript after manuscript from the drawers of Sarant's study in the small, spare flat. She handed me the typescript of "Charm and Death"; she gave me letters from Bellow, Delmore Schwartz, Alfred Kazin, and others. Letters came pouring onto the table where I sat. She handed me her deceased husband's phone books, with the numbers of relatives he had recently contacted; he had been, she told me, in the midst of a quest to learn more about his father. He had sat with Bellow one evening in Chicago speaking about Rosenfeld: "I felt how much he really did love my parents and also felt how terribly lonely he is," George wrote of the meeting.[8]

Claire gave me manuscripts written by George, too. They had started sleeping together while she was his patient; she added, wryly, that perhaps he chose her because she was the first Jewish drug addict he had ever met. George's training as a Reichian therapist was connected, he knew, to his desire to learn more about his father, perhaps to communicate with him since "channeling" was a skill perfected by his Reichian teachers. Among George's manuscripts was a brief memoir that described (in prose jarringly reminiscent of his father's) his inability to concentrate on his work as a doctor—he had graduated from the University of Hawaii medical school, trained as a psychiatrist, and worked in emergency rooms for a while—because all he wanted was to be "the emperor of pussy." Claire showed it to me, watching as I read. "He was a good writer, wasn't he?" she asked.

I sat in the living room at a large table now dense with manuscripts and letters, thinking about whether there might be a place in the neighborhood to photocopy the papers. (I doubted it.) A large dog, smelly and affectionate, pranced about at one point, jumping on the couch, its tail pushing the documents I read from side to side. Claire would call at it to stop: "Isaac," she would shout, "off the table!" A gaunt man entered the apartment with his own key. Claire introduced him as a friend. He called her honey. He limped (he had recently been hit by a car) and he, too, after brief introductions spoke freely about his addictions. I gathered up my courage and asked if I could take the material back with me to Stanford—where I was returning the next day—photocopy it, and send it back. Claire readily agreed. I called for a taxi, and neglected to give her the number where I was staying (I feared she might change her mind and ask for the material back before I had the chance to copy it). Leaving, I felt like an intruder, sensing that Claire's trust was too readily given, that it was made of the same stuff that had landed her in trouble: her addictions, her incapacity to sequester details, to withhold information, to hold herself back from the entreaties of her therapist, or from this new love whose hold on life seemed thin.

I knew this was the emotional terrain that Rosenfeld had made his own: anonymous rooming houses; sporadic sexual encounters; furtive, excruciatingly isolated people; good, hopelessly sincere individuals seeking to confess, to connect somehow, to regain something lost long ago. Here, in an obscure corner of the Bronx, was his legacy: his papers, a dog named for him, a daughter-in-law right out of the pages of his prose. Even Claire's lanky new lover resembled the charmingly afflicted Willy of Rosenfeld's *Passage from Home*.

That night I read Bellow's "Charm and Death" from

beginning to end and decided it was foolish to write a book about Rosenfeld. Though not Bellow's best work, it was better, more verbally inventive, and more humanly persuasive than anything Rosenfeld had produced. Its words cascaded, rumbled. Why write about a writer who didn't succeed—as much as he tried, and Rosenfeld tried hard—at what he sought to do? How to write about failure, particularly failure played out against the backdrop of Bellow—one of the century's most fertile writers—and his achievements? What to tell about Rosenfeld's life and work? Any life is packed, overwhelmed with small, inconsequential, messy details whose telling leaves even the hardiest skittish. We persist with literary biography because these details, presumably, connect us to texts that we cherish. How to do this with a writer whose texts have, on the whole, been buried, or left unpublished, or, even when published, remain obscure?

It was dusk in Claire's emotionally taut apartment—with its talk of addictions; the overlay of misspent time and random sexuality; and manuscripts piled, one after the other, on the table—that kept bearing down on me, reminding me that there was a story to be told about just this sort of messiness that weighed on Rosenfeld often and until the end of his life. While Rosenfeld understood that to write one had to protect oneself, what he sought to write about—as often as not—was the cost of such self-protection. That his son had started but never managed to ferret out all that much about his father, that he so desperately wished to do so that he persuaded himself to turn, in the end, to New Age cranks, made my own pursuit feel all the more pertinent.

I began calling the numbers in George's phone book and discovered far more material than I could ever have imagined: huge caches of unpublished manuscripts and letters, immeasurably more than the book I had envisioned could contain. Much of Rosenfeld's writing had been placed by George, with Bellow's help, at the Regenstein Library, at the University of Chicago. I returned there several times. But other material—unpublished, unknown, and in private hands —came tumbling in. Hundreds of letters to Rosenfeld's childhood friend Oscar Tarcov were saved by Tarcov's wife, Edith (a German-born Jew and the long-standing managing editor of *Dissent*), and I was given use of them. Tarcov's collection also included contemporaneous letters from many of Rosenfeld's other friends. I traveled to Chicago, New York, Austin, Waikiki, and Los Angeles to speak to people who had known Rosenfeld. I spent time with his daughter, Eleni, a Buddhist nun, a follower of Thich Nhat Hanh. I spoke with Rosenfeld's widow, Vasiliki, and with his first girlfriend, who was also one of his last lovers (they remet soon before his death), Freda (Davis) Segel. I met with Bellow, old Chicago friends, their wives, and ex-wives. His cousins soon felt as if they were my own cousins. Once, I picked up the phone to hear the voice of one of Rosenfeld's friends tell me that his tombstone in Chicago had fallen. She was collecting money to fix it and was calling Rosenfeld's closest friends. I sent a check.

Often I considered putting all this aside and returning to my work on European Jewish history. This, finally, became inconceivable as I wrote and rewrote this book against the background of the end of my own marriage, as I remet and fell deeply in love with the woman who is now my wife, and as I came to think more and more about the matters at the heart of Rosenfeld's own quest for clarity: in particular, his wrestling with how to live fully with one's mind and heart without losing oneself to either. This book felt, in the end, essential to write precisely because it demanded that scholarship be wedded, intimately, with some of the most basic, inescapable questions in life. But isn't this precisely what good, meaningful scholarship ought to be?

The insights of two individuals I met while working on this book—Rosenfeld's daughter, Eleni, and the dramatist and critic Lionel Abel—helped me best concentrate on why it was that I refused to give it up. Abel, by then old, frail, and uncommonly vain (he was reputed to have left one of his marriages by telling his wife he was going out for cigarettes and never returning), had urged me to come see him at his Upper East Side apartment, in Manhattan, when I first telephoned. He told me that he had much to say about Rosenfeld, but when I arrived, he admitted that he remembered little about him and talked about himself, his plays, his own life. He mentioned that it was a "rotten idea" to work on Rosenfeld.

Still, as I sat with Abel, feeling testy for having spent taxi money to listen to him rehearse the story of his life, the wiry, fabled narcissist offered an observation that came, eventually, to haunt me. If you're intent on writing about Rosenfeld, he said, the decision must have more to do with you than with him. Then, once again, he turned the conversation back to himself, his work and his achievements, and I left as soon as I could. Not long afterward, I was lecturing in France and took a trip to see Eleni at her Buddhist nunnery. When she made much the same observation as Abel had, it stuck with me. I had met Eleni before, while she was visiting her bedridden mother, Vasiliki, in Hawaii, and we had spent a couple of days walking around Waikiki talking at first uneasily but then quite freely, it seemed to me. A shy, bone-thin, and tense former nurse, she described her mother as frustrating, grasping. Her father, long gone, was a distant, august presence. We talked about Judaism (about which she knew very little), Buddhism, and what led her away from nursing. We browsed in a

bookstore where I purchased a few books for her Buddhist enclave. We ate meals together. Our time was mostly pleasant,
intermittently awkward and intimate. It felt as if we shared
the same exasperating relatives.

And then, a couple of years later, I saw her at Thich
Nhat Hanh's Plum Village, a remote spot a few dozen miles
from Bordeaux in breathtakingly beautiful countryside but
where Eleni lived in a compound stony and silent, surrounded
by signs cautioning appropriate deportment, a chilly place. It
was filled with a retinue of visitors who offered wide smiles
and long monotonous tales of how they found peace and happiness in the teachings of Thich Nhat Hanh. Most, it seemed,
bore the unease, the twitches, the palpable darkness of former lives that felt, despite their fervent pronouncements,
close at hand. It was hard to find anywhere to speak privately
with Eleni since she wasn't permitted to sit with me alone in a
room with its door shut. Her speech here was stilted; she now
claimed that she was unable to recall much about her father,
even her brother. "The killing of the Jews during the Second
World War was bad," she said at one particularly low point in
the conversation. The sentiment seemed so distant, so child-
ishly off-kilter, especially coming from the daughter of a
writer who had written so movingly about the horrors of
Nazism, that I remember turning away from her with something close to disgust. I can't imagine she didn't notice.

As the conversation grew ever more strained and the
room got colder (I recall leaning my body against the radiator
for relief), she glared at me and said: "You must decide what
this book means to you if you're to get it right." This was by far
the most direct, assertive thing she said all evening. I found
the remark unkind, and no doubt it was meant to be. I left
soon afterward, probably too abruptly, and spent an uncomfortable night at a nearby hotel, unable to sleep. The next day

on the train back to Paris I realized that Eleni was, of course, right. Abel and Eleni, two people as different from one another as any might be, had responded to our conversations about Rosenfeld in essentially the same way.

This, I knew, had come to feel like a story that I had to understand. Rosenfeld, a child of Chicago's (just barely Americanized) Jews, like my own West Side Chicago parents, pondered harder and more courageously than anyone I had encountered before what it meant to live with ideas. Written off by many of those who knew him best, he deserved better. When I read the first lines of *Passage from Home* ("and it seemed to me that I towered over the family. Life meant the family."), I felt that I knew what he meant. Rosenfeld saw ideas as intimate and familial. He was forever the prodigal son intricately meshed, even in his rebellion, with his own people. Much like Sholem Aleichem and the other Yiddish writers he admired, he felt he knew his own people's foibles, tics, and obsessions—which were also, of course, his own. He was certain that his intense, often combative relationship to Jewish life gave him access to just the sort of marginal perspective essential to seeing things clearly. He felt so intimate a relationship with Jewish matters that, as he saw it, he didn't need to think about himself as a Jewish writer.

True, some of his more radical notions scandalized many Jewish readers (he was in the late 1940s probably the most controversial of all writers on Jewish themes in the English language) and intellectuals closest to him often saw his Jewish interests as too pronounced. Anticipating the ethnically inflected 1960s, Rosenfeld denied that these were parochial or, for that matter, any less worldly or interesting or important than any of his other concerns, and asserted that he better understood the world because of—not despite—them.

He thought with honesty, with few evasions of human frailty. His willingness to acknowledge his own failures made him an unusually humane guide to life, work, and their complex, uneasy, and—in his mind—essential intersection. He yearned for fame, and believed that he deserved it. But Rosenfeld believed no less in the purity of art, and as messy as his life was, he remained uncompromising with his talents. He mused about cutting corners, about selling out, but he shunted these seductions aside and stayed true, much as he had been since his adolescence, to the belief that no real connection existed between artistic and worldly success. He knew, of course, that the reality was more complex, and he awaited the day when others would see that his writings were, indeed, masterpieces. Impatient and eager and ambitious as he was, he felt that there was no alternative but to wait for that day, and to continue to work much as he had done since his own passage from home.

There was still more that made it feel urgent to understand what Rosenfeld had understood, and especially what it was that had alternately crushed and animated his writing life. Few who write today, few who live amid books that they read so that they might write better, can overlook the assault on reading at the heart of contemporary culture—with its emphasis on the visual, its distrust of intellection, which itself is, arguably, among the more powerful legacies of the last century. Never, it seems, has the role of the writer felt so at odds with what is around us—despite superb writing that seems to speak to fewer and fewer. Other writers have in the past, of course, feared that theirs were times when the fate of literacy was at risk and such concerns have proven unfounded, off-kilter. No matter: now this sense of uncertainty feels warranted. For those, like myself, who early on found coherence in the world around us mostly through books, the uncertainty surrounding their fate today, their increasing marginality, feels ominous, one more way in which the earth is heating up right under our feet.

Books were for Rosenfeld a way out, the only credible way in which to clarify the dissonance, the incoherence, the furies of life. But he knew well how they could help one to hide. He insisted on confronting the limitations of a life spent with them; he refused to see books as the only way life might be understood, while, at the same time, acknowledging his undying reliance on them. I found myself wanting to speak with him about how he negotiated these tensions, what he did with them on—and off—the page. It was a long, open-ended conversation that I sought and this book is, in some measure, its byproduct. The impulses behind biographical work are many, but one abiding feature is, as often as not, the desire to meet one's subject, to hear the voice, especially when this is impossible. A. S. Byatt writes in her fictional meditation *A Biographer's Tale*: "I didn't want to hunt or penetrate Destry-Scholes. I wanted more simply to get to know him, to meet him, maybe to make a kind of friend of him. A collaborator. A colleague. I saw immediately that 'getting to know' Destry-Scholes was a much harder, more anxious task than hunting, or penetrating him would have been."[9]

Literary critic Theodore Solotaroff went to the University of Chicago shortly before Rosenfeld's death hoping to study with him but was too timid to meet him. Solotaroff recalled what reading Rosenfeld meant for him during a particularly rough, fallow period: "I spotted a copy of the *Chicago Review* that contained a posthumous essay by Isaac Rosenfeld on the experience of writing. I picked it up, began rereading it, and came to a passage in which he talked about feeling 'uncertain, alone, and much of the time afraid' when he began to write something. It was as though he had walked into the room, and sat down to counsel me in this terrible time."[10]

This book seeks to capture the immediacy, the stringency, of this voice. The writer, Rosenfeld explained in the essay that impressed Solotaroff, "will have to play the role that is not a role; to be the living man, the one left alone at three o'clock in the morning, when it's always the dark night of the soul; to be the man whom one encounters when there is no longer any uniform to wear . . . to be the man who is naked, who is alone, and the man who pretty much of the time is afraid."[11] He wrote these words soon before his death, at a time when his life—at least his writing life—seemed on the rebound. He was writing better, more fluently, with greater clarity than he had for many years and about themes that he himself knew best: about Chicago, about a King Solomon modeled after his old, ever more regal friend "Sol" Bellow, about the confounding demands of literature in a commercial age. Bellow, too, noticed that "during the last years of his life all the quaintness . . . was set aside. His wit was clearer and sharper."[12]

In this book I examine Rosenfeld's pained, circular quest as a writer, beginning with his essays and stories and continuing with *Passage from Home,* his odd, remarkable novel about fathers and sons. His fictional writing soon became more abstract. He sought to meld philosophy and fiction, trying to move beyond realism, to probe imagination, somehow, from within. But in the last couple of years of his life, he turned his back on such writing, it seems, and returned to themes he was arguably better equipped to write about: How to escape, and not escape home? How to embrace childhood and adulthood without turning one's back on either? How to embrace thought as well as instinct; mind and body; the rigors of intellection and the delicious abandon of sex; the purity, the innocence, of childhood, and the rest of life?

Rosenfeld wrote in his journals: "I feel this urge now—strongly, to discover, now at last in my 30th year, myself, the person, the living man, not the worried, over-anxious abstraction . . . I'm dying to write about myself, Vasiliki, the kids, the Village, my family . . . enough psychological abstractions—people, flesh and blood, reality!" He knew that he could write searchingly, perhaps brilliantly, about the details of life around him but he wrestled for many years as to whether this was what he wanted to do—and if this was the most accurate way of seeing the world: "Vasiliki's symptom of falling in love: sighs, distractions, unaccountable smiles, a clouded look in the eyes, the face full of embarrassment. All day long she hums one song: 'I'm as corny as Kansas in August . . . ' but stops short of the punch line, 'I'm in love with a wonderful guy.' Something guarded about her manner, as though she wanted to keep it sacred from any outsiders prying. The way she was brushing her teeth, her back slightly turned to the door, as if, even though I'm presumably asleep, she wanted to keep her feelings inviolate. Her voice when she talks with him on the telephone is soft, it has a depth in it. Her symptoms—exactly the same as mine."[13]

There is no way to know what he might have done had he lived, what his writing life might have turned out to be. How would his best work sound today if freed from the weight, the teleology, that has been imposed onto it? True, by his mid-thirties he hadn't lived up to his potential: he had been stunningly brilliant as a boy, a child-genius, and he stumbled, but then again, many do and get over rough patches. They overcome the disappointment of temporary failure, novels half-written, afternoons spent in dissipation, the fact that books written by their closest friends have done better than their own. If Rosenfeld's writing life weren't seen as a simple, steady decline, as a march into the abyss, how might it be viewed?

This question seems all the more crucial since much of Rosenfeld's work remains fresh, pertinent in its candid wrestling with the impact of books and the interplay between what it is that books give and what they take away. How, then, might his voice sound without the din of that tale of unsteady work, of a sudden death having sealed a graying, dimming fate?

CHAPTER ONE

Home

There will be a "Chicago School." But the point is that, no matter how we've changed and drifted, and no matter how many accidents have befallen us, that youthful idealism of ours, when we dreamed about writing and literature, has grown ahead, quietly working itself out. That's the biggest hope, and I say it for myself—for although my self-confidence, at the moment, is very low, I know that we all set ourselves right at the beginning, which is enough to provide for the end.

—Isaac Rosenfeld letter to Oscar Tarcov

ROSENFELD'S WAS A MISERABLE CHILDHOOD. AS A writer he saw childhood as containing life's best moments, yet his own memories were mostly dark, cramped, and unhappy. His father, Sam, was a closed man, easily bruised, with a vast capacity for recollecting hurts and slights. Hungry for love, he married three times (the third time to the younger sister of his second wife). Sam spoke English fluently and was well-off working as a buyer for a downtown fancy food store, but money he guarded. The Rosenfeld household was full of both the intrusions and the assurances of family. In the same apartment building lived Sam's two unmarried sisters, Isaac's fiercely loyal aunts—Rachel (or Rae) and Dora—who served as surrogate mothers and who figure, mostly grotesquely, in Rosenfeld's early fiction.[1]

Not much spoken about but ever present, looming as a formative influence for all that was wanting, was Isaac's mother, Miriam, dead of influenza at twenty-one when he was barely a year and a half old. Her photograph, with gorgeous, haunting Jewish eyes, is embossed, Russian-style, on her Chicago grave site. Rosenfeld's earliest writing—arguably, much of what he wrote for the rest of his life—was about her. "It must have been that when my mother died," he wrote in a journal in his twenties, "I was left in a state of suspended animation, the result of shock; which, except for intervals, has been my predominant state all through my life—under a clamp, fearful, deeply hidden in feeling. The little boy with the pale face and the large dark circles under his eyes, and probably underweight; who gives way to the stout adolescent always in a wide sweat under the arms." A few months after Miriam's death, a friend of Sam Rosenfeld visited the family apartment. Isaac was making noise and Sam yelled at him. Isaac turned to his father and said, in a mixture of Yiddish and English, "*fun a bissel tummel* [from a little bit of noise] the world comes an end."[2]

Rosenfeld wrote his first published short story in Yiddish at the age of fourteen. It was about a boy trapped for the summer amid a seemingly benign but actually terrifying, destructive family. "A Rich Boy's Autobiography" tells of a lonely, brooding child, his parents far away in South America. He yearns to join them but his aunts refuse—for reasons of their own—to let him go. "What—Henry, in South America!" The notion is too preposterous to consider, its declaration ample evidence of its absurdity. They seem, and perhaps really are, concerned for his welfare. Yet they're "cold as ice . . . with half of yesterday's smile." They intrude on him, they organize him:

he resents them more and more. The "hotter he got, the cooler his aunts became, cooler, colder, stranger. And it seemed to him that they were becoming larger, larger, and they began to sprout horns! Their devilish smiles pierced him like (sharp) horns! They are now altogether devils."[3]

Finally, redemption seems at hand. A car mysteriously appears, ready to spirit him away. "They didn't let me have any fun. You didn't let me go to South America and you interrupted all my plans. I have no freedom." He can't stay at home, where love suffocates, but he still hopes to be a good boy and reminds his aunts in a farewell note that nothing that happened was, in fact, their fault. And then, as soon as he grasps at freedom, it proves elusive: He enters "the wide world," never seems to locate his parents—who aren't again mentioned—but finds himself hungry, penniless, robbed of his belongings, longing to return. "Henry had already had enough fun."[4]

The story, startlingly mature and allusive, has Henry seem to want fun, to seek it desperately, at least for a while. What lures Henry most powerfully and without the prospect of resolution is his desire to join himself with a woman, silent, herself synonymous with the Moon: "Night—All is quiet. Sha, no one sees but the moon. She sees all. She knows all. She sees and is silent. She sees and smiles quietly. She, the Queen of the Night, the guardian of the quiet, God's witness. She sees how a piece of paper lies on a table. She sees how an empty bed lies alone. She sees how someone is going, all alone. A night wanderer? A nocturnal trip, alone in the darkness?"[5]

Isaac was a "rigid . . . nervous, fastidious" boy. He yearned by his early teens to get away, but he stayed on as the good, obedient, and brilliant son, a balm to his father, who wore the many blows he had suffered all too conspicuously.

"A white face, white-jowled, a sarcastic bear. . . . Among friends, his son had various names for him. The General, the Commissar, Osipovich, Ozymandias, he often called him," Saul Bellow wrote. After Miriam's death, Sam married Chana, who gave birth to a brain-damaged child named Mildred. Chana eventually died of cancer, Mildred was institutionalized, and Sam married Chana's younger sister, Ida, a Communist with a past who had lived on her own in New York. Sam suspected Ida of indiscretions, they had terrible rows, and he left her time and again. Isaac (his father's "secret weapon," in Bellow's words) tried hard to be good. In the graduation picture taken at the Sholem Aleichem school, whose yearbook published "A Rich Boy's Autobiography," the young Rosenfeld sits ramrod straight, a fixed, wide smile on his face, his hair slicked back with care; the ceremony was graced by the Jewish socialist Yiddish luminary Chaim Zhitlovsky. Rosenfeld was, by all accounts, studious, rigorous, and, at least publicly, happy.[6] In a poem he sent his aunts—as a young adolescent, or earlier—he demonstrated a deep preoccupation with Jews and their fate. Only a fragment remains:

> We are exiled, not from Italy
> But from history; Even a man
> With a lesser jaw
> And cleaner hands . . . [7]

An unpublished manuscript of his sketched the hidden life of a boy of thirteen, isolated, precociously bright, and afraid of the chaos, the unpredictability of life. Like *Passage from Home*'s Bernard, he spends nearly all his time alone in his room. When compelled to leave it, he goes to the public library, and once there, he hides in the toilets, mostly vacant

Isaac Rosenfeld's graduation class picture, March 1930, with his Sholem
Aleichem class. Chaim Zhitlovsky sits in the second row middle, and
Rosenfeld stands in the third row, second to right.
Photograph courtesy of Daniel Rosenfeld.

and blissfully cool rooms (the story, again like *Passage from Home*, takes place in the Chicago summer). For these excursions, he prepares himself with meticulous care: "This trip to the library, necessitating an early breakfast, a clear knowledge of the subject to which he would confine his research and the necessary and important books that had dealt with it, a sharpened pencil in case his pen ran dry, a note book; all this had to be assembled without haste and yet without delay. The trip itself, on foot if the weather permitted, followed by a consultation of the card catalogue, the wait at the desk, and the explanations with [sic] the librarian, whenever it happened—and it did quite frequently—that the books were out. Then a seat at the right table, in relation to light, drafts, and other people using the library. This was an exhausting ritual, especially to one who took it quite seriously, as the student did."[8]

The grinding terror of daily life ate at the young Rosenfeld, it seems, although he gave the impression at the time of a self-absorbed boy, too earnest, capable of being sardonic and quite funny, but mostly quiet, self-reflective, and hardworking. The fears he held at bay were, while apparently invisible, considerable: "My grandfather was a famous Talmudist," he wrote in a Dada-like pseudomemoir included in his journals. "My mother was an opera star. My mother died. My father was a chess player. My father began to play pinochle. I used to take clocks apart and they thought I was going to be an engineer. My father beat me, until I developed a love for stray cats; since then I have never broken a milk bottle . . . I have grown up and I owe everything to my aunt who used to invite me into the bedroom whenever she took a bath. My aunt is still a vegetarian virgin. I sleep all day."[9]

His childhood writings—and later his journal—with their jaunty, off-handed references to incestuous relations with his aunts, refer, it seems, to the absence of certain crucial boundaries in his home. His father's dark moods were imposed on everyone around him—this would figure into the central themes of *Passage from Home*. His aunts' love was no less intrusive, and Isaac often felt it to be more an extension of their own hunger to be loved than an expression of their feelings for him. Nowhere, not even in the bath tub, could he escape them. Insatiable, pervasive emotions figured among the facets of family life that he would circle time and again, seeking to understand on and off the page.

Emotional hunger incapable of being sated would form the core of Rosenfeld's imaginative terrain. He remained convinced that, despite its pressures, childhood offered a potential purity—perhaps most especially at the cusp of adolescence. He was certain that he had never experienced the pleasurable abandon nor the wholeness that he associated with childhood. He bemoaned the loss and longed to live it, perhaps later in life. He reflected often on the end of childhood, the time before the anguish and distractions of sex gave way to consummation. As he saw it, spiritual aspirations were the sharpest then, just before the onset of lust. "Sex repression is bad—so let's have freedom. No more Sturm und Drang, no more starved, embittered adolescence." Rosenfeld wrote, years later, in his journal that friends of his who spoke of the pleasure of such freedom forget "the value repression must have had in their own lives, the intensity and eagerness it produced, the over-evaluation of knowledge—the political activity, recklessness—in a word, idealism. The best, the purest, the freest moments. . . . Surely, as we look on our 'wasted youth,' our experience must tell us to be grateful."[10]

If asked where in literature these ideas were best contained, Rosenfeld would immediately have identified the Russian classics, which he devoured even as a child. The exploration of shame in Dostoevsky, the sense of something es-

sential irretrievably lost that pervades so much of Chekhov—
these were, as he saw it, the most persuasive explications of
the domestic life around him. Rosenfeld later spoke with
mock solemnity of how Chekhov had really written in Yiddish,
a fact concealed by his translator in an effort to save his reputation as a world writer. Bellow wrote of Rosenfeld's household: "[His] bullheaded father and two maiden aunts who
were 'practical nurses' with household patients (dying, usually) read Russian novels, Yiddish poetry, and were mad about
culture. He was encouraged to be a little intellectual."[11]

It was as an adolescent, around the age of sixteen, that
Rosenfeld first met Bellow. A genial, guarded young man two
years older than Isaac, Sol was popular, a track runner, ambitious even at that age as a writer but discreet about his aspirations. He was strikingly good-looking in contrast to the round,
unkempt Isaac, who was known to be oblivious to all but
books. ("I remember myself behind the counter in Hillman's;
selling salami and talking it up above the voice of the crowds,
by shouting the Waste-Land at the customers," Rosenfeld
portrayed himself in his journal.) His hair was sandy, his com-
plexion odd, yellowish; he seemed physically uncoordinated.
He soon started smoking, a lifelong habit. The school newspaper described Rosenfeld as a "short barber pole with
glasses." Friends spoke of him as sallow-faced, often breathless, with red marks on his cheeks (which disappeared by his
adulthood). As he later summed himself up: "I had no girl
friends, no frivolities. I had a Weltanschauung. This pleased
my father, but he kept his pleasure to himself." Rumor had it
that his IQ was 180. He was a skilled musician (he played the
flute beautifully) and he was reputed to know an immense
amount about nearly everything.[12]

Never before had Bellow encountered someone so
consumed by ideas, so thoroughly at home with what he—

less certain of his own intellectual ability—hoped for himself. Frequently, Bellow would insist that Rosenfeld was the more gifted of the two. Herbert Passin, one of their Trotskyist friends and later a Japan scholar, remembered that when Bellow first mentioned Rosenfeld to him, he said that he was a brilliant flute player and that he had read all of Immanuel Kant. With obvious unease many decades later, Bellow would remember hearing Sam Rosenfeld tell him, "Isaac will outshine you."[13] Bellow's description of his first impressions of Rosenfeld is as loving a portrait of another man as Bellow could ever bring himself to write. He wrote in "Charm and Death," where Rosenfeld is barely disguised Zetland:

> Yes, I knew the guy. We were boys in Chicago. He was wonderful. At fourteen, when we became friends, he had already worked out and would willingly tell you how everything had come about. It went like this: First the earth was molten elements and glowed in space. Then hot rains fell. Steaming seas were formed. For half of the earth's history, the seas were azoic, and then life began. In other words, first there was astronomy, and then geology, and by and by there was biology, and biology was followed by evolution. Next came prehistory and then history—epics and epic heroes, great ages, great men, then smaller ages with smaller men, then classical antiquity, the Hebrews, Rome, feudalism, papacy, renaissance, rationalism, the industrial revolution, science, democracy, and so on. All this Zetland got out of books in the late twenties, in the Midwest. He was a clever kid.[14]

Bellow introduced him to a lively group of talented boys, ribald and book-smart, none quite as smart as Rosenfeld—which probably pleased him—but more experienced in the ways of the world, much easier around girls. ("Weak boys, too undeveloped for whorehouses or gambling, sheltered by our fathers, we didn't have to worry about the Depression.

Our only freedom was in thought," wrote Bellow in a draft of *Herzog*.) These boys edited the school's newspaper, *Tuley Review*, which they sought—earnestly, foolishly—to turn into a major, local publication. (Soon out of school, the same group launched an ambitious, short-lived magazine, *The Beacon*, which they touted as "Chicago's Liberal Magazine.") *Tuley Review* carried cartoonlike maps of the terrain of James Joyce's *Ulysses* within days of the book's legal publication in the United States. Reading the famed Shakespeare and Company pirated edition provided these aspiring writers, or so several later claimed, with their first glimpse of how everyday reality could be transmuted into literature. They read vociferously, buying and stealing books: Rosenfeld's technique involved wearing bulky overcoats. They read their writings to one another and sketched brief, pointed biographical portraits of those around them: "Sam [Freifeld] who, in youth, flashed at us, through his eyes, smile, temple, his energy, high esteem of himself, inviting all to share in his being. Poet, revolutionary, lover, adventurer, a Knight of Division Street," Rosenfeld later described one of the group.[15]

Crucial to both Bellow and Rosenfeld, perhaps their dearest and most loyal friend, was Oscar Tarcov, a gentle, empathetic boy with intense literary ambitions that never came close to being realized and a gift for friendship deeper than either of theirs. He mediated bad moments between the other two, playing the peacekeeper, perhaps to his own detriment. Both confided in him, often in him alone, and their letters to him were among their most candid and unrestrained. He was a good, thoughtful man, a steadfast friend, and would later be a loyal husband and father, and a fluent but unsuccessful writer. (Tarcov certainly tried hard to be a writer, but he made a living doing Jewish communal work and produced an array of American Jewish tales, at least one play, and a novel, *Bravo,*

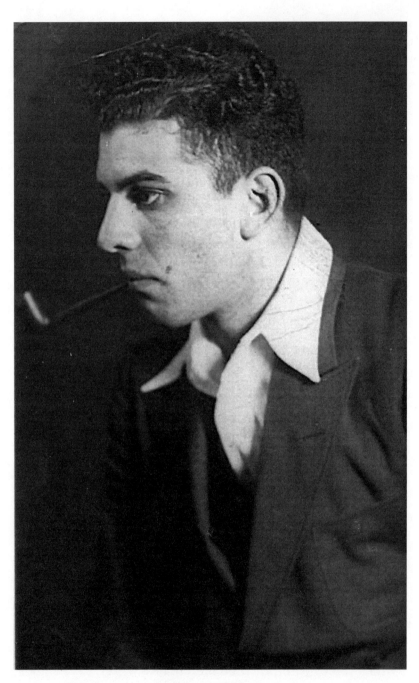

Sam Freifeld.
Photograph courtesy of Nathan Tarcov.

My Monster, an obscure meditation on the horrors of Nazi Europe.) Bellow, Rosenfeld, and Tarcov saw themselves as a trio: "In a way your enthusiasm reminds me that I have always been a sort of combination vanguard and experimental rabbit in the trio that includes both of us and Isaac," Bellow wrote to Tarcov in the early 1940s.[16]

But the friendship between Bellow and Rosenfeld was, it seems, unsurpassed. Bellow saw in Rosenfeld someone brilliantly insistent on understanding all of philosophy, a consummate intellectual whose vast, unsystematic reading of the classics underpinned a belief in the paramount importance of thought. Such intellectuals would occupy a central role in history. Bellow later sought to capture Rosenfeld's sense of what this might be:

> To be an intellectual was the next stage of human development, the historical fate of mankind, if you prefer. Now the masses were reading, and we were off in all directions, Zet believed. The early phases of this expansion of mind could not fail to produce excesses, crime, madness. Wasn't that, said Zet, the meaning of books like *The Brothers Karamazov,* the decay produced by rationalism in the feudal peasant Russian? And parricide the first result of revolution? The resistance to the modern condition and the modern theme? . . . The megalomania of the pioneers? To be an intellectual was to be a parvenu. The business of these parvenus was to purge themselves of their first wild impulses and of their crazy baseness, to change themselves, to become disinterested. To love truth. To become great.[17]

Rosenfeld—"Itzik," is what they called him—was prized in his high school years mostly as a budding philosopher and poet. In the *Tuley Review* he clashed with local Stalinists and published poetry, and sketches in the hoary, ele-

Oscar Tarcov.
Photograph courtesy of Nathan Tarcov.

vated style of British criticism. Together, this group of boys practiced erudite, ambitious talk on one another about the tasks of culture and their own group's indispensability in sustaining it. Much of it would reverberate, years later, in Bellow's fiction. Rosenfeld, too, tried hard to build it into his own. "Our Tradition," declaimed Rosenfeld to Tarcov, "is remarkably rich taking in a goodly segment of Modern Culture. Dali, Breton, Matisse, Picasso, Mann, Eliot, Huxley, Trotszy [*sic*] move across the pages of our history." These men, numbering a dozen or so, had, as Rosenfeld insisted in the same letter, their own "pantheon" (Farrell, Hook, Norman Thomas, John Dewey, and Irving Janis). "Sit at your typewriter," Rosenfeld wrote in another letter to Tarcov, "and be tortured. Remember everything you said, Saul said, Abe [Kaufman] said, when we used to talk to one another in more intimate days. Those were invaluable conversations and it all comes back to me, and after years. I think of what I want to do, and there are all those influences welling forth, fashioning my disgusts and ideals. . . . Now sit down and write, and the conversations will go on: about death, pity, love, sympathy, understanding, truth. . . . We are the hope to literature because we grew up teaching one another that above all it is necessary to understand the world."[18]

These conversations had the feel of extended monologues. No doubt the participants were eager to speak with one another but it seems they were more intent on the prospect of creating the building blocks for their own fiction, or philosophy. They were nervy and urban; steeped in street talk and T. S. Eliot; informed by Russian, but also English, French, and German, literature—all inflected in Yiddish. They dubbed themselves the "Division Street Movement," and other bookish boys beyond their ethnically diverse, mostly lower-middle-class Humboldt Park neighborhood sought them out. In his novel *Dangling Man,* Bellow called groups like theirs "colonies of the spirit" and insisted that they were the best bulwark against crudity. A decade or so later, when he was more worldly and less certain of the permanence, or influence, of such circles, Rosenfeld would still declaim (at the end of an essay on being a Jewish writer): "Artists create their colonies. Some day these may become empires."[19]

"If I were lying next to you in hell," wrote Bellow to Tarcov, "I would help you with all my power. But hell is for our ancestors. For us, nothing is so simple."[20] These conversations recall how Hermione Lee sums up talk in the Bloomsbury circle, with its comparable hubris, its sense of itself as a precursor of a convulsive, thoroughgoing change. There, too, one encounters "the sense of people alone, talking to themselves, unable to say what they mean or speaking sometimes quite different from what is in their minds. . . . Those conversations are really monologues."[21]

Many of these monologues were about politics, in particular about the Trotskyist movement, which split from Stalinist Communism when its leader was sent into exile from Russia in the late 1920s. For Rosenfeld and his closest friends, politics felt unavoidable—at least until 1939, perhaps a year or two later, when Trotskyism itself hopelessly splintered with the onset of the Second World War. They encountered Trotskyism in Humboldt Park, where they were (in the words of activist Albert Glotzer) "Spartacus people," or originally Socialist Party members. They became politically involved, once again, in college, where Rosenfeld and Bellow both fell in with Trotskyism. This put them at odds with the vast majority of the Left (Chicago was a major center of American radicalism), who remained faithful to Stalin and viewed Trotsky as a dangerous extremist, even, as Stalin would insist, a spy. "Gorky is dead," begins one of Rosenfeld's letters to Tarcov, "more now than ever . . . I can hardly wait for Bukharin's trial tomorrow. Before war we thought of death as screen-projection: self-in-trenches, bullet-pierced. I joined the movement and the dream changed: self underground, moving mole-sleek, airlessly, in long furry tubes like vulvas or subways or both—guns, knives, leaflets, bombs, dispatches, secret orders hidden on my person; Trotzy's [sic] face tattooed on my abdomen, my ears full of glycerin. Crowds of workers listen to me speak: they pass mc and I touch their eyes. . . . I used to

believe that a civilized man believes only in art. . . . You remember the time. Then we emerged from the jelly of rela-
tivism, having begun to grow spines. Now I believe that there
are things worth dying for."

Here Rosenfeld shows himself immersed in the by-
ways of Soviet politics and culture, reporting on these with
surrealistic inflections. The preeminent novelist in the Soviet
Union Maxim Gorky, he states, has just died after too many
years of deathlike obedience to Stalin ("dead more now than
ever"); Nicholai Bukharin, until recently the most influential
intellectual of Soviet public life, has fallen from favor and
is now charged with sedition. The letter imitates, probably
mockingly, Marxist calls for renunciation of liberalism's soft-
ness. Hence, it declaims the need to grow "spines." Fealty to
Trotsky cuts so deep, his supporters have all but tattooed his
face onto their abdomens, declares Rosenfeld, mocking this
political earnestness. Among the nicknames in college for
Rosenfeld and Bellow were Zinoviev and Kamenev, the pair of
closely interlinked, inseparable Russian Communist leaders
long tied to Stalin, then repudiated and murdered by him. Rumors later circulated that Rosenfeld was Trotsky's nephew.
He refused to disavow the rumor that he was related on his
mother's side.[22]

Trotskyist politics meant walking a tightrope between
veneration of the Soviet Union as a socialist state and criticism of it as a flawed, corruptive bureaucracy personified by
the monstrous Stalin. Trotsky taught that the revolution had
to be protected because once Stalin's tyranny was dislodged,
Russia would still, he believed, set the stage for the epochal
events put in motion in 1917. Despite its terrible flaws, the revolution—and the state created by it—had to be defended
since it remained the repository of the vaulted ideals of Bol-
shevism. Espousing an immensely complicated politics that

sat, mostly uneasily, between defense and condemnation of Russia—and that often sought to do both—Trotskyists set out to organize workers (who mostly ignored them), win student sympathizers (who tended, on the whole, to gravitate toward the Stalinists who unreservedly celebrated the world's only socialist state), and peddle periodicals (that slid, one after the other, into penury).

Although subtlety was on their side, the Trotskyists had neither political transparency nor much success. Stalin and his agents hounded their opposition; eventually decimating Trotsky's followers, they were probably responsible for killing his son (who ran the Parisian office) and certainly for murdering the "Old Man" himself in Mexico. Quite aside from these tragedies, it was often difficult for the movement's own ideologues to agree on what Trotsky meant for them to do. By the early 1940s, many of them, too, had split from the party to form their own separate groups, where they abandoned Trotsky while seeking to espouse politics in his name. Trotsky as a political leader was nearly impossible to obey but tough to ignore. Far larger than life, he was at the time of his expulsion from Russia the world's best-known revolutionary, and then its most famous political pariah. A bespectacled, bearded Jew, he was the least likely of all Russian military heroes but was an architect of the Red Army. He was a breathtaking orator, an outstanding expert on literature and art as well as politics. He wrote beautifully: his history of the Russian Revolution remains spellbinding. Rosenfeld's closest friends gravitated toward him, at least for a while, most starting as members of the Northwest Side Spartacist Youth League, an arm of Norman Thomas's Socialist Party. Thomas, Rosenfeld's first political hero, was a stalwart moralist, pacifist, and anti-Marxist who began his Socialist campaign to win the Presidency in 1928 and ran six consecutive times. Once

Rosenfeld and most of his circle were won over to Trotskyism, they sought to infiltrate the Spartacist Youth League, were expelled, and joined Trotsky's Socialist Workers Party. Rosenfeld attended the University of Chicago, and Bellow went to Northwestern, but the two spent a semester together at the University of Wisconsin, Madison; in all three places Rosenfeld and Bellow acted as political operatives of sorts, seeking out non-Stalinist leftists. "I am posing as a liberal, biding my time," Rosenfeld wrote in the fall of 1938. Their group took control of the Socialist Club at the University of Chicago; in 1939, when the already dwindling Trotskyist movement split over differing attitudes toward the Russian invasion of Finland, Rosenfeld joined the Young People's Socialist League (YPSL), headed by Max Shachtman, who would marry one of the boys' high school friends, Yetta Barshevsky. The "whole south side of Chicago section of the 4th International is thinking of going to Mexico," he wrote in 1938, some to carry on revolutionary struggle, "others for the climate."[23]

How deeply immersed in Marxist theory Rosenfeld was at the time isn't clear. Trotskyist devotees were expected to carefully read the movement's periodicals, to discuss them at meetings, and to promote their ideas. No doubt Rosenfeld engaged in these activities. But if Marxism drew him in, it didn't stick hard, or for very long. Neither in his letters nor in his first, published pieces in *Tuley Review*, nor elsewhere, is there evidence that Marxist ideology was a source of inspiration. What drew him to the movement was probably, above all, the relationship it afforded him with a small, intellectually beleaguered vanguard, the smartest of the neighborhood's Jewish boys and girls, superior in every way to the more numerous, conformist Stalinists. Their mentor, Trotsky, was shunned much as they felt they themselves were, and seemed, at least in this respect, familiar. He had been denied his rightful place as Lenin's heir by lesser men: he lived a contemporary epic, one that was Russian, and Jewish, and that pitted brutish evil against the austere and cerebral. Rosenfeld and his cohorts threw themselves into party work mostly in spurts, plugging the movement's periodicals (Anita, soon Bellow's first wife, was admired for her ability to peddle Trotskyist periodicals faster than anyone else), seeking allies among fellow students and professors, and judging anyone they dated on the basis of their attitudes toward Stalin. Oscar lost the exotic Ravelli (Rosenfeld wrote him letters imagining her breasts, her vitality in bed) because he finally admitted his Trotskyism to her.[24]

"Politics furnishes the best of all bases for secular culture," Rosenfeld would later claim. By mid-1941, both Rosenfeld and Bellow had moved away from political activities. Rosenfeld charged that the movement was "decadent" and distrusted its activists' impulses. "People who beat their grandmothers, always feed pigeons in the park," he wrote. He left at a time of increasingly intense sectarianism, when the tensions at the core of Trotskyism caused it to splinter into warring factions: Trotskyists split again and again between the Workers Party of the United States, the Appeal Group, and the Socialist Workers Party, which itself split. Battles started in earnest immediately after the 1939 Russian invasion of Finland, which Trotsky insisted was defensible and done to protect the socialist motherland. Many of his supporters—and his movement was quite small to begin with—saw the Finnish invasion as an inexcusable aggression. At the heart of this debate was a battle over how corrupt Stalinist corruption was: Trotsky still saw Soviet Russia as a socialist state—deformed, in the hands of a murderous dictator, but with legitimate reason to defend its borders. He handled the dispute with disdain, dismissing his critics, more than willing to isolate himself even from those who desperately wished to follow him. Rosenfeld and Bellow left his party in the midst of these disputes; Rosenfeld tired of them sooner than Bellow. Most of his closest friends were soon, as Rosenfeld put it, "intellectuals in retreat. So we are all honorable men."[25] In retreat from politics, Rosenfeld would search for other intellectual foundations, which he discovered, soon enough, in a distinctively personalized variant of existentialism.

Looking back at the movement, he was more bemused than impressed and saw timid people, enamored with abstraction, fearful of the merest prospect of power: "[S]ome day the world may actually fall into our hands! Then where would we run?" he wrote in his spoof "The Party." By the time Alfred Kazin met Rosenfeld and Bellow three or four years later, he found them "naked, loveable, human, without ideology." Still, politics had taught Rosenfeld what it felt like to live harnessed to ideas, and he remained convinced always that politics was an essential component of a coherent secular worldview. "He had learned, through political activity, to admire the vigor which a social orientation will impart to thought," Rosenfeld wrote in one of the first reviews he would produce for a national magazine, a piece on the memoir of a young, left-wing intellectual—Walter Morris's *Journal of a Generation*—in the early 1940s. It would seem that he was speaking from experience.[26]

By the time Bellow and Rosenfeld roomed at Madison in the summer and fall of 1937 (they soon moved into separate apartments close to one another), they engaged in continuous bouts of literary experimentation, with an emphasis on surrealism. They composed poems together ("Foaming rabbis rub electrical fish / Neckties declare the glory of God; while / A samovar is bled by a vaccinated horse / Othello delivers the flannel of offspring of tortured goats") and prodded one another, and their friends, to think and feel more intently. "For love of Proust," wrote Rosenfeld to Tarcov from Madison, "take time or aspirin and write an integrated subtle letter." They gravitated toward an eccentric, colorful visiting intellectual, the bohemian, Russian-born anthropologist Alexander A. Goldenweiser, a disciple of Franz Boas who studied race, sexuality, and Iroquois Indians: "Man Manifest," wrote Rosenfeld of him, "a separate act of creation . . . I rank him with Shish-Kebab as one of the finer things in life." Rosenfeld was working hard on his master's in philosophy: "I am expected to do . . . in a semester," he wrote to his aunts, "anthropology, ethnography, history (Spengler), economics (Marx, etc.), philosophy (Kant, esthetics, Spinoza)."[27]

Bellow wrote to Tarcov of how the two were "together most of the time. We both have colds, and conversations flagging we talk of our colds and sniffle with common accord." Bellow often berated Rosenfeld for his sentimentality, his being "virtually a Franciscan, a simpleton for God's sake, easy to cheat . . . I said he exaggerated everything. He accused me of a lack of sensibility. It was an odd argument for two adolescents." And he watched after Rosenfeld keenly: "there has been no . . . news of importance, with the exception of the renaissance of Isaac. Isaac is beginning to spring a little gristle in his marrow." Rosenfeld spoke lovingly to Tarcov, then at the University of Illinois, Champaign, of their long talks: "Saul and I have batted the old Surrealist ball around quite a bit." Around this time, together with Tarcov, they wrote a surrealist play called "Twin Bananas" that was later put on in the lobby of the University of Chicago's Harper Library. Rosenfeld spoke of himself, in an essay written in the spring of 1937, as "a surrealist at heart. His friend Raskolnikov wrote a poem about a comma spreading mustard on its sides."[28]

Kazin said that he had "never known intellectuals so close to my own heart." He recalled traveling with Rosenfeld and Bellow to Hoboken to eat at riverside dives, as they related their literary aspirations to one another: "There was an intellectual playfulness about them both, a gift for insurrectionary proposals. I saw them as characters from *The Possessed*—temperamental provocateurs in some nasty provincial town trying by force of their talk to raise a little dust. Chicago had kept them serious. They expected great things for themselves as creative artists, and showed it by their ease of speculation."[29]

There is a beauty, a longing bordering on the erotic, in Bellow's recollections of his coming of age with Rosenfeld outside the reach, finally, of both parental homes:

> It is an Indian summer, beautiful and somnolent. We have hired a canoe. I am getting in alone and find myself suddenly standing fully dressed in the water. A student runs down the pier and yells, "Hey, have you got a watch?"
> "Yes, I have a watch."
> "Give it here to me. You'll ruin it."
> I give him my watch. And now Isaac comes rambling by, abstracted, and I get his attention. I am sinking in the mud. He pulls me out and we go home to St. James Place. I change my clothes in the sun-filled room. We have a long conversation about *The Brothers Karamazov*.[30]

The most enduring collaborative effort produced by Rosenfeld and Bellow in this period was their never-published loose translation—in truth, a brilliant, hilarious, and savage parody—of T. S. Eliot's "The Love Song of J. Alfred Prufrock." Here they mixed modernism, surrealism, a mild, sardonic Yiddishism, and hostility for the cool distance in Eliot that they found dry, dangerous, even inhuman. They challenged head-on Eliot's terror of physicality, his dread of the human touch, and substituted a sentimental radicalism, a rueful Yiddish communalism. Their poem is packed with wet socks and dirty bedding; its women are "wives," not the desiccated seductresses of Eliot's imagination. In it, there are prunes, not peaches. On the shore, men air themselves in garish summer garb. Bellow always admitted that Rosenfeld wrote the bulk of the work. Already by spring 1937 some of their closest friends had memorized it. As literary critic Ruth Wisse observes: "If asked at what point American Jewish letters gave notice of its independence from Anglo-American Modernism, I would cite the day Isaac Rosenfeld, with the help of Saul Bellow, composed this parody. Calling it 'Der shir hashirim fun Mendl Pumshtok,' 'The Song of Songs of Mendl Pumshtok,' the poem was itself a declaration of their intent to remake contemporary western literature. They sought to reclaim it from the bastion of high culture, to free it from Eliot's antisemitism, to domesticate it, and, in their minds, to enlarge it. . . . What better way to credit [Eliot] as a poet and discredit him as an antisemite than by Yiddishizing the poet who so feared the Yid?"[31]

On the Yiddish stage, there was a long, odd, gloriously sectarian tradition of translations (of Shakespeare and other canonic works, most famously *King Lear*) that announced themselves as "translations and improvements." The T. S. Eliot translation was designed as an outgrowth of this tradition or, perhaps better said, a countertradition packed with hubris and irony and intended as exercises in imitation that were also reverential homage. Bellow and Rosenfeld knew this tradition from within and turned it inside out. In their hilarious, dexterous manipulation of Eliot's famous poem, which they knew no less well, they denounced their own exclusion as Jews from the English canon, which they saw as a travesty, and sought to underscore what they could bring to English if only it opened itself to them. Rosenfeld himself described soon after composing the piece how much he relished his notoriety as the poem's author: "He quotes his translation twice a day and pretends that he feels he is making a fool of himself so that people (who have already memorized his translations) will have to beg him to quote."[32] When asked to name the finest poem written by an American in the twentieth century, former poet laureate Robert Pinsky listed in 1999 as his first choice the Prufrock translation. He credited it entirely to Bellow.[33]

> Nu-zhe, kum-zhe, ikh un du
> Ven der ovnt shteyt uf kegn dem himl
> Vi a leymener goylm af tishebov.
> Lomir gayn zikh, durch geselekh vos dreyen zikh
> Vi di bord bay dem rov.

> Oyf der vant fun dem kosheren restorant
> Hengt a shmutsiker betgevant
> Un vantsn tantsn karahod. Es geht a gerorykh
> Fun gefiltefish un nase sokn.
> Oy, Bashe freg nisht keyn kasha, a dayge dir
> Lomir oyfenin di tir
> In tsimir ve di vaybere senen
> Redt men fun Karl Marx un Lenin

> Ikh ver alt, ikh ver alt
> Un der pupik vert mir kalt.
> Zol ikh oyskemen di hor,
> Meg ikh oyfesen a floym?
> Ikh vel tskatsheven di hoyzn
> Un shpatsirin bay dem yam
> Ikh vel hern di yam-moyden zingen khad gadyo.
> Ikh vel zey entfern, Borukh-habo

Nu, let us go, you and I,
When the evening stands beneath the sky
Like a clay golem on Tisha B'av.
Let us go, through streets that twist themselves
Like a rabbi's beard

On the wall of the kosher restaurant
Hangs dirty bedding
And bedbugs dance in circles. There is a stink
Of gefilte fish and wet socks.
Oy, Bashe, don't ask questions, why bother?
Let me open the door.
In the room where the wives are
Speaking of Karl Marx and Lenin

I grow old, I grow old,
And my navel grows cold.
Shall I comb out my hair?
May I eat a prune?
I shall put on white pants
And walk by the sea.
I shall hear the sea-maidens sing Chad Gadya,
I shall answer them: Baruch Haba.[34]

Among the most beautiful writing Rosenfeld did in the last years of high school and the beginning of college were his love letters to Freda Davis, one of the few girls who traveled as a near equal in his circle. Freda wrote for the *Tuley Review* and studied art, already in high school, at the Arts Institute. She was a bohemian from a working-class family of Orthodox Jews. She and Isaac had met as freshmen, but she became his girlfriend only two or three years later. A friend recalled sitting beside the two of them on the beach and spotting the pubic hair at the edges of Freda's bathing suit. "She was too much of a woman" for the bookish Rosenfeld, he remembered feeling at the time. In his journal, Rosenfeld would return, time and again, to the moments of their sexual initiation: "The young Freda and now, Humboldt Park, spring, the sticky yellow green buds and leaves—the sensations of first love, never (till now) recaptured, the flowered violets and yellow silk dress." In the draft of an unpublished story, "Paper Dolls," inspired, it would seem, by the same night, Rosenfeld wrote: "Our relationship changed after that night, awakening to impulses which her dreams alone could never have fathomed. She became more cheerful, less absorbed in phantasies [sic]. For she had found a new escape from soiled patterns of her family life. An escape in her own body." Freda would later insist that never in high school did they have sex, which contradicts Rosenfeld's own, often repeated recollections.[35]

His letters to Freda have a lightness of touch, a mock erudition, an earnest, playful preoccupation with the underpinnings of love: "For your information, [Matzoh] is an old Roman article of diet introduced into Roman life by POMPEIUS ATTLATICUS MANISHEWITZ in the year 57 B.C. The Romans used Matzoh for fuel, they built barricades and bridges out of it. Many of the bridges built by the early Romans out of Matzoh are still standing. Matzoh was also widely used as food and it formed the chief article of diet among invalids, prisoners, imbeciles, and Senators. The Roman Matrons of the Patrician Class found it indispensable to the instruction of their young daughters." Another letter describes his summer, spent at a resort in Benton Harbor, Michigan: "A rambling random landscape flecked with cows, running pigs and thin horses. Here and there a billboard, there and yon, a tree. Everywhere fat veinstreaked women supported on boneless, gelatinous thighs, big in loose bandanas, their husbands awkward in undershirts playing catch on the lawn, kibitzing at their wives' bridge games. . . . Everything dissipated, sunbrowned, dusty."

He proposes to write a novel about the country called "The Last Resort."[36]

Freda left him for another boy while they were in college. She thought better of it but too late—by then Rosenfeld had already met Vasiliki Sarantakis. Freda saved his letters, remet him in the last year of his life (by then a marriage of hers had broken up and he had left his wife), and they started sleeping together. She felt optimistic about their future but he, it seems, was torn and uncertain. She was the last person he saw before his heart attack. For years afterward, she spoke of him so often that her second husband came to loathe the mention of his name. (When we met, almost half a century after Rosenfeld's death, our conversations took place in the cafeteria of a motel near her condo in Orange County because her husband wouldn't permit me to talk with her about Rosenfeld in the house.) After their breakup in college, Rosenfeld brooded intensely over Freda and marked the date of her first marriage as the end of his childhood. The relationship seemed to be one that called on him sexually as well as intellectually. He strained hard when he wrote to her and did so with intensity. At sixteen, with aplomb and dense, sportive erudition, he criticized a lackluster letter of hers: "If Dido had once ventured to write thusly to Aeneas, if Penelope had submitted such an epistle to the wandering Ulysses, had Sappho listened listlessly to Beethoven instead of the lusting blood tumultuous in her temples, had Francesca dared tell Paolo that she was having a nice time and wish you were there—they would have forfeited their birthright of epic passion and found no solace. Can't you manage to feel yourself, even in the least, a tragic creature? O laundered Muse!"[37]

There is, already in letters written in his late teens, an electrifying tone, the ability to transmit the excitement, the nervy cadence, of his talk onto the written page. His hand-

Isaac Rosenfeld and Freda Davis.
Photograph courtesy of Freda (Davis) Segel.

writing was large, ample, looping, and easy to follow. He spent hours on some of these letters, pouring, as often as not, an immense amount of himself into them. Bellow felt he put far too much effort into them. Bellow's own letters were, even in his youth, uncannily mature, pithy, direct, and, not infrequently, self-pitying.

Rosenfeld bounced around for the next couple of years. These were odd, awful times, years of economic depression, bleak uncertainty, with few jobs available. Sam's marriage to Ida seemed on the rocks: he left her, returned to her, sought out his son's company in seemingly endless, aimless restaurant dinners. "My own paranoic papa is still giving us the run-around with his threats, suspicions and dreams." Having lost faith in Marxism, surrounded by economic devastation and rising fascism in Europe, Rosenfeld's friends found themselves in the midst of ever-deepening disillusion. The group fractured politically: one or two embraced anarchism, others adopted pacifism, some remained Trotskyists of one sort or another. Others, like Bellow, married young; in 1937 he wed Anita, an erstwhile Trotskyist stalwart, a beautiful girl with practical skills and the ability—unknown to the dreamy, ambitious Bellow—to organize everyday life. (They eloped in Indiana, so eager to do so that they crossed state lines to avoid Illinois-mandated blood tests, which would have delayed the ceremony.) Once the euphoria ended, day-to-day reality differed, of course, from early heroic dreams. Bellow recalled sitting, midday, at his mother-in-law's kitchen table, where he sought to write great fiction, staring at the empty, hot Chicago streets. "If I had been a dog I would have howled."[38]

Rosenfeld applied, unsuccessfully, to work for Chicago's *Yiddish Courier*. Instead he wrote reports—one, he said, was devoted exclusively to local pigeon racing—for the Works Project Administration. In a 1939 letter to Tarcov, Bellow described Rosenfeld as having returned from Madison to Chicago "sour and sick but prepared to resume his twenty-second straight year on the same set." Rosenfeld admitted that he was in a funk: "Just eat, sleep, walk in the afternoon, book at night, now and then a girl." Abe Kaufman, a friend from Tuley High, wrote to Tarcov asking, in December 1939, "Has Isaac given you cognizance of his rendition of Rabelais into classic Greek! It's quite a feat. With Slavonic infusions." As Bellow revealed, "Ever since he began his paper on the Absolute as conceived by Josiah Royce, Isaac has been intolerable. . . . One can predict even less for Isaac than for me."[39]

Rosenfeld seemed to gravitate to apartments that were unusually cramped, and grim. He lived, as he described it, in "a sort of attic" with a slant roof, a small window that left the room, essentially, in perpetual darkness. It was to this room that he would bring Vasiliki Sarantakis, whom he met in December 1940. "She is a girl of twenty-four, short (4′ 11 3/4″), slender (32), lithe (118 lbs). . . . She has brown eyes, perfect white, even, excellent teeth, a classical Greek profile, small hands and feet. She wears earrings, looks Jewish, acts crazy, and I think the world of her." They met at the convocation ceremony for Chicago students; they sat near one another since seating was alphabetical. Soon they went to bed and were together, in effect, from then on.[40]

Vasiliki was a savvy girl two years older than Rosenfeld who probably knew less than he believed her to know about books, life, even sex. She was tough and streetwise but less sophisticated than she liked people to think. Bellow later remembered her as a "pagan beauty" and "the type of woman who would dance on a table with a rose between her teeth." Others described her as more excitable, perhaps more calculating than intelligent. Both she and Rosenfeld wanted to escape the bonds of family, and of ethnic sectarianism; both fell

From left to right: Sam Rosenfeld, Ida, Isaac's half sister Annette,
Isaac, and Vasiliki.
Photograph courtesy of Eleni Rosenfeld.

into their love with a velocity that might have given them pause. But they seemed to feel—they admitted as much— that they were immersed in a sublime drama where they, two Midwestern provincials, now played the leading roles. In a thinly fictionalized portrait, William Phillips, editor of the *Partisan Review,* portrayed Vasiliki as "short, plump, rosy, and full of youthful energy that was mistaken for intellectual curiosity. She was girlishly pert and pretty, and her shining eyes and delicately fleshy nose aroused mixed feelings of sensuality and tenderness." After they met, Rosenfeld spent four days, on and off, writing a letter to Tarcov about her. It was nineteen handwritten pages. "Vasiliki," he wrote there, "is the beginning of my maturity."[41]

"Sunny afternoons, Vasiliki and I in bed. . . . Our clothes are thrown over the table and the chairs, covering our books; it is between classes or after class. And the light plays on our naked bodies." Rosenfeld's writing had always been infused with deep longing for love, a desire for an intense sexuality that engulfed him entirely, the sort that he had for many years associated only with Freda and feared he would never recapture. Perhaps the most powerful lines in his poem "A Season of Earth" are devoted to recollections of love gone:

> Shared in the nightside
> In blind touch making runs
> Of known arms, Remembered:
> Her hairscent. Pulsebeat
> And as in earth
> Molemute, mourns
> Her voice.[42]

Love he craved, sex he hunted for relentlessly. "I spend my days waiting for the moment when the Bourgeois Bubble of Sex shall be at least burst. . . . It is too bad that it should be the only thing I truly want," he wrote to a friend. Now he was convinced he had found someone "deeply sensuous, unusually cheerful, light spirited, spontaneous," with "uninhibited sex qualities," gloriously skeptical of academic abstractions (Vasiliki graduated Chicago with a degree in social work). By May they had decided to marry and Rosenfeld committed himself, fervently, to the idea: "Isaac is dead set on marriage," Kaufman wrote to Tarcov. "I find it difficult to believe he really thinks the world of her; to adjust to a girl, adapt, feel tender, even love—this is understandable in a virtuous man. . . . But to believe [in marriage]!"[43] Vasiliki had intellectual aspirations of sorts, but it wasn't clear how much she really cared about books or ideas, or how comfortable she was with them. She tried hard on this score, at least intermittently, and would continue to do so for years. She wrote to Oscar's wife, Edith Tarcov, in the mid-1940s about her impressions of *Anna Karenina*: "Oh, oh, I just finished reading Anna Karenina, and including, naturally those chapters you had indicated. I enjoyed Anna immensely and my only dissatisfaction lay in the fact that I had expected it to be better than War and Peace and it wasn't. Have you read War and peace? [*sic*] It's a far superior novel, wider in conception of plot, more definitive characters, and more satisfying than Anna. What amazed me is that War and P was his first novel and that's why I was disappointed in Anna, bec. [*sic*] generally speaking, an author's first novel is rarely better than those which follow. Isaac liked Kitty in A.K. whereas I thought that Anna was better delineated."[44]

Vasiliki possessed other gifts, a vivid knowledge about things physical, not cerebral—Rosenfeld remained convinced of this always. On knowing her, Rosenfeld's writing—

certainly his letters—were buoyant; happiness spilled all over them. He wrote to Tarcov in April 1941: "A bright Sunday morning, the birds sing, the slender-legged, small-jelly-breasted girls are walking in yellow and green through the firm and elastic ether. . . . The sky is clear and ringing like blue China."[45]

He continued to vacillate between literature and philosophy. As an undergraduate at the University of Chicago, he studied English and won the John Billings Fiske Prize for "A Season of Earth." But graduate studies he devoted to philosophy and he wrote a master's thesis on "animal nature" in Dewey and Santayana, the divide between body and soul as reflected in animal impulses. A work of some one hundred pages—clumsily written in part but fluent and interesting on the whole, it examines the transcendence of moral dualism, the prospect of mind and body "never in conflict because they are never rivals." It is full of lively metaphors and flights of fancy, and preoccupied with many of the same themes that would haunt Rosenfeld long after he abandoned the study of philosophy. In it he explained Dewey's ideas in terms eerily similar to those he would seek to integrate into his own life, especially once he moved to the Upper West Side of New York, and then to Barrow Street in Greenwich Village, where he sought to embrace a life that scanted neither literature nor love: "Wicked or not," as Dewey understood the sensations of animals, "there is no rest for the creature. But in its rough life it can attain some replenishment, and exhaustion does not come on all at once. There are islands of experience, moments as well as transitions, and for pain there is also ease." It is an abstract work, an explication of philosophical texts with prose that seeks to stretch beyond abstraction: "If it is a flying squirrel we shall want to kill and mount it; but if it is a bat we

Abe Kaufman.
Photograph courtesy of Nathan Tarcov.

shall let it be. . . . Metaphysics is collapsed into epistemology and methodology, logic into biology, objects into knowledge of objects, truth into warrant. The world is too much with us."[46]

With Vasiliki now with him, Rosenfeld's fortunes seemed to have turned. ("Isaac I see at school and hear whistling loudly in the halls," a mutual friend wrote to Tarcov in the spring of 1941.) He was accepted, with a small stipend, to study in the graduate program in philosophy at NYU. Deliriously in love, Rosenfeld felt his achieving perfection in work and life—at the core of the Division Street Movement's beliefs—to be at hand. His relationship with Vasiliki made the study of philosophy all the more feasible because, as he now told himself, she kept him closely connected with life's instinctive side. Soon, in New York, staring out of his tiny, dim apartment's window at the Hudson, in bed sick with pleurisy reading *Moby-Dick,* Rosenfeld claimed it was then that he abandoned philosophy for fiction. He became convinced that fiction was the best route to philosophical knowledge. He felt terrified on giving up his NYU fellowship, but also hopeful as invitations to write for leading literary magazines came, suddenly, one after the other. When informing Tarcov that he had sold his first short story and also a poem to *The New Republic,* he added, "I wish something of Saul's had appeared too." It seemed that he had left Bellow in the dust.[47] Now, as always, each measured success with reference to the other.

Bellow wrote years later—after Rosenfeld's fall, as he saw it—of his friend's heroic entry into New York. In his unpublished novel about Rosenfeld (one section of it, which included this passage, was published as the novella "Zetland: By a Character Witness"), Bellow turned this trip from Chicago into an epic of sorts, with Isaac and Vasiliki making their journey draped by gorgeous skies, flashing waters, carrying with them, perhaps as signs of the unwieldy emotional burdens

they would soon confront, cups grainy, and heavy with meaning: "Zet and Lottie swam into New York from the skies—that
is how it felt in the Pacemaker, rushing along the Hudson at
sunrise. First many blue twigs overhanging the water, then a
rosy color, and then the heavy, flashing of the river under the
morning sun. They were in the dining car, their eyes heavy.
They were drained by a night of broken sleep in the day coach,
and they were dazzled. They drank coffee from cups as grainy
as soapstones, and poured from New York Central pewter.
They were in the East, where everything was better, where objects were different. Here there was a deeper meaning in the
air."[48]

Oddly, Bellow had long insisted that Rosenfeld's tendency to romanticize daily existence was a weakness that
could hurt him as a writer. Yet here, in his fullest portrait of
his friend, Bellow does just that. His description of Rosenfeld
in New York, the most intimate we have of him, is one of a genius on the skids and in it we see an extraordinary man who
came to distrust his greatest asset: his mind. Especially once
Rosenfeld moved from his first address on the Upper West
Side to Greenwich Village, the city sapped his intellectual energy; it reinforced the worst in him and made him suspicious
of what he could do best. Suffusing Bellow's "Charm and
Death" is an acidic view of bohemia, its self-absorption, its inability to do more than celebrate the moment, to revel in it at
the expense of all that is lasting. Rosenfeld, too, distrusted the
self-indulgence of bohemia but could never quite cut himself
off from its promise of freedom, and the prospect it offered of
emotionally untangled, redemptive sex. Despite its excesses,
which he loathed—at least when he considered them abstractly—it offered the most readily available route to com-
bining the perfection of life and work.[49]

He and Vasiliki first lived in a two-and-a-half-room, ground-floor apartment on West 76th Street, near Riverside Drive. The bathtub was in the kitchen. "In the morning," wrote Rosenfeld, "when there are still mists in the river, and the houses on the Hoboken side stand on the cliffs," the place is magical. By no means was the place always magical. It was "so full of bugs that we couldn't sleep. And it is so full of heartbroken, crying, and ashamed Jewish landlady, that we couldn't move out." They killed the bugs, one at a time, with their hands, "imagining each bug was Hitler."[50]

He admitted that they let the place "happily go to ruin, the drawers are overflowing, and dishes lay around unwashed." This was carelessness, childishness. Still, he was also convinced that it represented a statement of sorts. (He later acknowledged he couldn't be attracted to a woman unless she had a stain on her dress.) Bellow recalled a surprisingly fierce fight in the apartment, over Rosenfeld's unwillingness to kill cockroaches: "In the morning Isaac and I sit at the breakfast table until noon, and we have a flaming quarrel over cockroaches. Isaac had become mystical about our right to take life and he will not lift a hand against the cockroaches who are running away with the place." Rosenfeld reveled in all this, and yet when he started work on *Passage from Home*, he subjected bohemia's empty, aimless self-absorption to merciless scrutiny. The bleakest characters in the book resemble those with whom he and his wife partied as a free, unfettered couple. By the time David Bazelon, a Chicago Trotskyist later turned social analyst and legal expert, arrived in New York in early 1943, Rosenfeld introduced him to nearly everyone he knew of intellectual importance. Rosenfeld seemed willing to give more of himself than others around him, or so Bazelon felt; he managed to endow everyday reality with a rare glow. Being with Rosenfeld, as Bazelon put it, "you could take your life seriously, any part of it you wanted, and he would really help—he really wanted to help."[51]

Rosenfeld's entry into the literary life of New York's left-wing intellectuals happened rapidly. While still a philosophy student, and within a few months of his arrival in New York, he poured most of his energy into his fiction and essays published in *Partisan Review* and elsewhere. He tried to persuade himself that he could succeed at both school and literary life: "For the past days," he wrote to Tarcov, "regardless of how I may have been disliking school and wishing I were free of it, I have been noticing that on my way home from school, walking the several blocks from Washington Square to the subway, I have been experiencing some of the deepest and most spontaneous reflections I have ever had."[52]

After about a year, he left school and, relying mostly on his wife's earnings as a secretary, picked up small writing gigs. (These included pieces for a trade magazine for ice cream and tobacco, and radio skits for the American Jewish Committee; Rosenfeld also boasted that he made money writing pornography.) He won a fellowship at the Cummington School for the Arts, which supported him for a couple months. He admitted to Tarcov that he felt uneasy about having given up the study of philosophy; he felt puzzled as to why he hadn't managed to do more to "find a decent compromise . . . but it bored me, and I couldn't fake my responses." He mused that his father may have been right all along, that he was simply lazy. But publishers, as he told Bellow and Tarcov, had already contacted him seeking book manuscripts. Much as in Chicago or Madison, he quickly became the subject of local folklore in the circles he cared about most. The story circulated that the first time Rosenfeld came to the Greenwich Village Astor Place office of *Partisan Review* looking for Lionel Abel—

whom Bellow and Rosenfeld had befriended in Chicago—he was mistaken for an FBI agent and tossed out the door.[53]

It was then, in the early 1940s, that he was embraced as the "golden boy" of Irving Howe's memory. In 1944, he won the first *Partisan Review*–Dial Press novelette award for a Kafka-inspired novella "The Colony." With it came one thousand dollars. Rosenfeld's reviews were startlingly precocious, agnostic. He perfected—beginning with his first published essays, which appeared about a year or so after his move to New York—the ability to capture a reader's attention with a powerful, memorable opening sentence. True, his literary tastes could be surprising; he found most of what he read wanting but he had now learned how to be gently persuasive, not commandingly erudite. His pieces in *The Beacon* in the late 1930s had been strained performances, even a bit childish, but he now knew how to win trust, to take readers by the hand and skillfully guide, not push. In essay after essay, he revealed a breadth of erudition marked by an equal measure of generosity of spirit, a palpable excitement about literature and culture that showed, above all, a commitment to engage in serious, unencumbered intellectual exchange rather than to force acquiescence. Soon Rosenfeld captured the attention of some of New York's leading critics, and almost immediately after leaving NYU he savaged on the pages of *The New Republic* the work of his own teacher, the distinguished Marxist thinker Sidney Hook, then the leading anti-Stalinist socialist intellectual in the United States.[54] Savagery was much valued by Rosenfeld's new intellectual circle.

A great deal has been written about the New York intellectuals Rosenfeld fell in with on arrival in the city. Some, indeed, would embrace him for a time as the most likely candidate for the mantle of the next great American writer, someone who would produce a European-style American litera-

Isaac and Vasiliki Rosenfeld in 1947.
Photograph courtesy of Daniel Rosenfeld.

ture, philosophical and self-reflexive, and redeem American culture now that Europe was in decline. Much was seen as riding on the emergence of a master of fiction among the writers close to the *Partisan Review,* which saw itself as the epicenter of all that was new, meaningful, politically progressive, and culturally avant-garde. Other magazines didn't quite count: *Partisan Review* writers appeared, for example, in *The New Republic,* but mostly for the cash it paid and the attention it generated; its politics were seen as flaccid, insufficiently anti-Stalinist. *Commentary,* started in 1945, was respected, part of the intellectual stable, but a curious hybrid because of its sponsorship by the American Jewish Committee. *Partisan Review,* a child of battles within the Communist Party, split from the Party in 1936 and reconstituted itself as an independent journal the next year. It had only a few thousand subscribers, appeared on rough paper, and looked somewhat like a college publication. This minimalism meshed with pride of place—its sense of itself as the only credible place for the smartest to publish. No longer politically active, its editors retained their old, vaulted sense of their indispensability, their essential rightness. "They had been for some time more or less inactive politically," wrote Mary McCarthy, "and their materialism had hardened into a railing cynicism, yet they still retained from their Leninist days . . . a notion of themselves as a revolutionary elite."[55]

Partisan Review sought to disseminate some of the most crucial aspects of the political and aesthetic radicalism of the 1930s while shedding the scars of the dogmatic Left. To American readers it introduced Sartre, Orwell, and Silone, and helped resurrect the reputation of Henry James as a fictional master no less sophisticated than the Europeans. It consolidated a reading public for Kafka (it was among the very first English-language periodicals to publish him) and translated Isaac Babel. It relied on Trotsky as an important influence not so much for his politics but for his insistence that the best radical literature was interconnected with the avantgarde. Probably no less crucial was T. S. Eliot.

These intellectuals were, as Harold Rosenberg famously described them, a "herd of independent minds." They valued intellectual journalism and political reportage above all else but understood that their cultural preeminence was dependent on their producing the next great American novel. Fiction, they felt, was critical to consolidate their role as indispensable to American intellectual life and they hoped to produce an American Dostoevsky or Tolstoy. This was part of the grand plan, as devised by *Commentary* editor Elliot Cohen and *Partisan Review* editor Philip Rahv, for the Europeanization of America, their recasting of postwar intellectual life in a skeptical, anti-Communist, culturally radical vein. Fiction was the best vehicle for the widespread dissemination of their ideas. It was, on some level for both, of utilitarian, not intrinsic, value; hence, those most respected by Cohen, Rahv, and their followers were the preeminent critics of the age, intellectual synthesizers such as Edmund Wilson and Lionel Trilling. If writers of fiction were taken seriously in these circles, it was mostly because they could also write essays—in short, they could think as well as feel. Fiction writers in this stable—Bellow, Rosenfeld, Delmore Schwartz—felt, with justification, that their own contributions took backseat to literary and cultural criticism. Bellow recalled sitting in the *Partisan Review* office after the mail arrived and listening to Rahv inform William Phillips that nothing important had come in, "just fiction."[56]

Yet the dream was for a writer—at first it seemed it might well be Rosenfeld, then Bellow quickly came to the

fore—to emerge out of this milieu and capture the biggest literary prize of all. On the eve of the appearance of *The Adventures of Augie March,* Bellow's first, unabashedly American
fiction, "[t]here was the sense" among the intellectuals close
to *Partisan Review* and *Commentary,* wrote Norman Podhoretz, "in which the validity of a whole phase of American experience was felt to hang on the question of whether or not
[Bellow] would turn out to be a great novelist." Once Bellow
was anointed—with the publication of *The Adventures of
Augie March* in 1953 and the acclamation of him as a major,
widely read writer—New York intellectuals would savage him,
too. Bellow complained about it, and thin-skinned as he was,
his complaints weren't off-target. Critics in this circle wrote
devastating reviews of many of his books and seemed to want
him to stumble. (When Alfred Kazin in 1942 published his
lavishly intelligent study of American literature, *On Native
Grounds,* still another book from this camp that was enthusiastically embraced by a wide range of readers, they did much
the same to him; the worst review it received was in *Partisan
Review.*) Rosenfeld, alert to how his new friends had pitted
him against Bellow and how they pitted themselves against
quite nearly everyone else, summed up dinner parties at
Rahv's as evenings spent "throwing darts." The impact of this
ferocious competitiveness on the already amply rivalrous boyhood relationship between Bellow and Rosenfeld would continue to haunt both until Rosenfeld's death. It remained with
Bellow long after that.[57]

Why this circle was so eager for their own to succeed
and so unkind to any that did remains puzzling. They often
acted, wrote *Partisan Review* editor William Phillips, "as
though they were in a primitive struggle for survival." In his
memoir *A Partisan View,* he described a group "torn by personal and political differences—by vanity, temperament, and

Saul Bellow.
Photograph courtesy of Janis Bellow.

conviction . . . it was not known for its loyalties." They were, of course, all quite new to American life outside the dense neighborhoods of Jewish immigration. Few had gone to college, fewer still to elite universities, which continued to hold Jews at arm's length. No one better personified the group than Philip Rahv, the dominant figure at the magazine. Erudite, European-born, profoundly troubled, Rahv was brilliantly perceptive, capable of great enthusiasms and quick, devastating judgment. Rahv never managed to write a full-length book, but judged the books of others with the calculations of a stockbroker, and he maintained an emphatic, uncannily precise sense of who was on the rise and who was on the fall.[58] William Barrett, a philosopher and *Partisan Review* editor, described running into Rahv one afternoon in the late 1950s, and as they walked around Gramercy Park, Rahv "began ticking off one by one some of the people we had known and their initial hopes, ending always with the refrain, 'It wasn't in the cards.'"[59]

Mary McCarthy depicted Rahv in her 1949 novel *The Oasis*: "Facts of any kind, oddities, lore, local history intoxicated . . . this realist, whose own experience had been strangely narrow—a half-forgotten childhood in the Carpathian mountains, immigrations, city streets, the Movement, Bohemian women, the anti-Movement, downtown bars, argument, discussion, subways, newsstands, the office. This was all he knew of the world, the rest was hearsay. . . . Practical jokes were anathema to him; they belonged to an order of things which defied his power of anticipation, like children, birds, cows, water, snakes, lightning, Gentiles, and automobiles."[60]

These were self-made men, essentially self-taught, with their learning picked up in prodigious fits of reading at local public libraries, or during long, dull stints in the army.

They had little to fall back on, except for their willfulness, their hubris, their ambition. "One can only speculate about the forces that added a jungle morality to a sense of community," wrote Phillips.[61] Still, their achievements were considerable: they expanded the range of American literary culture, brought it closer to Europe, and helped introduce, or more widely circulate, American writers—Poe, Hawthorne, James, and a few others—who would remain emblems of a cerebral, self-reflective American literature.

Rosenfeld was enthusiastically celebrated at first, and then—by the late 1940s—he began to grate especially on Rahv, even though he remained quite productive through much of this period. Rosenfeld's much touted Jewish preoccupations probably contributed to the slippage; Rahv saw these as sentimental, a distraction from serious work. But, as time passed, a greater impediment was Rosenfeld's skeptical stance toward rationalism, his doubts, expressed openly and often, regarding the unassailability of scientific knowledge. (Rahv loathed anything irrational, more, it was said, than he hated Stalin.) Rosenfeld began scrutinizing rationalism critically as soon as he started writing for New York's magazines.[62] His exact attitude toward rationalism remains scattered, and much of what he wrote on the subject was characterized more by discomfort than by clarity. But this remained one of the most persistent themes in his writing life, and he would weave it into the core of *Passage from Home*. What it was that he, and his friends, saw as his preoccupation with metaphysics was built around a perhaps vague but much repeated belief of his that life—writing or sex or politics—without spiritual preoccupations would be bankrupt: "Comfort Saul, if you can, and bring him to peace with himself," Rosenfeld wrote to Tarcov in 1941, just as Bellow's first marriage was beginning to unravel. "Let him find comfort in himself, and not feel bad be-

cause he has failed but feel glad because he has good pur-
poses, love in his heart and a mission in life. Do I sound
wacky? It's very hard to explain what I mean without falling
into religious phraseology because religion has been the only
(practically the only—but, of course, there is poetry) discipline that has spoken of these matters, and maybe religion is
right. I will say to you and to Saul, and to everybody, believe in
God. That means believe, have faith in yourselves, love." He
then quoted a line from a short story he was working on, "Joe
the Janitor": "'Others find peace in sleep, but I find it exalta-
tion.' That's the simplest way I have of putting it. If it brings
across my meaning, paste it on Saul's forehead, paste it on
your own . . . I wish I could fill you and Saul with my state of
mind."[63]

These convictions meant for him that the "jungle
morality," the aggressiveness of the mean-spirited, if brilliant,
intellectual circle in which he was now a part, conflicted with
his core beliefs and these may well have sharpened as he became more familiar with this scene. Its hardness, its calcula-
tion, its unremitting unkindness—these pushed Rosenfeld
to define himself in opposition, and more and more he embraced categories (spirit, faith, transcendence) associated
with theology, not politics. He also insisted on openly exhibit-
ing these convictions, declaiming loudly the warmth and
goodness that he was certain must be at the center of any real,
lasting cultural transformation.

Hence his insistence on helping with odd chores, ex-
pending time and energy and precious daytime hours on ac-
climating newcomers to the city, lavishing attention on the
battered and the unhappy. It was this generosity of spirit combined with the belief that he was destined for literary greatness that so many found beguiling. This is why Rosenfeld was
anointed a "golden boy" by Howe, Kazin, and others who were

awed by his wedding of humanity and talent. Yet the same men who in the mid-1940s embraced him would a few years later—in no small measure because of many of the same qualities they first found so attractive in him—abandon, even shun, him.

In sketches written soon after his arrival in New York, Rosenfeld sought to capture his belief in (what he insisted on calling) spiritual values as embodied in the spare, but potentially rich, emotional lives of "little men." His protagonists were, as often as not, janitors; Rosenfeld had worked while in university as a janitor at Chicago's Billings Hospital, and believed, or at least wished to believe, that those who cleaned up after others, the anonymous drones of the working class, were the most susceptible to human empathy and transcendence. In these stories, he sought to emulate the Russian classicists—especially Gogol and Dostoevsky, both of whom he had devoured since childhood. These were stories of desperate men, eager for love, without the capacity to attract it; eager for sex because of their hunger not so much for sensation as for the connection it promised with human beings.

The first of these stories, unpublished until after Rosenfeld's death, was "Joe the Janitor." Joe is a "mild-looking man, a little below average height, with watery eyes and an ear for music." He dreams of women and his dreams are in Russian despite the fact that he doesn't know the language. He imagines sitting at day's end with his beloved Ninotchka, turning to her at dinner's end, admiring the sunset together, and "I, after looking at it, turned to her and said, 'Ninotchka, it is beautiful, it is a work of God!' 'Yes, it is very pretty,' she would say, 'But why do you always have to drag in God?'"[64]

Joe has finished college, has a few graduate credits under his belt, and works as a janitor. There is, of course, no

Ninotchka in his life. His coworkers mock him, he lives in a furnished room, he has suffered a breakdown, sometimes he talks to himself, and he dreams of young, naked girls, "clean, brimming with life. I clasped her to me, trying to enter into the stream of life and share her undying beauty." At a Tchaikovsky concert that he happens to hear on the campus where he works, he is alerted to the prospect of transcendence. He stares not with envy but with affection at couples on the grass, at the bald and middle-aged, at the young and supple, and he recognizes: "We were all one substance, one stuff, one soul." Going home, his bed feels perfect, his sheets cool, his solitude comforting. "It was good to give myself back to life, to precious, delicate life, knowing that I might always give myself, without fear, and with belief in my yearning."[65] Yearning, as Joe sees it, is made of much the same stuff as religious faith. Tchaikovsky offers him entry into knowledge inconceivable purely through reading. Rosenfeld here identifies a source of meaning beyond written truth, a source of beauty hidden from the view of most but accessible, at least potentially, to everyone, and perhaps all the more so to the miserable and outcast. There is in the story an overt didacticism that renders it clumsy as fiction, but all the more revealing of his convictions.

Rosenfeld used much the same material rather more successfully for a story that he placed in *The New Republic* in 1941, "My Landlady." Here too the protagonist is a janitor. He gives money to a poor stranger, a woman visiting a sick child at his hospital, then goes to her dingy apartment and leaves her with an unkind husband. The janitor returns home and flirts innocently with his landlady—"a stocky, middle-aged woman"—dancing to music she is playing. "Shoeless, her large, round bosom thrust forward." He stands and watches her, she smiles at him as she dances and continues to do so until her husband, astonished by the scene, walks in: "Then she bent down and began putting on her shoes. I looked into her husband's face . . . and I looked at his thin, spent figure; then I looked at my landlady, her dark face flushed and her eyes flashing . . . I sensed the embarrassment between them, but I was ready to leap for joy for the vision of goodness I had had."[66] Shame and ecstasy, simplicity and transcendence— these would, time and again, be the issues Rosenfeld circled around, that he sought to open up. In "My Landlady," much as in "Joe the Janitor," what most intrigued Rosenfeld was the prospect of exploring yearning, for him the only metaphysical preoccupation still possible.

By 1944, when he published "The Hand That Fed Me" in *Partisan Review,* Rosenfeld had moved closer to perfect- ing the voice of an underground man, a superfluous post-De- pression, postpolitical man, "bare, pared," and writing letters sent essentially into the abyss. (No other story of his is built around letters—the expository form in which he excelled— and this is among his best.) Its tone, as Ted Solotaroff de- scribes it, "combines a Jewish sensibility with the new exis- tentialist one," and what obsesses its narrator, Feigenbaum, is the tension between his aloneness, his freedom, and his fero- cious desire to escape both.[67]

"The Hand That Fed Me" is made up of letters written by Feigenbaum over the course of ten dreadful days. He sends them to Ellen, a girl from a Russian family who, we soon learn, had flirted with him three years earlier at a WPA office. She invites him home; he meets her family and brother, eats a Russian lunch, and never sees her again. His letters, written with mounting intensity, are ignored until she writes a casual note, a Christmas card. He examines it endlessly, turning it over again and again for hidden meaning.

He recalls the moment of their encounter with exquisite detail. He is waiting in line to report to a WPA clerk in a room packed with old, listless men. Just then, Ellen, pencil in her mouth, catches his eye and sticks her tongue out at him. "First the pencil, then the tongue. Ellen, Ellen!"[68]

Ellen lingers until he finishes at the office and then invites him to lunch ("Even now I can hardly believe that I should ever have received such gifts of kindness") and serves him borscht. He learns that she is Russian—all the more marvelous, packed with meaning since he, too, considers himself Russian. ("As a Jew, I am also a German, an Italian, a Frenchman, a Pole. I am all Europe—but a Russian, foremost.") Perhaps, he now speculates, they broke up because he is Jewish; or maybe it was because he reminds her of the WPA, and its humiliations. He writes to her again, explaining why he persists in humiliating himself by writing to her despite her spiteful, inexcusable silence: "I live in what I consider to be a state of exile." He seeks her out at her home and, though not permitted inside, declares his love for her: "And why do I love? Because you came to me. Because in the basement of the relief station you noticed me before I noticed you, and because your flirting was not in response to an act of mine, but an overture, an opening entirely of your own. For this, all my gratitude. Because, at a moment when you did not exist for me, I already existed for you. Isn't this reason enough?"[69]

In the story there remains more than a residue of politics, certainly in the narrator's fevered internationalism. Still, politics won't alter his misery; only human fraternity can do that. While he yearns for Ellen sexually, what this "superfluous man" of Rosenfeld's wants most is the promise of human communion the family lunch augurs. More than he wants sex, he seeks to eat at the family table, to share convivial conversation, to be embraced by people who simply want to be with him. It is the distance between his (pathetically modest) aspirations and their inconceivability that gives the story its poignancy. It resembles something of an extended Yiddish joke, and while Rosenfeld leaves his protagonist's humanity intact, this is because we see him as someone whose unhappiness is intractable.

All the heroes of Rosenfeld's first stories—antiheroes, of course—are loners, reclusive, obsessive readers marked by their furtive habits and poverty. But they manage to transcend their gray everyday lives or, at least, glimpse something brighter when they encounter music, or feel the prospect of love, or experience the beauty of raw, humble, decent folk. It's not rational argumentation, nor even political action, that will create the basis for transcendence, as Rosenfeld sees it, but random moments of goodness, of human decency.

Ironically, Rosenfeld wrote these grim stories at a time of great happiness. The fellowship at NYU had made him feel "less shadowy." He declared his love for New York, and for Vasiliki; he yearned to see himself reunited with Bellow, still in Chicago, and Tarcov, in Champaign. The womanizing he would soon fall into, especially once he moved to Greenwich Village, was still in the future; he seemed to relish his life with Vasiliki, and his friendships with Bellow and Tarcov remained fertile and pleasurable. By early October 1941, he told Tarcov he had finished half a novel that he planned to send to Simon and Schuster. "Some day," he wrote to Tarcov, "may all our voices thunder together. And I say it now. It is no mere accident that we are what we are—we have an identity as a group. Are you writing anything?" "The sweetness of this chocolate life," is how Bellow described this time in Rosenfeld's life. The intense joy of his daily life now spent with a woman whose physicality, whose capacity for sensual pleasure, continued to impress him deeply; his belief that his fiction was beginning to explore the interplay between thought and heart in new, innovative ways—these persuaded him that he was now, finally, pushing beyond the artistic and human boundaries that had so long absorbed him. His new friends in New York were aware of Rosenfeld's distrust of pure intellect. As David Bazelon wrote to Bellow at the time, "He is strong because he pays homage to desire and needs. His weakness, I think, is that he does this, and often too directly, too non-intellectually."[70]

The clash between intellect and emotion was then widely believed to be at the core of the conflict between liberalism and the Right and, indeed, at the forefront of contemporary politics and culture. On the European continent, the most alluring ideology by far was fascism, with its espousal of the preeminence of the intuitive and nonrational. Fascism had already ravaged Spain, captured Italy and Germany, and scored major victories elsewhere with reverberations such as Father Coughlin's lurid radio programs, broadcast from Michigan and close to home. Its political solutions, as Rosenfeld knew, were ludicrous, but its ability to speak directly to human yearnings, to address needs scanted by rationalism, had to be confronted if the political Right was to be challenged. Fascism, much like the Catholic Church, recognized —far better than did ideologies on the left, as Rosenfeld saw it—how passion, not mind, exerted the most persuasive power. Rosenfeld had long been convinced of the failure of logic: "His talent for abstraction displeased him," wrote Bellow. "He was afraid it indicated a poverty of his feelings, an emotional sterility."[71]

These would be themes at the heart of his novel, *Passage from Home*. Its heady adolescent protagonist is a mess of incoherent impulses, sexual and otherwise. Still, he begins to face, sporadically and painfully, some of the basic truths about life that leading liberal philosophers—like Rosenfeld's former NYU teacher Sidney Hook, whom he attacked in a 1943 essay—chose to ignore. The interplay in Rosenfeld's work between the themes of *Passage from Home* and his assault on Hook couldn't be clearer. Both insist that reason and insight are by no means identical; both disparage reliance on reason alone as deaf to life's deepest, and probably most inexplicable, mysteries. Rosenfeld's piece on Hook, which appeared in *The New Republic,* was a reply to the philosopher's *Partisan Review* article "The New Failure of Nerve" (part of a symposium with John Dewey and Ernst Nagel), which had examined the impact of contemporary loss of faith in science as revealed most potently in the spread of fascism. Hook saw the phenomenon as a byproduct of a "failure of nerve," of panic in the face of confusion. Irrationalism, as Hook viewed it, was dark, bad, and unsettling; it was embodied in political reaction, the cults of mysticism and obscurity, the flirtatious mythologies of quasi-fascism, and the doctrines of the Catholic Church. The presumption that there were alternatives to science, or rational thought, for those opposed to reaction was, simply, "intellectual and moral irresponsibility," argued Hook, one more way in which Hitler's blight could, in turn, infect his own foes. Hook's essay, according to Rosenfeld, was an attack on intuition, on the contemporary tendency to validate "every mode of experience" as authentic, and it insisted that the tendency to conflate visceral reaction with knowledge was precisely what allowed for "the ravings of an insane mind."[72]

Rosenfeld spoke in his retort of the attractions of the Right: "the motive for man's allegiance to the obscure as well

as the doctrine of obscurity itself." Science is emotionally impoverished, as is liberalism, and both must be made to confront the anxieties of life, the reasons for the failure of nerve.
Science must be liberated from its simple-minded empiricism
and become better aware that rational explanations will never
do away with irrationalism. It is fatuous to seek to simply wish
away anxiety, or fear, or lack of nerve; and disapproval in the
name of science or reason cannot do away with the fears at
the core of political irrationalism. The "intellectual panic" described by Hook is real enough, but its solution cannot be
found in dismissing the afflicted, who will otherwise never be
led back to (what Rosenfeld called) the "watershed of sanity."
Fear can lead to dreams of immortality, or God, but the same
impulses can be the seedbed of credible, essential political
transformation.[73]

It is insufficient to point out reaction's mistakes ("men
live primarily by their mistakes," observed Rosenfeld), and it
is irrelevant that the Church's teachings can be proven
wrong. What must be better understood are the impulses that
have drawn so many to disprovable ideas, and it is the desire
to know God that must be understood if humanity is to be
taken seriously by liberalism. Yearning may not lead to clarity,
but unless it is understood, rationalism will never compre-
hend the world: "There is a narrowness of doctrine in the official position of empiricism, which the more difficult emotions
betray into perplexity. Normally taking little into account of
esthetic, imaginative data, of the sources of poetry, art, and
playfulness, as well as of suffering, the official position fails
both in its assessment of the causes of the failure of nerve and
in its appeal to sensibility. . . . Somewhere it has missed the
richness, the variety, pleasure, tragedy, the sheer possibility of
experience. It has overlooked man's legitimate spiritual or-

phanage in attacking the false asylum of the Church. And it
has had its own failure of nerve—or better still, a failure of
verve."[74]

Rosenfeld described *Passage from Home* in much the
same way: "My own desire to acquire insight," not mere
knowledge, he wrote in a letter to Tarcov. He worked on the
plot on and off for three years, discarded much, but then
wrote the final version quickly, in 1944, prodded by his publisher, pressures for money, and hunger for fame beyond his
own circle of admirers. He admitted this openly in letters to
Tarcov, and acknowledged his fear of Bellow's response to
the manuscript while also desperately seeking his approval.
The two sometimes read their manuscripts aloud to one another—Bellow was at work on a brooding, existentialist novel
about identity and antisemitism, *The Victim*. Vasiliki and
Anita, Bellow's wife, later reported that often both would nod
off at these sessions—they worked full time to allow their
husbands to write—but rarely did the men notice. The birth
of Rosenfeld's daughter, Eleni, also called Nitza, in 1943, made
the pressures Rosenfeld felt that much greater but he was
convinced that he was now all the more alert to life's intuitive
pull, to how "the revealed man is revealed through the imagination." He scrutinized Eleni's responses to life with great
care in his journal, and promised himself that he wouldn't
smother her emotionally the way his father and aunts had
smothered him. Her birth made the writing of his coming-of-
age novel feel all the more urgent. In *Passage from Home* a
Chicago boy like him is on the verge of adolescence and the
beginning of quite nearly everything: sexuality, shame, knowledge of women and of his father, distaste for bourgeois pro-
priety. He wrote half of the book, some fifty thousand words,
between late June and early October 1944. By then he had already won his prize for the novella "The Colony." His reputa-

tion was growing, and much was expected of him: "There lives the Jewish Kafka," Delmore Schwartz recalled William Barrett telling him, in 1947, as they passed Rosenfeld's Barrow Street apartment in the Village.[75]

Rosenfeld claimed that he had already sketched out the beginnings of four novels. The first, "mostly imaginative," was *Passage from Home.* He told his relatives before it appeared that it was an *"oysgetrakhte mayse,"* a "made-up tale." The second was to be about his family; the third about the Division Street Movement ("our gang"); the fourth about God.[76]

An early version of *Passage from Home* was turned down by a New York publisher. "I was not depressed by the rejection of the novel, indications to the contrary," Rosenfeld wrote to Tarcov. "I was exhausted, just tired after a long siege of four o'clock nights and days spent thinking every word and page of it. . . . For several days I did nothing but tremble." He then announced in the letter as openly as he ever would his immense ambitions as a writer: "I want to write so that light spreads from my pages, and every thing I touch takes on reality. I know why people want immortality. You just haven't got time enough in this world, and the possibilities of human perfection and happiness are infinite . . . I find that there is destructive art and healing art. Destructive art, both in its creation and appreciation, tears the soul apart, injures and exhausts. Healing art brings peace and energy. My novel has been destructive, so far. But it has to be—only the last half is healing. To undertake to heal, restore, revitalize the world—our contemporaries are afraid of that."[77]

Rosenfeld summarized his work-in-progress for Tarcov: "My novel is not very much about myself—which is an accomplishment in itself. It's equally about old folks as well as adolescents. It traces a young man's breaking away from home—his going to live with a friend in a rooming house, and

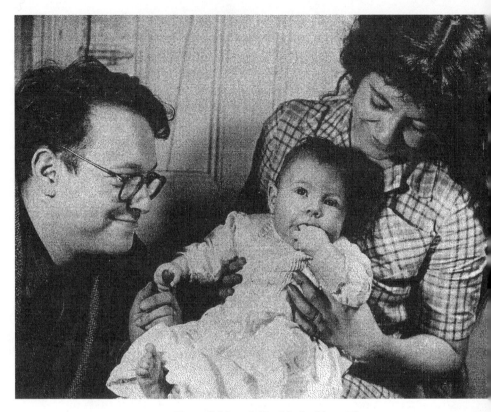

Isaac Rosenfeld with Vasiliki holding Eleni.
Photograph courtesy of Mark Shechner.

a love affair he has in which his closest friend makes a cuck-old out of him. That's only the shell; it is actually very compli-cated (a real plot)—all I can state briefly is the theme—the theme is: man's resources against humiliation." These re-mained the themes, more or less, as the manuscript evolved; perhaps a year later, the book now accepted by Dial but still only about half-finished was, he told Tarcov, about a "kid . . . and his love for two older members of his family. He becomes involved in their lives and the whole thing forms a chapter in his sexual, moral and intellectual autobiography. I am natu-rally pouring a lot of my present concerns into it—such as my desire to acquire insight, opposed to the feeling I have that purely human knowledge is insufficient."[78] Aspects of the story kept changing but at its core it stayed much the same— a tale of shame and its origins, of the inadequacy of mind as a reliable way of charting one's way through life, of the unbridgeable chasm separating insight and knowledge.

Like so many other writers, Rosenfeld published only one novel, a slim book that sold fewer copies than expected. *Passage from Home* was built around a medley of familiar themes: Jewish family, unease with a redoubtable European-born father, adolescent desperation and quest. Yet it was an uncompromising, deceptively simple book written in straightforward prose that spared none of its characters. It left its reader with no real, concrete answers to the dilemmas it posed, wholly internal ones about the origins of shame and self-knowledge. Originally Rosenfeld thought he would call it "Through a Glass, Darkly"; he placed the Corinthians 1:13 citation at the book's frontispiece: "When I was a child I spake as a child, I understood as a child: but when I became a man, I put away childish things. But we see through a glass, darkly."

None of the book's characters is flat, or predictable. The middle-class home of the narrator Bernard's family is unbearably dull, but also a place of integrity. The apartment of his aunt, Minna, looks at first like a haven, a splendid, bohemian enclave full of life and beauty, but by the book's end it is little more than a tense, passionless place. The book's most charming character, the hobo Willy, is listless, faithless. All of life's most self-evident choices are found to be compromised, including bourgeois respectability, rebellion, embrace of and flight from family. Rosenfeld admitted to Tarcov, just before finishing, that he had no idea how to bring the work to a close.[79]

Life's best moments, its rare, transcendent moments,

are located, as its protagonist Bernard finds them, in the most unlikely places. Reading the Bible, he hungers for direction and ponders the story of David and Bath-Sheba with its sexual allure and murderous seduction. His closest glimpse of spiritual transcendence is in the Hasidic synagogue of his grandfather, where he sees simple folk abandoning themselves to God-inspired joy. Passover is evoked lovingly in the book as an earthy festival, filled with wine, bawdy-sounding songs, and emotionally promiscuous conviviality: "Done with this we sang about a kid 'which my father bought for two zuzim'—a song in the manner of The House that Jack Built. It grows like a rolling snowball, picking up verses on its way, each devoted to a cat, a dog, a stick, fire, water, an ox, and a ritual slaughterer—until the angel of death comes and with the stroke of the fierce and tribal Jehovah sets things right by ending them. Then we sang the same song over again, with variations. . . . No wonder it took us forty years to cross the desert." The rituals of Judaism seem, as Bernard looks them over, to offer at their best an entry into the more elemental sources of pleasure, ties to family, connection to forces beyond oneself.[80]

In a novel devoted to escape from home, oddly the warmest moments of life are those with family. The book begins with a robust celebration of the primitive pleasure of family gatherings. Bernard, then fourteen years old, describes cousins, grandparents, aunts, and uncles sitting drinking tea, eating honey cake, children romping in a West Side apartment on a Sunday. This is, as he puts it, "the year when I first felt respect for human intelligence. I was fourteen, a precocious child, as sensitive as a burn." Bernard's interior life, the novel's true focus, is a swamp of mostly unidentifiable, hopelessly messy responses. It is crucial that these be understood precisely because of the uncertainty surrounding his father's emotions, a man stifled by hurts whose shame spills out endlessly and darkens all around him. His father broods, he embarrasses, he depletes; most of the others take in life more easily. Indeed, in sharp contrast to his father, most of the family is open, warm, and accessible: "We loved noise, loved the banging of doors, the sound of dishes in the kitchen, the swirling of water in the bathroom. But we also had a capacity for silence, a quiet feeling and respect for the family's presence. . . . The men, especially, had a great love for these silent, meditative hours in which, they felt, the whole heart of the family lay."[81]

Bernard finds himself at one point alone with his cousin Essie, a precocious girl well aware of his interest in her bosom, "pretty, in the way of the family, having to endure a privation of natural resources." Her makeup has been applied probably under the exacting instructions of her mother. She is round, she is young and flirtatious, and yet "already she had her mother's air of dispatch and authority; her eyes had the young girl's naïve liveliness, but in their depths you could see the clubwoman's stare."[82]

The story takes place during a single summer: repulsed by his father, Bernard gravitates toward Willy, a relative through marriage whom Bernard hopes to bring together with his aunt Minna, his dead mother's youngest sister. For reasons at first mysterious, Minna lives beyond the clutches of the family, and hers is a solitary life on the North Side in an apartment vastly different from the homes of everyone else: she has a fireplace (something wild and untamed that Bernard associates with gentiles), she has books, her living room has a blue lamp. She is thin (all of the other women in the family are round), she has jazz records, and, perhaps most important and alluring, she is cool, distant. When Bernard tries to kiss her, she pushes him away and then flirts with him; she offers him a glimpse of a sensual world beyond the clammy confines of home. He sits in her small living room and revels in its half darkness. The room contains "the world": "The low ceiling, sloping at the corners under the pitched roof, enclosed me in its friendly, personal angle. . . . Here dwelt that spirit which we barred from our lives, and in its freedom it was friendly, not raging, and not destructive, but liberal. This was its natural home."[83]

The book's emotional center is Minna, described with acuity as someone who parades a freedom she seems unable to enjoy, and who so seeks personal joy untainted by responsibility that she is left to live out her life pathetic and alone. For her, "even love was an intrusion. Another breathing her air would only pollute it." In her appearance, she reminds Bernard of a picture of his dead mother in his father's drawer. But while her face and perhaps her mannerisms resemble those of her sister she is but a pale version, without any trace of family devotion. Still, his belief in this resemblance is critical to his interest in her, one that because of his adolescence gives way to sexual impulses but is born of feelings still more basic. For all of Rosenfeld's presumption in how sexuality indelibly shapes life (and he would, by the late 1940s, become a highly vocal devotee of the sexual pioneer Wilhelm Reich), he also believed that sex was but one of a large medley of human reactions and by no means the most powerful. In *Passage from Home,* Bernard has no greater urge than his insatiable longing for his mother, and when he searches Chicago's streets for Minna he is really trying to locate someone else, irrevocably gone. Once he turns his attention firmly on Minna, what he finds instead of individualism is a clotted self-regard, a quality turned in on itself and emotionally fatal: "Proof of this was her nervous self-concern, as if she knew her restlessness needed watching, lest it do herself, or another, some injury. Sometimes her smile had a fine, cutting edge; she had made it a weapon for defending herself. More frequently, she wore a frown, taking care against its becoming permanent, a mar to beauty, by relaxing occasionally all expression from her face, pressing her hands to her cheeks and drawing her fingers across her forehead. She had no normal defenses—her skin was so delicate, white and clear as to seem permeable."[84]

In a dreadful scene at his father's birthday, Minna arrives uninvited and announces that the reason she fled the family was that Bernard's father had tried to seduce her after the death of Bernard's mother. Bernard leaves home to join her and finds that Willy has already moved in. Their relationship, forged right before Bernard's eyes, disintegrates quickly. Camped in the kitchen, Bernard now begins to see bohemia differently: the apartment is bug-infested, its self-absorbed adults pay him little attention, and life is aimless and lonely. He meets Minna's closest friend—the furtive, sadomasochistic owner of a local dive named Mason, to whom, it turns out, Minna is secretly married. Rosenfeld's description of Mason is a grim depiction of bohemia: He is "about twice as broad [as Minna], the outline of a sack of sand. . . . He was bareheaded and bald; his scalp curved down over his head and around a fringe of graying, reddish hair like a flap of a baseball. . . . The folds of his sweater sagged at his breast, suggesting loose flesh everywhere; his eyes were blinking and sliding, but whether in slyness or restlessness, pain, perhaps, I had not yet determined."[85]

Bohemia is, of course, made of many different parts and promises freedom inconceivable in bourgeois life. Certainly Bernard sees this, too. He carefully watches the very first steps in Willy's courtship of Minna and sees how their mutual bitterness, their frustrations, turn suddenly to sexual attraction:

They circled around the room, smiling, talking to each other. I could not hear them but, I thought, they must be saying nice things to each other, they seem happy. His face was wide with a grin, and he held one eye half-shut in the expression of competent wisdom. . . . It occurred to me that this, which was now before me, must be the very event I had so desperately wanted to bring about, and I tried to recall my feelings on the night soon after the Seder when I came to Minna with the still not fully conscious intention of bringing her together with Willy. I could not re-enter that earlier evening, the emotion of that time was gone, and I therefore had nothing with which to compare my present state. But I remembered the awkwardness which the grace and freedom of her life had brought out in me, the penalty I had paid for my happiness and for venturing to express it . . . I watched Minna kicking her feet about, sliding and whirling, her heels flying, and Willy moving with her, less skillfully, with none of her grace and ease and yet perfectly in rhythm, and I felt, though I did not know how to dance, that I should very much like to be in his place. [86]

All ends badly. Willy is humiliated, Bernard returns home more tolerant, but soon to be disappointed by his father once again. Bernard understands that he will forever feel the intrusive presence of shame. He wishes that life could be packed with moments just like those he saw in his grandfather's synagogue with "people . . . remaining fixed to the best moments of their lives." Most of life is different, and this recognition terrifies and fascinates him: "I felt myself on the verge of a shame and an enticement that I had never suspected to exist."[87] Returning home, he knows he can't recapture a childlike veneration of his father: "I felt myself suspended over the unmade declaration, the postponed scene of final understanding. . . . Now, I thought, it was too late."[88]

There is a claustrophobic feel to *Passage from Home*.

Rarely are we permitted beyond one of a cluster of rooms (Bernard's or Minna's, his father's or grandparents'), and never does one view things except from Bernard's own perspective. But this is also a source of the novel's strength: before Philip Roth's stories and novels, this was the most psychologically probing fictional analysis in English of the making of a Jewish intellectual. It is a study of what it feels like for a thinking person to come of age, to become aware of the grim cost of self-awareness: its erasure of childhood, the dismantling of the old-style Jewish patriarchy, the move into a life of freedom that is enticing and also, almost invariably, lonely. In the novel, Rosenfeld managed to capture something of the eagerness of an adolescent intelligence made up as much of flesh as of mind. He was right to feel that it was a triumph.

Still, the irresolution at the novel's end might also be read as an acknowledgment of Rosenfeld's inability to describe all that he had hoped to on the pages of his first fiction—to create, as he had hoped, a transcendent prose that captured something no less essential about life's mystery than did the religious literature of the past. That he failed in this respect ought not to surprise, but then again, his aspirations were vast: "Now," he wrote in the book's last sentence, "there would only be life as it came and the excuses one made to himself for accepting it." Was he lamenting Bernard's—and his own—sense of the limitations of life as well as art, concluding that the novel itself, no less than its protagonist's own future relationship with his father, would never quite meet one's prior expectations?[89]

Bellow recalled the book as a disappointment. He told this to Rosenfeld and it put great strain on their friendship. Rosenfeld felt that *Passage from Home* was unfairly ignored. He complained bitterly about how *A Tree Grows in Brooklyn,* published in 1943—a mediocre novel in his view—garnered such attention while his book languished. Some friends recalled their surprise that the book was less engrossing than they would have expected from such a brilliant storyteller. In an hour-long radio tribute broadcast in Chicago made by his admirers soon after his death, the novel was described as only a "minor success."[90] Still, many others around him celebrated *Passage from Home* as having captured more effectively than any other book their own first bouts with the world: with reading and sex and freedom. *Passage from Home* was praised as a work of painful, startling recognition. Some critics insisted, in fact, that what it achieved was previously thought to be too complex or elusive to be captured in literature. "I can think of no one now writing fiction in whose development I have greater confidence," declared Diana Trilling. For sociologist Daniel Bell—who wrote a long essay built around the novel—it was "the fullest articulation of . . . generational conflict between Jewish fathers and sons." Irving Howe admitted that "One tries without success to recall a novel written in the last several years as rich and warm, as pliant and amenable to a variety of meanings, as perceptive of the internal areas of existence."[91]

The discrepancy between Howe's retrospective recollections of the book as minor and his contemporaneous sense of it as momentous is instructive. Howe acknowledged years later that the work had a lasting impact on him. As a socialist agitator writing for sectarian publications and thinking about what he might want to do with his life, he read two of Rosenfeld's works at more or less the same moment. First he read Rosenfeld's long, discursive short story "The Party," a brilliant takeoff on the self-destructive margins of American Trotskyism in which Rosenfeld had long been involved and which still occupied much of Howe's time. (He was for a time editor of the movement's magazine, *Labor Action*.) The story quite nearly pushed him over the edge, recalled Howe, and felt "like a finger pressing secret wounds . . . [it] hurt to the point of rage."[92]

But *Passage from Home* left a far greater imprint, and Howe's review of it is full of wonder and gratitude: "Rosenfeld is primarily concerned . . . with the relationship between external act and internal meaning, their mediation, conflict, reconciliation, and ultimate gap. His theme is particularly and poignantly suitable to this purpose; for it involves the eternal pattern of conflict between father and son given concreteness in the immigrant Jewish family where it takes on especially sharp form."[93]

The section in the novel that moved Howe most is when Bernard returns home from his stay at Minna's: his father enters his room and stops beside his bookshelf. He looks at the books, staring at them as the clearest representation of the irretrievable distance between father and son. It was the father's money that bought the books, he wanted them purchased and wished for his son to be educated by them, but they provided the most visible proof of the gap between generations. "Nobody," wrote Howe, "who has been brought up in an immigrant Jewish family and experienced the helpless, tragic conflict between the father, who seeks in his son the fulfillment of his own unformed intellectuality, and the son for whom that very fulfillment becomes a brand of alienation . . . nobody, I say, who has known this can read this passage without feeling that here is true and acute perception, the very stuff of which literature is made." True, Howe admitted, the novel's plot is "slight," relying too heavily on psychological rumination, not description. Still, he insisted: "Its very difficulties and shortcomings are themselves indications of the dimensions of Rosenfeld's talent. The novel is not merely a promise, though it is certainly that; it is a fulfillment."[94]

A few months later Howe published yet another essay in *Commentary* on Rosenfeld's work, a long, uncharacteristically personal piece that was so intimate he later apologized for its content in his memoirs. He would never include the essay in anthologies of work that comprised quite nearly everything else he wrote and he knew well that it was for him an exercise in unrestraint, unfettered inspiration. As Howe wrote in his memoirs,

> In late 1946 I picked up a novel by Isaac Rosenfeld, *Passage from Home*. What drew me to it was probably the fact that its author had once been in our movement. I was curious about the terms of passage. The novel itself, sluggish as story but bright with intelligence, described the inner experience of a Jewish boy, "sensitive as a burn," breaking out of family and entering selfhood: from dark to dark. Upon me it made an overwhelming impression, no doubt because it touched elements of my own experience that I had willed to suppress.
>
> The day after finishing the novel, I sat down and wrote two thousand overwrought words about it. I wrote with hardly a thought of publication, pouring out unused feelings that the book had released, as if the circling return of this young writer to the days of his adolescence in an immigrant family made it legitimate for me to venture a smaller, less-considered return.[95]

Thus began Howe's career as a literary critic. He sent the article to *Commentary*, where it appeared in its entirety, it seems, under the title "The Lost Young Intellectual: A Marginal Man, Twice Alienated." The essay, contrary to Howe's retrospective assessment, is a beautifully crafted, perceptive

work that uses Rosenfeld's novel as a springboard for an astute, and acutely personal, analysis. He captures the main
thrust of Rosenfeld's novel and sums up the Jewish angst of
young men and women like himself and Rosenfeld:

> He suffers, of course, from the same sense of alienation that
> besets Jews as a group. Even when he succeeds in detaching
> himself fairly completely from Jewish life, he continues to
> exhibit all of the restless, agonizing rootlessness that is the
> Jew's birthmark. He feels in his flesh the brand of his peo-
> ple: echoes of the endless trek of a people that could never
> find a home ring in his ears; the tradition of a people always
> living on its wits and on the precipice of disaster, he finds
> fulfilled in his own life; the highly literary quality of his reli-
> gious tradition with its semantic nuances that produced a
> thinned-out verbal refinement, he finds characteristic of his
> own literary activity; and the traditional mock-hero of Jew-
> ish life, the luftmensch, of whom no one knows how he
> lives, our intellectual finds recreated in his own being. . . .
> He has inherited the agony of his people; its joy he knows
> only second-hand.[96]

Howe received soon afterward—"scrawled in pencil
on brown butcher paper"—a letter from Rosenfeld that
stated, simply, that Howe had "shown that the Marxist
method could be used with undogmatic flexibility in literary
criticism." (By now, Rosenfeld found those like Howe who
were still immersed in Marxist sectarianism more than a bit
suspect, certainly less than fully flexible intellectually.) Howe
wrote: "I was as bewildered as I was pleased. Not only was I
now pronounced a literary critic, but I even had a 'method.'"
The relationship between the two, quite close for a while,
started then with a somewhat paternal message from Rosenfeld regarding Howe's piece on fathers and sons, an indica-
tion to the younger writer that he was on the right track.[97]

Daniel Bell, then a sociologist at the University of Chicago, also wrote in response to *Passage from Home* a ruminative piece of some twenty pages in length; Bell's essay, published in the Labor Zionist magazine *Jewish Frontier,* inspired a long, pugnacious response from the young Zionist thinker Ben Halpern. Bell's essay is more discursive, less patently personal than Howe's, but it too insists on *Passage from Home* as a crucial text in understanding the present-day Jewish dilemma and, more so, contemporary alienation. The novel was, as he put it, "A Parable of Alienation." Starting with Arthur Koestler and Clifford Odets and leading up to Rosenfeld (now, with the release of the novel, "a major interpreter of the perceptions and emotions of the young Jewish intellectual"), Bell argued that in Jewish life all rests on family. In modernity, these foundations are increasingly tenuous, and hence a novel like Rosenfeld's explores the central dilemma of present-day Jewish existence. *Passage from Home* is all the more impressive, as Bell saw it, because it is a tale that is wholly internal and preoccupied with "the inner thread of meaning." At its heart is a retelling of the tale of the prodigal son who returns home to discover that there is no prospect for true homecoming. "The Jew," wrote Bell, "cannot go home. He can only live in alienation." Like Howe, Bell admired the novel's spareness, its insistence on examining not the external lives of immigrants and their offspring but "the quest of the young adolescent to find understanding. . . . He treats the young Jew as a sensitive person trying to face the implications of maturation. . . . Being a Jew . . . was a simple, undramatic, accepted fact of life. There was a knowledge of being different. But this was taken for granted."[98]

Diana Trilling concentrated in her uncharacteristically glowing review, in *The Nation,* on just this point. A critic who lacerated without pity books she didn't like (and she liked very few) and who loathed Jewish fiction especially, she noted at the very beginning of her review that the book stood out precisely because of Rosenfeld's ability "to use its Jewish background as a natural rather than forced human environment." It is a work of "profound universal meanings," not simply a "Jewish genre novel." Being human, Rosenfeld knew, is "sufficiently complicated," and, like Bell, Trilling admired the way in which being Jewish was handled by the author as "simply another facet" of life. Much of the review, in fact, is an attack on lesser novels of Jewish content, which for Trilling represent, at best, resistance or acceptance of a larger world outside Jewry or, at their worst, personal aggression. In her view, Jewish subjects don't seem to lend themselves in American culture to "heroic fiction of growth."[99]

But Rosenfeld, a writer with a "high order of . . . novelistic gift," understood how to examine the nascent adult within the child, the turbulence, permeability, and lack of stability that prevail as the child makes way for the adult. Trilling compared Rosenfeld's gift, and the novel's thematic structure, to Henry James, to *What Maisie Knew* and *The Pupil.* In its "preoccupation with the moral nature of the early educative process," *Passage from Home,* as she read it, probes with rare acuity what it means to take "life at so high a moral pitch."[100]

"There was," wrote Howe, "an air of yeshiva purity about Isaac that made one hope wildly for his future when I knew him in his few happy years after the war. Isaac made me feel the world was spacious."[101] Perhaps nowhere would Rosenfeld depict quite what he hoped life would be as he did in a letter to Tarcov, written while at work on *Passage from Home.* Rosenfeld described meeting Marc Chagall walking Madison Avenue with his new friend Alfred Kazin. When they spotted

Chagall, the two men stopped him and spoke for a few moments. Rosenfeld was mesmerized:

> Light really comes out of his eyes. There are few such people; but the many legends of saintliness are based on actualities. He is not as old as you would think him to be, much huskier and healthier. He has silver fillings in his teeth, and can't speak a word of English. We talked French, Russian, and Yiddish. He's the only man whose Russian I can understand and as for his Yiddish (I was stupid enough to ask him if he could speak the language) it's the kind that Moses spoke. We asked him to have a drink with us. . . . And he explained that it was Yom Kippur. I hung my head in shame . . . I resolved, and repeat it now, henceforth to fast. The whole meeting lasted 3 minutes. I went away raving. He is, believe me, one of the few really good and great open souls: the only man who could paint those pictures. A tzadek, one of the 39 [sic], for whose sake the world continues to exist; without a beard, but a patriarch from the day of his birth, a man who has conversed with Abraham.[102]

Rosenfeld dreamed, he yearned, and he wrote fiction about the prospect of a life infused with moments such as this one. There would be no need in such a world to deny one's urges, but these, too, would be transmuted into something pure, transcendent, larger than life itself. He sought, desperately, to describe moments in his fiction like the one he experienced at Kazin's side, but his descriptions became increasingly bare and abstract with the stories underlying them ever sparser as he reached deeper philosophically but farther from the actual world around him. He wanted to write about sensations at the core of life, those beyond immediate view, the magic in everyday reality. More and more, as the years passed, concrete reality disappeared in his prose: what remained were his increasingly abstruse reflections about it. He had fled the study of formal philosophy for fiction; he had sought to write a philosophical fiction concentrating his attention, at the outset, on the daily yearnings of average women and men, but these came to bore him as he became desperately aware.

His eminence dimmed quickly. He had amassed a rich pile of awards by the mid-1940s, but soon they stopped coming in. In 1944, he won his *Partisan Review*–Dial Press award on the basis of "The Colony." *Passage from Home* appeared in 1946. The next year, he won a Guggenheim Fellowship to expand "The Colony" into a novel. But the book was never finished, and neither were the others he started. Soon many of those around him grew impatient with his literary experimentation and uneasy with his descent into bohemia. They ceased to think of him as a "comer" and began to look elsewhere for the great American novelist. William Barrett noted Rosenfeld's fall from grace and heard Philip Rahv making disparaging remarks about him. Wallace Markfield recalled witnessing, in Rosenfeld's apartment, the Viking Press editor Monroe Engel rejecting the expanded, book-length version of "The Colony." Rosenfeld, he remembered, had a tough time fighting off his tears. And as if things weren't bad enough, it was Bellow, by 1947 the author of *The Victim* as well as *Dangling Man,* who was embraced by *Partisan Review.* Even before he garnered an enthusiastic international reading public for himself with the 1953 appearance of *The Adventures of Augie March,* he had become the new young novelist to watch. In the meantime, Rosenfeld wrote a great deal, eventually producing a small mountain of incomplete manuscripts that he knew to contain nuggets of the brilliance for which he was reaching but that he couldn't sustain.[103]

He wrote by day, sometimes in rooms shared by writers, artists, and musicians at the edge of the Village, on Hudson Street. There he became good friends with the anarchist novelist and theorist Paul Goodman, a wildly candid bisexual both charming and insufferably self-absorbed. Rosenfeld eventually spent large parts of his days avoiding his writing, chasing and sleeping with women, playing his flute, and hoping to avoid becoming a Village "character." He wasted long stretches of time: "He minded kids for graduate students. He cooked for the sick. He looked after people's dogs and cats . . . and shopped for old women," wrote Bellow of Zetland. He could be ridiculously candid: Ralph Ross, his new boss at NYU and chairman of its humanities program, recalled how surprised he was when at their first lunch together Rosenfeld announced that he and his wife had an open marriage. "He was not a great talker, but a lively and eccentric one," said William Phillips. Already now, in his mid-twenties, he would admit things to friends, even passing acquaintances, suddenly, in ways that unsettled even Village diehards. He spoke openly about his affairs, and also about Vasiliki's. He admitted how his feelings about his own children ran uncomfortably hot and cold. George was born four years after Eleni, in 1947. Their needs, he acknowledged, he all too frequently shunted aside, even overlooked, as he and Vasiliki fell into their bohemian routine. Sometimes night after night the Rosenfelds threw parties, and they became a well-known couple in the Village. Their apartment at 85 Barrow Street—where they had moved in 1943—acquired the standing of a legendary bohemian enclave. Eleni and George slept in a small bedroom within ready earshot of the hubbub that regularly enveloped the flat. By all accounts, both children hungered for the attention their father dispersed only sporadically, far more willingly to George than Eleni. Rosenfeld's friend Sidney Passin recalled witnessing a homecoming of Rosenfeld's when both children were quite small: they ran to greet him but Isaac embraced only George, not Eleni, and she looked crestfallen.

Already painfully shy as a little girl, in contrast to her charismatic, handsome brother, Eleni was easily overlooked. Rosenfeld worried often about whether he ought to have had children; he sometimes felt that he was better with those of others. "I have been cruel to George on several occasions when he's waked crying, in the middle of the night," he wrote in his journal. "I've been rough as I picked him up, have cursed, sworn, pinched him. I've been ashamed of myself and vowed never to do it again."[104]

Rosenfeld threw himself eagerly into his parties, which he took quite seriously. An especially popular pursuit of his was the "Dostoevsky game," where guests were invited to confess their most sordid acts. Animals filled the apartment—an ailing dog Smokey, a cat, snakes, and other reptiles. Once settled in the Village, Rosenfeld fell in with a circle of fast-living, fast-talking men. They called themselves "the boys," and often talked through the night, drank prodigiously, and picked up women. Seeking, perhaps, to resist these allures, the Rosenfelds moved to St. Albans, in Queens, in 1949, but they soon returned to the same Barrow Street building (now to the ground floor, where guests could climb into their parties from the window). Often all that the Rosenfelds provided at a party was a jug of cheap wine, besides warm, lavish conviviality, of course. Isaac would sometimes leave the living room for fifteen or twenty minutes in the middle of a party, and guests would hear the sound of typing in his tiny nearby study.[105] Wallace Markfield fictionalized an account:

> [Their] living room lighted by candle stubs in colored glass.
> A party of parties by its own right a being and a becoming.
> Where no drink went stale, yet none were seen drunk.
> Where no ashtray was out of reach. Where platters of marzipan cookies shone with a toytown brilliance and fresh bowls

of potato chips and salted peanuts were magically generated. Where all seemed of one kind and one heart, yet each
was what he himself wished to be: warmer, wiser, wittier,
calmer, surer, more playful, capable, energetic, potent, attractive, straightforward and sensible than in life. Where
scholars who had mastered Kant and Hegel, dour young poets and senior fellows in schools of letters recited dirty lim-
ericks, sang the ballads of Bessie Smith and imitated James
Cagney, Charles Laughton and Bette Davis. Where the
heavy-footed danced flamenco and the poorest of singers
sustained impossible notes.[106]

"Whom shall I imitate today?" Rosenfeld asked in a
journal entry of the late 1940s. These were his bleakest years
as a writer. His Kafkaesque experiments, a primary focus of
his in this period, are his least regarded works, despite the fact
that the first of these, "The Colony," seemed quite promising.
In his review of *Passage from Home*, Howe referred to "The
Colony" as a "remarkable novelette." Yet the manuscripts Rosenfeld now wrote seemed meandering and ponderous. (It is
curious that Rosenfeld sought so hard to imitate Kafka, who
had left him cold when he first read him.) Soon he more than
embraced Kafka, aiming to make himself into his prime, contemporary disciple. He would also seek to become a follower
of Reich, Gandhi, and Tolstoy while jealously protecting his
individuality. It was tough to combine his stubborn independence with discipleship, and his fictional characters now felt
wooden, more metaphors than descriptions of people, with
their terrain ever more foreign (set in India, or Russia, or a de-
personalized future), but always in much the same terrified,
unremittingly internal backdrop. Throughout this period his
journal contained, side by side, riffs on *Crime and Punishment*; analyses of friends, his wife, lovers, strangers on the

street; and, with great frequency, daydreams about sex. These daydreams intruded on his literary work: "I see two girls in the street," he wrote in his journal, "one a red head . . . obviously from Jersey, the other a lovely mulatto, whose skin of a shade no deeper than the Bronx, though her hair is coarse and stringy. I stare at them. They stare at me, all three of us curious. Their curiosity is aroused, probably, by the Chico Marx hat I wear; mine, by their paint and powder, golden hoop earrings, by their greasy, but very likely hot and genuine sex . . . I glance back and they are looking at me as they pass." He threw himself as fervently into these activities as he did into his writing, which, as often as not, he left unfinished and unpublished. Often he showed this work to friends—he would read it aloud at nighttime gatherings—and many recalled it with little short of reverence. As Kazin once put it—unkindly but accurately—in these years he inscribed "his signature on the air."[107]

Kazin—a dear friend of Rosenfeld's, a superb critic, and a man whose pettiness far outstripped that of nearly anyone in this clamped, envious circle—wrote Rosenfeld a letter, on May 22, 1946, that analyzed, with eerie accuracy, just what he failed to achieve in *Passage from Home* and what would prove to be his most exasperating challenge as a writer of fiction. The letter was meant to be an affectionate, even adoring document, and expresses much of the sense of self-identification that Howe and Bell both felt when reading *Passage from Home*. But the letter also reveals some pique at Diana Trilling's comparison of Rosenfeld with the vaulted Henry James —not named here but alluded to with palpable, hushed awe. Still, what Kazin pointed to in Rosenfeld's fiction as his tendency to "explain rather than to demonstrate" isn't off the mark. All the fiction that Rosenfeld would now write, and rewrite, year after excruciating year, and that he couldn't manage to place with publishers would be plagued by just the sort of problems highlighted in this letter. Kazin wrote:

> Reading your novel has been a tremendous double experience for me. To begin with, I forgot—somewhere around the 10th page—that I was reading a novel by my friend Isaac, forgot that I had read much of it before on yellow paper, while Smokey was gnawing at my instep. I was reading the work of a novelist, so mature and finished a novelist, that the suspension of my knowledge of you, or relations, was the most perfect tribute my admiration could pay you. I wanted, as the saying goes, only to know how it could come out.
>
> But if I forgot about you as a person while reading it, it reawoke me at every point to a deeper confrontation of myself. So much of the life, so many of the experiences, so rich and inflowing is the Jewish home flavor, that under handling it became, almost for the first time in my reading experience, the shaping by art of a life analogous to my own. But how strange and wonderful, I thought, that the sense of correspondence should be through a work of art! I mean, in the past it was the heroes of Joyce and Proust, and Mann and you know what else, with whom one could identify oneself. Now it was a hero, a true hero, and all the more lovable because he was in a setting so much like your own.
>
> Yes, Diana Trilling was right when she spoke of the tribute that must be paid to you because of the high moral pitch at which you have taken life. It is that quality that gives the book its extraordinary unity; the form is admirable, because the perception which molds it is integrated, stubborn, and wise.
>
> But from that, too, follows my criticism—my only criticism. It is that you allow your total realization, your eloquence, your ability to turn experiences into perception, to do your novelist's work for you at times. So much have your [*sic*] realized of yourself, and of your material, that one

could hardly ask you to abandon this analytical and sum-
mary gift. But at times you tend to ride with it; when it
should be only the q.e.d., it sometimes becomes the syllo-
gism. The tendency to explain rather than to demonstrate
comes, I suspect, from a fear that there won't be enough,
rather than from any fear that you can't demonstrate. You
are so skilled and so supple a novelist that I wonder why you
don't invent more, let your gift take you along. . . .

    With all this, however, the book seems to me a gem of
feeling, of understanding, and of true writing; and it points
to so much maturity in yourself, and so much order, that I'm
torn between envy, admiration, naches, and a kind of secret
pleasure that out of experiences which have brought so
much confusion, pain, and uncertainty, there should have
been made such an exquisite and proud work of art.

    Kazin signed the letter: "With love to you always, Al-
fred."[108]

    There is no evidence of Rosenfeld's response to Kazin.
No doubt he did react (the two men remained close friends in
the mid-1940s), and Rosenfeld's responses to criticisms were,
with rare exception, guarded and defensive. But since Kazin's
comments were couched so carefully, even evasively, and because his qualms about the novel were tucked away in a letter
that set out to praise it, Rosenfeld may not have been offended. Otherwise, it is unlikely that he would have saved it
among his papers. Rarely, it seems, did he save letters in a life
that was so chaotic, disorganized, and, once he left Vasiliki,
transient.

    At the core of Kazin's criticism was Rosenfeld's ten-
dency to rely too heavily on abstraction. Despite this stric-
ture—and, eventually, Rosenfeld would at times level much
the same criticism at himself—his work now slid more and
more often into just this sort of writing. It was inspired for

several years, in the late 1940s and early 1950s, by the psycho-analytic theories of Wilhelm Reich, themselves an influence unlikely to deepen his fictional ability to "explain rather than to demonstrate." Prodded by Reich's ideas, stultifying for him as a fiction writer but surprisingly fertile, it seems, for his essayistic work, Rosenfeld remained throughout these years—perhaps the most painful in his life—acutely self-aware of his achievements and failures and left behind a copiously detailed record, especially in his journal and in letters. These constitute a remarkable account of what it means to produce and not produce as a writer, how to calculate the cost of success and failure in artistic or intellectual life, how one melds life and work, and what it feels like not to succeed for long, painful stretches of time at either.

CHAPTER TWO

Terrors

What can be done? Isaac labors with the same difficulty. He has not reached the level where he can thunder. Like myself he is somewhere in the trees. In the trees one rustles. You know whence thunder comes.

—SAUL BELLOW, as quoted in Atlas, *Bellow*

WHEN ROSENFELD RESIGNED IN THE SPRING OF 1944 as assistant literary editor of *The New Republic* and gave up a weekly salary of fifty dollars to work on a barge as a "captain" (everyone who worked on these boats, he admitted, was called "captain"), it seemed to his friends a colorful decision, offbeat, unexpected, but not bizarre. Wartime conditions meant much was unpredictable (Rosenfeld was excused from service because of bad eyesight), and the group's engagement in left-wing politics, as well as the Depression, cut asunder their assumptions about conventional employment. Later, Rosenfeld would again hold down jobs at universities and magazines. In 1946, he would be appointed the first literary editor of *The New Leader* (it required that he work one day a week at a starting salary of fifteen dollars). He didn't spend much time on the barge, no more than a few months, but the brief stint would come to be seen by those close to him as emblematic of his descent into eccentricity.[1]

Bellow reacted positively to Rosenfeld's stint on the boat: "His color was generally poor, yellowish. . . . But during the war he was Captain Isaac, the entire crew of a barge in the New York harbor, he had good color. He read Shakespeare and Kierkegaard on the water and found it agreed with him to be in the open air. . . . It was impossible not to be attracted . . . by the good nature of his face, and I assume his ineptitude with ropes touched the hearts of the deckhands on the tugboats."[2]

"We have a sort of floating city here," Rosenfeld wrote. "There are about thirty boats tied in . . . off shore, a big rack runs down the length of the city, jutting out down stream, room for more boats. The inside barges have their heavy ropes out, fastened to the rack, and the others are tied on to their neighbors. We are not tied very neatly. Some of the ropes have slipped . . . [with] . . . sometimes a space of five feet between boats. But the general idea is that of a city, with streets, alleys, and thoroughfares, and rows of housing standing on their wooden lots."[3] Then he added: "There is no way of getting ashore while we're here. I wonder how many of the captains feel bored."[4]

Here was his opportunity finally to break free, to flout convention—including those that dictated that one never gave up a job at *The New Republic* to work on the harbor. His boat and twenty-five others were docked nightly on an inlet between Staten Island and the New Jersey coast. He had a "small cabin, containing bed, table, chair, and stove and several blankets. The boat rocks very quietly," he wrote to Oscar and Edith Tarcov. Now, like Melville, he would work on a boat and spend his days with strange, darkly different people. The first page of "A Barge Captain's Log," a 101-page handwritten manuscript, describes how a Jamaican, who first smiles at

Rosenfeld and then "solemnly raised his hand, showing the pink underside," all of a sudden breaks into a jig: "He threw his head up, waved his arm about, spun around a few times and went back to his cabin." Immediately Rosenfeld is reminded that this is an altogether different world—savage, uncerebral, elemental, and precisely what he had sought to discover beyond Chicago on the streets of Greenwich Village.[5]

The log has a promising beginning. Rosenfeld describes the citylike character of the floating armada that is now his daytime home, and he manages to transmute his new, peculiar surroundings into something that he can understand—an urban scene like, say, Chicago with its alleys and countless monotonous buildings. This was just the writing he had said he hoped to produce. Yet in the log's first entry, and immediately below the vivid description of the dancing Jamaican, Rosenfeld admits that already he is bored, edgy, and unable to concentrate on what is around him on the ship. He labors on for a while, and captures with precision the new terminology he encounters: "One never says bed, but bunk. It's line and not rope, and a very thick one. . . . One of the captains came up to me today and asked if I knew how to splice. I told him no, politely, remembering to call him 'cap.'"[6]

Lines continue to cause him much trouble. Once he is told that he must begin to splice and admits, again, that he does not know how, he encounters his first bout of disapproval: one of the veteran captains "deliberately spat on my deck, landing a brown splatter from his quid sparely on the guard rail . . . I practiced bowlines and square knots all day with a small piece of rope. It's not much of a line, so I suppose I may call it rope. Still don't have the hang of it." His companions soon begin to disappoint him; rarely susceptible to political dogmatism, Rosenfeld balks at the indifference to May Day on the boat, noting that although the doors of the other captains' quarters are shut, the men seem to be playing cards. He goes to sleep, gloomy, chilled, dulled.[7]

By May 3, the log takes on a quasi-fictional mode. Rosenfeld begins to act as if he is writing in the same ledger as did ship captains before him: "[Captain] Bertelsen favored pencil, and most of his work, I'm afraid, has been lost to us. He had a weary scrawl, and what little I can decipher of the black, smeared pages shows him to be a man of simple, declarative style, sparing in his words, not much given to detail, but with a wonderful eye for essentials." He imagines Bertelsen with a "pair of horn-rimmed glasses on his nose, the kind you buy in dime stores." And already Rosenfeld is suffocating at the purposelessness of his activities: "[W]e all lie here in our floating city and never move. I'm jealous of my predecessors. . . . They've been to Port A or Port B, have towed, have carried tires." His greatest fear is not waking in time to leave for the night and being "left here overnight, all alone. Being with myself I really dread most."[8]

Instead of seeking adventure, Rosenfeld persuades himself to luxuriate in the new experience of urinating without a toilet: "You pick a spot where the wind is right, select some object on the shore to aim at. . . . It's a way of getting back at civilization." He enjoys the sheer act of boarding the little tugboat for the barge at 8:30 or so, which is for him quite early: "the boat rocks and sways, but ever so gently. . . . The earth spins from west to east . . . but only water reminds you of it. Little wonder that Heraclitus took the river for the measure of reality." He begins to wrestle with how he might, finally, write about this experience, as he sticks "his head out and [opens] his eyes to the sight" of "sunlight, motion, water, sea spray, mists, a few gulls":

We cut across the bay. . . . An industrial landscape lies in front of us—smokestacks, train yards, oil refineries; behind us are the sun and the grimy wharves of the base; to the right are what the newspapers call the towers of Manhattan—I don't care for them much. The sun catches them through the morning mist and gives them a good coating of light and gold, which, in my opinion, they don't deserve. To the left is the ocean widening beyond the barriers and the steamers going out [to] . . . repeat the experiment which convinced Columbus that the earth is round. . . . It occurred to me this morning that . . . nothing in particular happened—that I might, at some indefinite future time look back precisely on this morning and remember every detail of it. Why shouldn't a day become in memory something indivisible like a single act? A gesture remembered from childhood—the first time, say, that I patted a girl's hair.[9]

He seeks, persistently, to capture the simple, meandering beauty of daily experience, and asks himself, "Can it be that I live only for happiness?"[10] He writes: "Today, it is so. The wind blows through my cabin, there is an odor of marine spice in the air, a scent of clover from the seas. . . . Due west of where we lie, a bridge rises. . . . Today it is clear and I can see finches hurtling through the air; the steel girders are like threads. . . . Today, everything is right."[11]

Soon enough, things sour. He befriends Louie, a genial barber who is also a captain, but Rosenfeld barely listens to Louie's questions, and his mind wanders when his new friend talks. Louie has "skin . . . mahogany red from the wind and sun," he plays Spanish guitar, and claims to be able to play Bach on it. He is "a good person . . . sweet and kind and genuinely so, without motive or hypocrisy." He is the sort of decent man about whom Rosenfeld had been writing since arriving in New York, and while Rosenfeld knows this, he is dulled by his presence. "I should like to tell him . . . that he is a remarkable person and that his character is of that (high moral) type which inspired writers to create their gentle peasants . . . their dreamy cab drivers and philosophical barbers." Somehow Chekhov and Gogol did far better with the same human material. "[H]is good, kindly, boring nature puts me to shame."[12]

Rosenfeld dwells on Louie, turning him into a father figure ("he is old enough to be my father") and also courting him, much as he might a woman. Rosenfeld places Louie "in the position of a woman, which disconcerts me"—what he means by this Rosenfeld leaves unsaid. Only when he reminds himself that Louie is a "character . . . a piece of literature, out of the pages of Steinbeck, or Saroyan" does he manage to revive an interest in him. Rosenfeld locks himself away in his cabin to read Chaucer; he records the cadences and appearances of fellow captains who are Filipinos or Norwegians ("vast . . . with eyes of a sort of cooked-out blue, like steamed clams"). Never does he grow accustomed to the "universal ignorance of the gang. They know very little apart from matters connected with sailing . . . very little sense of society beyond their immediate space." Once he brings a typewriter onboard, some ask him what it is; they've never seen anything quite like it and can't imagine why anyone would use it. He overhears one of them say, "All I ask is my daily bread and a piece of fried meat on Sundays."[13]

And then the text turns starkly surreal, indeed, into a sustained nightmare. Rosenfeld grows more and more disenchanted with the crew, their narrowness and pettiness. He seems drawn, uneasily—he can't help writing about this, he seems to do so obsessively—by the presence of male bodies stripped to the waist all around him, day after day. The first intimation of more than mild discomfort in the presence of near-naked men occurs in the presence of a captain he finds truly dreadful: "A spiteful man, but otherwise like any other captain, dressed as they all were, in rough, simple clothes, that conveyed an unassuming swagger, a fullness of experience which was childlike, rather than full grown in so far as it attached itself to so little that was really meaningful in life." The man curses rats, he swears at seagulls; Rosenfeld dubs him the "rat-hater." His diatribe about seagulls is, Rosenfeld is convinced, in fact a veiled monologue about Jews. As Rosenfeld waits for the tugboat one day, "leaning against the cabin, port side, near the stern, watching a fair day develop over the bay," he overhears the voice of the rat-hater: "The lousy Jews, the goddamn f—— Jews."[14]

Rosenfeld walks over to the group, stares at the "anti-Semite," and spits over the side of the boat as he glares at him. People around pretend not to see what is happening. "I was *aufgeregt* [distressed] all morning," Rosenfeld writes—this is his first use of Yiddish in the text. He throws himself into his work, sweeps the whole length of the deck, trembling, trying to "burn away" his hostility. He recognizes that all along he has expected this sort of thing to occur: "my fear and expectation were certainly among the things that were making me so uneasy."[15]

He talks about the episode with the other Jewish captains (there are five of them), including one barely articulate man, a "furious" card player: "as he plays he shouts, swears, spits, slaps his cards down and groans and exults with his losses and winnings." Rosenfeld begins to recognize that whatever happiness he has felt onboard, his keen desire to live "for my happiness alone" is rendered cheap by the terrible fact that "millions of people have been slaughtered in this war. . . . Your own people have been marked for doom. And you are standing by. You who live only for your happiness—what have you to show for it!"[16]

And then, on June 17, he records a "strange sight":

One of our captains, stripped to the waist and his legs bare,
in shorts—his whole body tattooed like a savage's. I boarded
his barge, on some pretext, to get a better look at his decora-
tion. I was shocked to recognize him as the rat-hater, the enemy of seagulls.

Not a clear inch of skin anywhere on his body. His
arms, beginning with the wrists, his shoulders, his back, all
of his relatively hairless chest and legs, are covered with serpents, dragons, anchors, crosses, beasts pierced by arrows,
naked women, initials, names of cities, dates, sailing vessels,
flowers—all thrown together and interlaced with blue-green
and red hues. An air of surly indolence about him as he sat
in a deck chair, his legs crossed, the sun glinting in his
glasses, his eyes shut. He opened his eyes, looked at me,
seemed to remember me, and shut his eyes again.[17]

The rat-hater is now difficult to avoid. On hot days,
Rosenfeld can't stop watching him, "naked in his finery"; he
waits for the other man to show his true colors. "My suspicion
of him grows. I know what he meant by seagull." And then, on
July 8, there is the inevitable explosion: An elderly captain is
struggling with his rope; he loses control of it while the "seagull hater"—Rosenfeld learns that his name is Rudolph—
watches him, contemptuously, and blurts out, "Look at that
fat Jew up there. Scared of his life."[18]

"He directed this remark at no one in particular; it was
meant for the man at his side, for the fellow sitting opposite
him, perhaps also for me." No one says anything and Rudolph
goes on puffing at his pipe. Rosenfeld realizes the moment
has arrived: "I walked over to him and shouted, 'You shut up,
you son of a bitch!' . . . I spat . . . and walked off to the other
end of the boat. I was churning with rage, I was biting my lips,

and my hands, clenched into fists, were trembling and it was impossible for me to calm myself." As soon as the day ends, Rosenfeld follows him, grabs hold of him, drags him through the gate outside the dock. "His muscles flexed, solid and hard against my hand. I dug my fingers into his arm." Rosenfeld refuses to relent, holding onto the man. He asks whether he has "any more cracks you'd like to make?" It is only now that he realizes Rudolph is "elderly"—"in his middle fifties and somewhat shorter than myself." Rosenfeld still wants to hit him, but realizes that without further provocation he can't. He shouts, longing to "punch him . . . at the same time fearing to do so." A crowd forms, but still the antisemite says nothing. Rosenfeld continues to follow him, to hound him. Rudolph insists that his only objection to the old man who couldn't handle the rope is that he is too rich, that he doesn't need the job. There are "lots of Jews like that," he says. "Rich bastards that grab up everything. Now that's a fact. You ain't gonna deny a fact."[19]

Rosenfeld tries to provoke a fight; he even tries pushing Rudolph but the other man eludes him and responds by offering to buy Rosenfeld a beer. They enter a dirty waterfront bar, sit amid captains who witnessed their fight and who are puzzled by Rosenfeld's presence. Little by little, the room empties and they are left alone. "Rudolph orders me to get him another beer. I told him he could damn well get his own." Once again, the two start arguing. Rosenfeld feels that his opportunity to get back at Rudolph is slipping away; he still wants to hit him, to smash him with a beer mug. Rudolph figures that he won the battle; "the longer I remained stuck impotently at his side, unable to revenge myself, the deeper his insult sank in. I felt as if I were paralyzed in a dream, longing to strike out at him, but unable to move." Rudolph gets up to leave, says his goodbyes with exaggerated courtesy. Rosenfeld tries to block his exit; he follows Rudolph into the street, pushing and shouting. Somehow, Rosenfeld follows him to his apartment and spots the name Rudolph Kramer on the mailbox. The apartment is no more than a small room, "lit by a single bulb which was shaded by a paper bag." Clothes are scattered about the room, it is very hot, and both men are perspiring. Rudolph seems to fear that Rosenfeld has a weapon and he tells the intruder: "Come over here! Sit down on the bed!"[20]

The text now feels even more like a confounding, disjointed dream. Rudolph's response to Rosenfeld's presence in his apartment is: "You can take off your hat now." Rosenfeld then writes, "I saw my reflection in the mirror above the dresser as I spoke, seeing what I must look like to him. I wondered if I shouldn't after all be capable of fulfilling the part he had assigned to me." Rosenfeld reassures him that he doesn't mean to kill him. Hearing this, Rudolph grows calmer, his confidence restored. "He settled back on the bed, more comfortably, leaning his head against the wall, and crossing his legs. There were the serpentine tattoos once more, encircling his ankles."[21]

Rosenfeld says that he understood that Rudolph feared he had a gun. "But we [Jews] don't carry guns," he explains. He wants nothing from him except an apology, and he declares that Rudolph has blood on his hands: "Jewish blood! The blood of five million Jews in Europe. The slaughter that's going on right now. . . . Doesn't that mean anything to you? Can you stand here and see innocent human beings cut down in cold blood? In gas chambers? With live steam turned on their naked bodies? Doesn't it mean a thing! The screams? The mothers begging to leave their children spared? The children begging. . . . Doesn't it? Do you mean you can picture it and you still don't care? You can still stand there with that filthy grin on your face?"[22]

The manuscript, a fragment of what was intended to be a longer work (Rosenfeld was still picking at it, listlessly, five years later) ends with the following observation: "It was late when I came home. I sat down in the chair at the window in my dark room, still as in a dream, paralyzed, unable to cry out, still suffering the unappeased longing to hit out madly, to strike and maim and release myself." He crossed out: "in the ecstasy of violence (I sat at the window in unfulfilled longing)."

Then, "Suddenly, a light flashed on in the window across the court. I saw a naked girl run in tip-toe to the refrigerator and took [sic] out a plate of food. I knew that her lover was with her and that she had come out of bed, hungry to refresh herself. The window went dark again, but for a long time I could see her naked body going swiftly out of the room and on its errand of love and peace."[23]

Rosenfeld had sought to record, in detail, the lives of simple people in rare moments of rapture, much like those people he had written about since coming to New York. Meeting them, spending days with them, had flattened him; he ceased to see them as truly, if obscurely, intriguing. Rather, he felt shamed at the boredom he experienced in their company. He couldn't manage, hard as he tried, to make them into something more than what he saw.

He hoped, perhaps, to use the log as a springboard to a work of fiction. He leaned on *Moby-Dick* and there are repeated allusions to it in his text. Rosenfeld had kept a journal on and off since adolescence, but this resembled none of them—his journals were filled with jottings, random observations of his moods, descriptions of his wife and children, what he read. The narrator of "A Barge Captain's Log" expresses much of the intense, aimless desire for fulfillment that characterizes fictional figures like Joe the Janitor. The dark room where he sits at the end, musing about his time on the bed with Rudolph and staring, with hope, at the naked girl across the courtyard isn't the place on Barrow Street. It isn't loud, packed with children, full of friends at night. It was conjured out of Rosenfeld's imagination, out of his nighttime horrors, as, it would seem, was his jostling with the naked Rudolph, who sought to make Rosenfeld into a subservient at the bar, into someone who fetched his drinks and with whom he fell into bed in that wretched apartment.

Much of what is recorded in this log is Rosenfeld's struggle, nowhere articulated more clearly, to draw on day-to-day experience, to take the lives around him seriously and turn them into the basis for his writing. He wrestled with his weakness for "metaphysics" (as both he and Bellow called it), his inability to concentrate on the everyday world. He was keenly interested in the people around him, and while he projected just this impression, he admitted in "A Barge Captain's Log" that it was often a facade, that his mind turned so dulled that he had no idea what Louie was saying to him.

But why Rudolph Kramer?

It is certainly possible that something akin to the incident actually did occur. There may well have been an anti-semite on the boat, and perhaps Rudolph was his name. In the text, Rosenfeld credited the man with stock notions about Jews: their mendacity, their control of Hollywood, their selfishness, and their debilitating, ridiculous fears.

Still, the likelihood that Rosenfeld stalked this man, followed him into a bar, into his apartment, and then into his bed seems preposterous. Never in his journal—where he speculated, often meticulously, on his own responses to the lives of others around him, on the near suicides of friends, on other matters of potential embarrassment, even his homosexual impulses—did he allude to this incident, or to anything similar. It seems certain that this part of the manuscript was a fiction. What had started as a log, as a realistic, factual document, had veered off at some point and become a horrible, haunting fiction.

Rosenfeld's first glimpse of Rudolph, of his savagelike body, evokes the opening of *Moby-Dick*, where the narrator, Ishmael, ends up in bed with a tattooed savage. But why did Rosenfeld bring himself into Rudolph's room, and then into his bed? Why did he speak afterward of his need for "release" and "unappeased longing," and why were these feelings sated, somewhat, by the sight of a naked woman feeding herself and then returning to her lover?

He would write often, with great discomfort, in his journal about homoerotic responses. He wrote there about "fairies" he encountered—waiters, and others, whom he disparaged—and then, as often as not, admitted shame and contrition. He had close friends who had sex with men while living as heterosexuals: Paul Goodman, for example, and James Baldwin. (It is unclear whether Baldwin spoke with Rosenfeld about his homosexuality, but Goodman talked with nearly everyone about nearly everything he did.) In the last year of his life in Chicago, while working at the university, Rosenfeld also became good friends with Allan Bloom, a closeted, then-married homosexual. Rosenfeld wrote in his journal that his homosexual fears were sated, temporarily, whenever he slept with a woman other than Vasiliki. (Having sex with Vasiliki helped somewhat.)[24] Perhaps this is why he reassured himself by watching the young woman walk in the dark between bouts of love. He would frequently ask himself whether his obsessive need for other women might have been fueled by a desire to cast aside unwelcome, unruly passions. Never did he pose the question more emphatically than in "A Barge Captain's Log."

He never managed to finish the log nor did he mention it in his journal. Writing to Tarcov soon after he had left his work on the ship, he noted that there are "3 things I'll want to do at once—more on India, something on the barge-captaining and something on pregnancy, childbirth, parenthood, life and death." Little more was said about the barge manuscript. Other unfinished texts he mulled over or criticized. He dwelt on these failures and had trouble pushing them out of his mind. Yet "A Barge Captain's Log" he rarely mentioned, giving the impression that its mere existence was for him a source of uneasiness.[25]

The most explicit terrors at the heart of this manuscript are those of the war, in particular, the mass murder of Europe's Jews. Most of the intellectuals close to Rosenfeld were at the time unable to speak directly about the Jewish catastrophe that they later acknowledged as having had a profound but uncertain influence on them. Their fear, or inability to air sentiments that seemed too insular or the product of special pleading, their abiding universalism that itself was, in some measure, an expression of a discomfort that their circle was overwhelmingly Jewish (Edmund Wilson called *Partisan Review* the Partisansky Review), stopped them from speaking candidly about even the most basic details of the destruction of European Jewry.[26] In her novel *The Oasis*, Mary McCarthy summed up the coddled response to his Jewish background of a character modeled on the *Partisan Review*'s Philip Rahv:

> A kind of helplessness came over him when he became conscious of his Jewishness, a thing that seemed to reduce him therefore to a curious dependency on the given. He was not

a defiant Jew or even a rebellious one. At such moments, he felt himself to be a mere mass of protoplasmic jelly, deposited by the genes of his parents, which could only quiver feebly in response to a stimulus that society sent through him like an electric current.[27]

For Rosenfeld, terror remained the most sustained interest of both his fictional and essayistic writing, and an inescapable feature of his thinking about such horror—and, indeed, contemporary culture as a whole—was murder of Europe's Jews. Repeatedly, he insisted that it was modernity's central experience. Others close to him—indeed, nearly all of those now seen as leading figures in the New York Jewish intellectual milieu—felt an emphasis on Jewish catastrophe could diminish them as actors in the larger drama of postwar life. Rosenfeld refused to take seriously that such a choice must be made. He praised screenwriter Ben Hecht, in 1944, for his passionate *Guide for the Bedeviled,* in which Hecht assailed all Germans (this Rosenfeld deplored) but also Jews—especially the powerful Jews he knew in Hollywood—for their indifference to Jewish suffering: "Ben Hecht has done well in picturing the anti-Semitic underworld of goons, loons, and shady Napoleons and in assailing the Jews who reject Jewishness," he wrote in a *New Republic* review. Rosenfeld sought to write novels that directly confronted wartime horrors, including a book-length manuscript, "Mother Russia," set in a Stalinist regime. In his view, terror left most numbed, or complicit, including those who sought to oppose it; terror afflicted even its fiercest opponents with hopeless feelings of compromise, guilt, and remorse. The most courageous are those rare souls—this would emerge as one of his most persistent themes—able to stay their doubts, to harness their neuroses and their damaged souls, to create some basic, credible political good. The power to achieve this begins with an awareness of the essential ugliness of one's own instinctual responses.[28]

In his writings, such themes would increasingly be wedded to what would become a long-standing preoccupation with Wilhelm Reich, the controversial, errant Freudian who rose to great, if short-lived, prominence in the 1940s. More and more, Rosenfeld spoke of the necessity of "hegemony" over one's instincts, the necessity of achieving this skill as a prerequisite to political or social change. According to Reich, "character armor" stopped most people from realizing their potential "full genitality," which was achieved through an unblocking of free, unstifled sex. "Orgone energy," as Reich called it, could be harnessed quite literally in a box, an accumulator known as an orgone box, a metal enclosure whose basic components, strictly dictated by Reich, were layered rock and steel wool. Reich's pseudoscience, eventual mounting megalomania and insanity, and the quackery associated with the orgone boxes he promoted and that Rosenfeld and others embraced, have made Reich's teachings seem patently ridiculous. This box came to be the prime prop in stories of Rosenfeld's decline. Kazin wrote of him looking lonely in there, "as if he were waiting in his telephone booth for a call that was not coming through."[29]

Years later, James Baldwin provided an especially cogent assessment of the Reichian craze of the 1940s, which he saw as a credible response to the confounding nature of war. Reich, as Baldwin explained, captured the imagination of many on the American Left in the immediate wake of the Second World War with his insistence that he had discovered in erotic repression the psychosexual origins of fascism, and with his prescription in the form of a box he had designed to neutralize the toxicity of its users. In this context, Reichianism offered answers about humanity and its prospects for re-

demption. Baldwin wrote in his essay "The New Lost Generation":

> It was a time of the most terrifying personal anarchy. If one
> gave a party, it was virtually certain that someone, quite pos-
> sibly oneself, would have a crying jag or have to be re-
> strained from murder or suicide. It was a time of experimen-
> tation, with sex, with marijuana, with minor infringements
> of the law. . . . It seems to me that life was beginning to tell
> us who we were, and what life was—news no one has ever
> wanted to hear: and we fought back by clinging to our vision
> of ourselves as innocent, of love perhaps imperfect but reci-
> procal and enduring. And we did not know that the price of
> this was experience. We had been raised to believe in formu-
> las.
>   In retrospect, the discovery of the orgasm—or,
> rather, of the orgone box—seems the least mad of the for-
> mulas that came to hand. It seemed to me . . . that people
> turned from the idea of the world being made better through
> politics to the idea of the world being made better through
> psychic and sexual health like sinners coming down the aisle
> at a revival meeting. And I doubted that their conversion was
> any more to be trusted than that. The converts, indeed,
> moved in a certain euphoric aura of well-being, which would
> not last. . . . There are no formulas for the improvement of
> the private, or any other, life—certainly not the formula of
> more and better orgasms. (Who decides?) The people I had
> been raised among had orgasms all the time, and still
> chopped each other with razors on Saturday nights.[30]

As Reich saw it, liberalism's upbeat understanding of
human nature was superficial, and fascism (which he had
seen up close in both Vienna and Berlin) mobilized more elemental human drives such as sadism, envy, and greed. He
preached a return to the most basic traits, a quasi-biological
wisdom unleashed by sexual freedom without neuroses, or

taboos, and without the consequent social and political per-
versions that destroyed Europe. Reich taught a body of essential truth that preceded, as he insisted, the insights of psy-
chotherapy: "Go back to the unspoiled protoplasm."

By the time Rosenfeld discovered him, Reich espoused
an unencumbered self-expression with the aid of a science
in which the achievement of total orgasm was the key to
personal and societal health.[31] Both Bellow and Rosenfeld
sought out Reichian therapists; Rosenfeld's therapist was
Richard Singer, who had an office on the East Side of Manhattan. Chicago friend Sidney Passin built the orgone box for
them both. (Devotees were supposed to purchase them from
Reich's followers, but for the sake of economy Bellow and
Rosenfeld had theirs built for the cost of a few dollars each.)
Zetland's therapist, as described by Bellow in "Charm and
Death," disgraces him, compels him to relive childhood miseries, to scream, to kick; he calls him a pig, insists that he sim-
ulate copulation, and Zetland leaves with bruises. The view of
Rosenfeld in the manuscript is a pathetic one—he is aimless;
he is in the grip of a relationship with a doctor whose expertise, perhaps hold on reality, seems shaky; but he can't move
beyond childhood terrors more real to him than his day-to-day
life. Zetland's writing life feels permanently on hold. Bellow
might have felt this to be too dour a description of Rosenfeld
to allow himself to publish it; perhaps this explains why he put
most of it aside.[32]

The most disturbing portraits of Rosenfeld are those
that deal with this long, fevered bout with Reichianism.
Reich's teachings had, speculated Bellow, an especially powerful impact on Rosenfeld since he felt that "he was haunted
. . . by an obscure sense of physical difficulty or deficiency, a
biological torment or disagreement with his own flesh."[33]
Bellow tended to shrug off his own, lengthy involvement with

Reich, saying that he joined in only to stay in touch with his friend. This distancing from Reichian enthusiasms is something that Rosenfeld never sought, and in the end, he appeared to have been something of a solitary devotee of Reich. By no means was this the case. Perhaps he was a more persistent and spirited follower than Bellow and others close to him, but many of them were deeply involved in Reich's ideas, too. Still, the stories about Rosenfeld's fixation stuck fast:

William Phillips remembered seeing at Rosenfeld's house in the St. Albans section of Queens, where the family lived in 1949 and 1950 until moving back to Barrow Street, "a little pastoral orgone box to vitalize his vegetable garden. [Vasiliki and Isaac] had the usual suburban tomatoes, peppers, string beans, peas, and lettuce, but kept the seeds in the orgone box before planting them, and he was sure that the orgone rays stimulated the growth of the vegetables."[34]

According to the recollections of the psychologist Laura Perls, cofounder with her husband, Frederick, of Gestalt therapy: "[Rosenfeld] was forever on the look-out for gadgets and devices to improve his powers of reasoning and phantasy, to support what could stand stubbornly enough on its own feet and flutter so amusingly, soar so amazingly on its own wings. He would squeeze himself into an orgone box to be irradiated by mysterious currents with intensified vitality and powers of concentration, and we could perhaps prove to him for one relaxing moment, but never convince him in the long run, that he could perform the miracle entirely on his own, without external devices."[35]

Bellow remembered how Rosenfeld, influenced by Reichian notions of sexuality, would urge his son, George, then four or five, to touch the vaginas of little girls with whom he played in Washington Square Park. Bellow recalled walking with them to the park and hearing Rosenfeld urge George to engage in free, sexual experimentation. In a letter to James Atlas, George confirmed Bellow's description of the scene: "[Bellow] added the story about being at Washington Sq. Park with Isaac and me. And Isaac encouraged me to play with the little girls in the sand box and that it was ok to touch them, that it was good. That he'd encourage me to put my hands down their panties. I asked Saul [Bellow] what the mothers did and he said they didn't know that was going on."[36]

By the late 1940s, Rosenfeld's interest in Reich had reached its greatest pitch. What drew him to Reich is clear—its (wacky) scientism, its unorthodoxy, its uneasy but emphatic connection to the political Left, its promise to crack the mystery of sexual desire. Its teachings were, as Baldwin affirmed, widely embraced at the time by those in Rosenfeld's circle. Lionel Abel recalled sitting at a party in New York sometime in the late 1940s or early 1950s when the woman next to him declared, suddenly: "This is orgone weather." What puzzled those close to Rosenfeld was why he stuck with Reich so long, and so passionately.[37] Rosenfeld justified his allegiance, insisting that Reich's ideas provided him with access to mysteries otherwise believed to be the sole province of faith. As Solotaroff astutely put it, Reich sharpened for Rosenfeld "one's instinctual life, to educate . . . feelings . . . to struggle against the pettiness and defensiveness and prevarications of the ego for the larger claims and possibilities of existence."[38] Rosenfeld's journal is packed with Reichian speculation. He mused on the impact of orgone box "irradiations of the vagina," on heat and cold in his and Vasiliki's erogenous zones. He understood the skepticism that some felt about Reich's notions and how some close to Rosenfeld might "smile and shake their heads on hearing that it is of benefit to sit in a box." He thought best sometimes, he was certain, in his accumulator box; he gauged his orgasms, sought to gauge the extent to which he had changed. "Violent trembling of the lips, jaw, neck, muscles, chest, and thighs . . . all in the first session of therapy," Rosenfeld noted. "And the hands and face go numb, and the neck. . . . Amazed from the point of view of the usual dignity of the self, to find it so soon shattered and helpless. But let it die—and let the warmth which suffuses the trembling body with the flow of energy take over and stay." He watched Vasiliki with attention, even during those periods when he was engaged, as he often was, in sleeping with other women: "I remember the previous burst of tears, when V[asiliki] and I that Saturday afternoon 'had it out' with each other . . . and I see her continuing frowning and old-womanishness, the flight of life. . . . How good it would be to love!"[39]

He also cast about widely for thinkers, aside from Reich, who might provide guidance about life and work. Rosenfeld could celebrate with as much energy as he criticized, and Nietzsche and Kafka both provided him with a deeper appreciation of contemporary society, especially its terrors. By the early 1950s, he also embraced Tolstoy and Gandhi because, as he explained, each had confronted psychologically disfiguring flaws, deep personal imperfections that they acknowledged openly, and both showed how to triumph over one's worst instincts. For politics to be meaningful, he insisted, it had to explain how to achieve such triumph—this lesson he credited to Reich. The sources for this thought were eclectic, never fashionable. He reveled in antiorthodoxy. Still, there remained in his writings a certain thread, a consistency that animated much of what he wrote in these years as an essayist as well as a novelist, and this was that the war cut asunder beliefs previously irrevocable. Anyone unable to understand this was simply caught in the grip of self-denial, hopeless illusion, at best, nostalgia. In the old days, there were simply good and evil; now, in the wake of Hitler's destruction of the Jews, one had to confront the ever more pervasive horrors of terror.

Few close to him seemed quite as thunderstruck by news of the Nazi horrors against the Jews. Certainly no one else in his immediate circle wrote about it as much nor, it seems to me, as astutely. It is a theme to which he returned time and again. He sought desperately to deal with it as a novelist. As an essayist, he articulated his fear that the catastrophe constituted a new chapter in humanity's sense of itself, and that in the wake of the Nazi calamity a line had been crossed that can never be denied: "We still don't understand what happened to the Jews of Europe, and perhaps we never will." This is how he began a remarkable essay, "Terror beyond Evil," published in *The New Leader* in February 1948. It is not a question of knowledge: "By now we know all there is to know. But . . . we still don't understand. Most carry on like before, as if nothing has changed; most are numb, and in this respect onlookers are no less morally culpable than the murderers themselves who . . . were oblivious to the screams around them."[40]

It seems incomprehensible, wrote Rosenfeld, that these screams weren't heard. "How is this possible? How can such things be?" The best accounts of such horrors are the most straightforward, the least stylized. He admired, for example, Jacob Pat's *Ashes and Fire,* a simple, direct book written by a Yiddish writer who went to Poland to speak to its Jewish survivors, to hear their stories about rebuilding their lives. Pat appreciated that there was no prospect of reassurance in a book like his; nor did he seek to provide an explanation for the horrors. No book can. All that can be done is to look squarely at the catastrophe with no reassurance, and with no confidence about the impact of enlightenment. The war shattered such beliefs: "Anything else stops short of presenting it in full,

[it] leads nowhere, bogs down in the wilderness of our usual assumptions—the wilderness of good and evil, of ethics and morality, of reason, science, method, history, sympathy and mercy, the whole human world, or what was, until now, human. All this has been annihilated. . . . There is only terror."[41]

Only once laughably discredited ideals—goodness, philanthropy, revolution—are abandoned can the horrors of the last war be faced, along with the reality that there is no prospect for enlightenment. Understanding isn't the antidote to terror; this can only be found in joy, which is something far deeper than mere, transitory pleasure. "Terror beyond evil and joy beyond good: that is all there is to work with, whether we are to understand what has happened, or to begin all over again."[42]

In January 1949, Rosenfeld came back to these issues and provided in "The Meaning of Terror," published in *Partisan Review*, a series of propositions both whimsical and grim. What these propositions reveal, above all, is how Rosenfeld sensed—more emphatically than others around him—that the killing of Europe's Jews constituted a fundamental rupture in history, and how exasperated he was by the apparent inability of other intellectuals to confront these implications with sufficient seriousness.

In the wake of the horrors of the war and what it showed about man's capacity for terror, the human ability to destroy the lives of others must be seen not as an anomaly but as the norm. Hence, as Rosenfeld stated, "Terror is the main reality. Pleasure cannot be seen as its alternative: it is too innocent, and, increasing, it is unattainable in a world fraught with horror. Pleasure eludes, terror surrounds humanity, and, indeed, it comes to define the dreams as well as the concrete, daily realities of humanity."[43]

The concentration camps did more than devastate European Jewry, wrote Rosenfeld. They demolished the prospect of belief in the power of culture as a redemptive force. With all traditions broken, all culture dead, with nowhere else for human beings to gain inspiration, we live at a moment of utter discontinuity with human values everywhere "violated and denied." The cultured person today is utterly isolated, with his humanity all his own: "the cultural form that conveyed humanity and assured the transaction from one man to the next has been destroyed."[44]

Basic information about the concentration camps—which, as Rosenfeld acknowledged, is readily available in the press and films—has done little more than offer simple, stark distinctions between the nightmares of Buchenwald and the good dreams of Hollywood. These are timid, useless notions, out of step with the overriding horror. All must now ask the following questions:

> How is this possible? How is it possible that thousands of men, women, children, and infants should be lined up in a field, to be shot before an open ditch, and that their screams should not be heard? That furnaces should be stuffed with human beings? That a thousand should be marched into airtight chambers, to be gassed, or steamed to death, their naked bodies stuck together by the pressure and the heat? The death-schedules are possible: efficiency, the salvaged hair, gold fillings and wedding bands: industry. But that no one heard the screams? We cannot understand, we are as numb as the perpetrators of the crime. Our knowledge should shock us, it should stir us deeply, it should make our old life impossible, subjectively, as it is impossible in fact.[45]

The terror of the concentration camp and its capacity to subjugate completely puts to rest all belief in tradition, culture, or goodness. The only alternative to such terror is joy:

"Everything else," Rosenfeld insisted, "is privation." The abstractions of the past—including belief in morality, the redemptive power of politics, the prospect of a good life on earth—are old, and decrepit. "Men will go on to seek the good life in the direction of what is joyous; they know what is terrible. May the knowledge of joy come to them, and the knowledge of terror never leave!"[46] Only those alienated from the world's values are capable of living in it, Rosenfeld pronounced. This he would argue, in various ways, for the remainder of his life.

Kafka provided the most stringent portrait of what it feels like to live with terror, Rosenfeld argued in an essay in *The New Leader* in April 1947. In "The Metamorphosis," as Rosenfeld saw it, Kafka understood terror in terms both cosmic and intimate. For Kafka, terror was a byproduct of the inability to believe in God ("man's whole fallen estate before God," as Rosenfeld put it) and human beings' incapacity to live with their own, horrific failings—which, in Gregor Samsa's case, include sins as humiliating as incest. Samsa's death restores his parents and his sister to life in much the same way the terror of the Second World War was trumpeted as a purging force that obliterated millions so that others might be liberated.

Consequently, Kafka's isn't a symbolic fiction. Its depth is the product of its basic, inescapable reality. Kafka's power lies in his ability to speak concretely of issues that theology describes abstractly: "It was his genius to see the world's unity; even if we take a single aspect of his symbolism, say, man's struggle for Grace, it at once reveals something of the moral, psychological, social, and even political structure of the world in which man lives." All Kafka's fiction is constructed around things, not ideas or symbols; his mysticism is "secular" and there is "no other modern writer whose subject matter . . . is so broad." What distinguishes Kafka's work from philosophy is precisely that it isn't preoccupied with ideas as it is "a kind of realism" whose depiction of relationships is "objective." In Kafka, "the world, as in a mystical system, becomes a visible legend"; portraits of terror are rendered in the form of realistic parables.[47]

Kafka's brilliance is thus in his ability to combine aspects of the human experience otherwise considered separate: the struggle with God and the conflict within the human soul. He manages to understand faith without succumbing to belief, to examine what freedom means while appreciating the madness of the unfree world around him. "Kafka begins where he ends, with an understanding of the limitation of human freedom, and an effort to transcend that limitation to achievement of as much peace as one can reach in mankind."[48]

Rosenfeld would seek to imitate such realism, but with little success. In his daily life, too, the freedom he sought—mostly through illicit romance—eluded him. Joy at his writing desk became less and less frequent as he explored terror in his fiction and became increasingly unable to match expectation with reality. His fictional writing until the mid-1950s grew constrained, elliptical. Terror supplanted all else as its major theme—and he devoted more and more attention to it in his journal, where the bulk of his descriptions were of the terrors of domestic life and of how his marriage was tearing apart.

Exactly what pulled him and Vasiliki together and then drew them apart bedeviled him. He pondered this question for years; he continued to mull over it in journal entries he wrote at the time of his death. They seemed an ideal couple at first and remained so in the eyes of many until the late 1940s, and even later. Yet they fought ferociously and engaged in sexual trysts in full view of one another and their children. Both George and Eleni asked themselves repeatedly why their parents had ever married. From the time she was in high school, Eleni was acutely preoccupied with avoiding pregnancy, convinced that she would be a dreadful mother much like Vasiliki.[49]

Their father they remembered as doting, affectionate, playful. Vasiliki often told them after his death that he hadn't wanted children ("a twenty-year mortgage," she said he called the prospect), but once they came along, he fell deeply in love with them and managed to show his feelings more transparently than she was able to do. But Eleni recalled awful battles, including one in which her mother hit her head against a doorknob, with screaming followed by reassurances from Isaac that the children were still loved, followed by more shouting.[50]

In his fiction—and especially in a series of sketches built around life in the Village—Rosenfeld sought to capture the inner contour of these domestic terrors. In his journal he detailed his obsessive need for other women, and Vasiliki's dalliances—which weren't "indiscretions" because she seemed to work so hard at making them public. He bemoaned the emptiness of their sexual life together, and reveled in their rare moments of sexual abandon with one another. He studied her constantly, subjecting her smallest moves to a scrutiny that must have felt stifling. At times, the couple seemed almost deliriously happy; at other times, miserable.

Just as views about their marriage differed widely, descriptions of the two were increasingly diverse, even contradictory. Rosenfeld continued to be seen by many as the warmest of his circle of New York intellectuals, blessed with generosity of spirit, eager to share mind and heart. Others viewed in him the traits of an emotional predator, a chronic gossip too eager to collect and dispense secrets, a man who used friendships without investing much of himself in them. While admirers described him as an American Gogol, as the writer who would produce the great novel about the Village, there were those—more and more with the passing of time— who decided he was more a talker than a writer, that he promised much and delivered little. Views of his capacity to negotiate New York's competitive literary world also diverged. Some saw him as adept, and canny, with the ability to milk contacts, to get places no one else could; others insisted that he was an impractical boy lost in the big city.

Opinions about Vasiliki varied no less: some celebrated her as sensuous and exotic while others dismissed her as uninteresting, an intellectual mediocrity, something of a flake. Bellow remained deeply impressed with the comfort she felt with her own body, her ability to feel pleasure deeply, and continued until the end of his life to speak of her with admiration. A newcomer from San Francisco, Janet Richards, the wife of the writer Manny Farber, remembered the couple warmly as she described the turmoil of Village life in her memoir:

> The Rosenfelds lived around the corner . . . opposite a bakery that sold fruit tarts for five cents apiece. We all loved those tarts, but Isaac above all, and now I speculate lamenting that his daily consumption of them almost by the dozen may . . . have contributed to his death. . . .
>
> Isaac was fat and short, with a round, rosy, amused face and sardonic eyes behind twinkly glasses. . . . He liked to talk about books chiefly, but also he could get carried away into an imaginative investigation of somebody's character and mind that usually culminated in a flight into a Dostoievskian laying bare of the soul.
>
> He was invariably cheerful, greatly aided by his Greek wife who . . . was so gorgeous in appearance, having a classic Greek face, dark, heavy lidded, fine of feature and crowned with thick, lustrous long black hair, and was so

given to shouting with spontaneous bursts of merriment or fury, and so generally charming that she would cheer anyone up.[51]

Richards's views contrast markedly with those of a writer who knew Isaac and Vasiliki well. In Wallace Markfield's thinly disguised 1964 novel, *To an Early Grave*, the characters Leslie and Inez Braverman are closely modeled—as Markfield readily admitted—on the Rosenfelds, and both, especially the wife, are dreadful. Inez manipulates everyone, from her children to friends, grocers, and lovers: "She was the old Inez, the charmer, the wheedler, the one who could promote and operate and take good care of herself." Her smile is "hard, professional, like an airline stewardess or a chorus girl." She tells embarrassing stories to all who will hear about her estranged, now dead husband. And the husband—"a figure, a talent, an original"—who possessed limitless capacity for feigned empathy, would spend hours and hours comforting the miserable, the desperate, listening to their stories, storing up these details, and then later, once the unfortunate confessors had left, would regale those closest to him with these same heartfelt tales.[52] The Bravermans had the ability to win trust, which they then squandered for the sake of a good, devastating laugh: "Always, some busted-up character, someone on the verge of divorce, someone who had the look of a potential suicide or an alcoholic. Wandering near one of the bedrooms you could make out the sounds of his weeping, or Leslie's voice, soft, tremulous, counseling and cajoling. Later . . . the boys would stay behind, a small, permanent cadre, while Leslie, spreading out on the sofa, gave them the full story. . . . Leslie's studied Talmudic air . . . gave the warning that it could be dangerous to put yourself under his power."[53]

Markfield's protagonist recalls that he met them as a student in one of Leslie's night classes. Leslie had praised, a bit too much he felt, a paper of his on *Anna Karenina*. They spoke after class, went for coffee, and then Leslie brought him home. Though it was late, Inez made him French toast. They fed him Polish sausage and an eggplant spread, and he talked to them about everything through the night. By morning he was enthralled.[54]

Leslie, in Markfield's account, is alternately appealing and aggressive. "From each Leslie had taken and gotten! Wherever there was a foundation. Wherever there was a grant. Wherever there was a publisher to hand out advances." Even Inez describes him, on the morning of his funeral, as someone willing to take anything from quite nearly any woman: "Look, kid, maybe he had standards in literature, but when it came to you-know-what it was just a question of what could fit on a mattress. If Greta Garbo came along—fine! And if Rose Dreckfresser turned up—also good!"[55]

A still more devastating portrait of the two was produced by short story writer Evelyn Shefner, a onetime assistant editor at the *Contemporary Jewish Record* who also knew the couple well. She was a friend of Rosenfeld's back in Chicago and he found an apartment for her at 85 Barrow Street. She and her husband, Harry, are often named as a couple in Rosenfeld's Village stories. In Shefner's story "Monday Morning," which appeared in the *Hudson Review* in winter 1955, Rosenfeld was transmuted into a lightly fictionalized monster, a man of boundless narcissism, appetite, and brutishness.[56]

The story begins with the protagonist at breakfast, buttering his hot cinnamon bun. It's a winter day and he sits at the breakfast table furious at his wife because she plans to go to Mexico with a divorcée friend. From the story's start, we're aware that he is ungainly, inattentive to his appearance or health, someone whose most taxing activity is the walk he must take from home to the university where he teaches a writing class.

His wife stares at him, initially, in silence. She is enveloped with unhappiness that clearly is the product of far more than this one unpleasant conversation. Once beautiful, she has been disfigured by bad behavior seemingly endured over a long period of time: "The face beneath was blanched and naked, the skin white and heavy-pored, with lines of tension running from the nose to the corners of her pallid, willfully sensual mouth."[57]

They argue about her use of the telephone in the small apartment where her husband must devote his mornings uninterrupted, trying to write. She insists that he acts like a tyrant, that she must tiptoe around the house fearful of disturbing him. Their friends have no respect for her, she declares; they presume that she is a "moron" because she creates nothing new and all she does is to bring children into the world. His responses to her are, in turn, ponderously, hopelessly self-preoccupied: "'My God!' He banged his fist on the table, thunderously. 'Can't you even admit that your telephone calls are of secondary importance? You say people look down on you for not being an artist. But you're the one who seems to get an indecent satisfaction out of depriving a working artist of the few hours a day he has free, at his disposal. Isn't it enough for you that I have to spend every afternoon teaching and most of my evenings writing reviews? Do you want me to give up everything! Haven't I sacrificed enough, already?'"[58]

All weekend they had quarreled about small things that escalated. The arguments grew steadily in fury. The couple had slept in separate rooms, or in the same bed but rigidly apart. Now that the children are off to school, the fight erupts again.[59] The morning slips away; it's 11:15 and still he hasn't started working. He begins to shout at her, to forbid her to leave, and she insists she will go anyway. She taunts him that she, too, like her friend, might well pursue a divorce; she has sufficient grounds. They argue about the fate of their two children if she leaves him. He sits in the kitchen, asks himself why he had ever married her, and muses on the wintry scene outside: "When he was a little boy his grandmother had entertained him with stories of travelers lost on the Russian steppes, the faithful horses steamy and exhausted, breathing white huffs into the frosted air, the furred men sitting in the lonely troika while the circle of starry-eyed wolves ranged in."[60]

When he first met her, twelve years earlier, she had been "gifted with unusual lightness and grace, a pure bodily outline of beauty that had excited him immeasurably. In a weak moment, he once told her she reminded him of an Eastern dancing girl. . . . His own figure, middle-aged now, had never been so different. The grace and flexibility of his wife had appealed to him as a contrast to his own burgher solemnity. Also, he thought privately, living with her, he might be able to incorporate some of these graceful qualities into his writing: so that one might have said he had fallen in love with an idea."[61]

He admits he saw other women, picks them up at parties he attends with his wife ("If they were willing and they were not absolute pigs, he made arrangements, discreetly, in the hallway."). He dreams of freeing himself, finally, from his wife; he dreams of finishing his next book, which could rid him of the need for teaching and book reviewing. And he realizes that he must make up with his wife; she settles him, is essential to him: "Between them, those two, they defined a reality, held a world trembling in balance."[62]

Both now wild with fury, she starts screaming at him,

and as he watches, and listens, he feels mounting excitement and nudges her in the direction of the nearest room, where he has a cot. "Her body was arched back, her breasts were tossed and pointed up to him like two flaring serpents." He calls her a "bitch" and "filthy whore," then checks the time—the children are returning from school in half an hour. Finally aware of what is happening, she demands that he let her go.[63]

> All at once her muscles unlocked and an indecent smile of complicity melted her face. He did not push her onto the bed, she toppled. Lying there, white, flaccid, her limbs sprawled and unhinged, she welcomed him with the smile of a corpse seducing its murderer.
>
> But before plunging in, he had the presence of mind to mutter, "You won't go then? You'll stay."
>
> After, there was only the ragged sound of breathing.[64]

Shefner's story wasn't intended as a memoir, of course, but the domestic scene it describes roughly resembles that in Rosenfeld's journal. How truthful or, better said, how truthfully characteristic journal entries are, is unclear: angst, displeasure, and self-loathing surface there with far greater frequency and volatility than in life. "Journal entries," according to Cynthia Ozick, "those vessels of discontent, are notoriously fickle, subject to the torque of mutable feeling, while power flourishes elsewhere." Rosenfeld used his journal to speak of inadequacies: his inability to produce sustained prose, the intractability of childhood phobias, the unraveling of his life with Vasiliki, his failure as husband and father. As a genre, journal writing fascinated him: he reviewed Gide's *Journals*, comparing them unfavorably with Chekhov's *Notebooks*, insisting that although Gide sought hard to capture the mundane details of his life, Chekhov appreciated that the only true theme of a writer was "the revealed man [as] revealed through the imagination."[65] In his own journal, Rosenfeld set out to probe the origins of his literary life—especially its torments—and hoped that by writing them down he might purge them.

Beginning in childhood, with sometimes lengthy breaks thereafter, Rosenfeld kept a journal. The first, a standard school notebook, has pictures of teachers' faces, line drawings of male genitals, and quotations from the classics. In the mid- and late 1940s, he wrote in the journal often. He stopped around 1951 (he kept small notebooks with jottings, calendar reminders, syllabi), and returned to it in the last year of his life.

Among his more persistent themes is his fear of homosexuality. He connected it to his aggression toward men, his jealousy, his incessant womanizing. This fear meshed with periods of dark depression. He fell ill with maladies that seemed psychosomatic, suffering flus and fevers that were often accompanied by frustratingly long periods of listlessness. He sought to cure these maladies with Reich's teachings, and it was his journal writing that provided him with the closest he would come to classical therapy.

Such writing—to which he would sometimes devote several hours daily—provided a ready substitute for fiction; it was also a place to display writing that wasn't ready to be called a draft. The angry, terrible passages in the journal— filled with loathing for others, sometimes Vasiliki, but mostly himself—are not infrequently accompanied by passages scrutinizing how to extricate himself from the morass:

> I have attacks of hatefulness during which I see only evil in others and I am overcome in fear. It seems to me everyone has designs on me. Women I do not fear so much because I can handle them. But men make me feel self-conscious,

spiteful, timid and suspicious; I feel homosexual influences. I feel homosexual impulses stimulated in their presence and suspecting the same of them, preparing myself for an act of aggression or of love. At such times I think all men are unconscious murderers. . . . Then there are the nightmares, like the one the other night . . . I looked up; people began to stream into the room. There were several women among them, but I was aware also of men among the intruders, the brutal antagonists who populate dreams. I was seized with fright. I couldn't look; at the same time my vision and my consciousness were blurred as during an orgasm. I wanted to scream, but couldn't, and woke up.

I notice that these fears subside when I have slept with a woman other than Vasiliki, and a happy time with her makes them fall off, though not so sharply.

I don't know, of course, what all this means, nor can I expect to find a root explanation by myself. My uneasiness with men, I imagine, has to do with my relationship with my father . . . Dora, who became my "mother" when I was two, also has something to do with it. My father's open hostility to her must have puzzled me as I identified myself with him. I also turned against her love. This may have made it difficult for me to place myself in competition with men, for just at the time when I had grown to expect it, suddenly my father turns against the mother object. As a result, my attachment to the mother-object is incomplete, my identification with father also incomplete, and has never properly worked itself out, as it might in the case of simple competition. Never having had the full mother attachment (2 stepmothers followed Aunt Dora) I don't know what I want with women or with men and remain puzzled and vaguely guilty about it all.

But one thing I know, my hatefulness must come to an end. (Perhaps it grew out of this: that I felt my father's disapproval whenever I showed love for mother Dora; and do still feel guilty in loving a woman.) It cannot go on this way.[66]

Throughout the journal, his sex life with Vasiliki is described at length, sometimes with excruciating precision. He found her a remarkable and also a ridiculous woman, a fountain of sensuality and a narrow-minded shrew. "The smells of sex, the smell of arm pits and breasts . . . the warm life of it." By the late 1940s, both made their dalliances as public as possible: Rosenfeld documented an academic party that started with "the usual dull conversation, canning vegetables, botulism, the relation of modern and ancient Greek" and evolved into party games. Vasiliki began to flirt, declared her love for the college town somewhere outside New York City, and urged people there to find Isaac a job. She drank some more, declared, "On Reich: Isaac is the theoretical one. I put it into practice," and then announced, "I want to make love to a man other than my husband."[67] She went off with someone, and although Isaac waited for her, Vasiliki didn't show up until nearly five in the morning, "disheveled, blouse messed up. . . . He's impotent," she informed her husband.[68] Incidents like these are interspersed with moments of affection:

> Next morning, vomiting, migraine, remorse. Nothing will stay in her stomach. I take care of her all day. She has no recollection of what happened at the party.
>
> So, entering a new world. She looks younger, prettier, the hair shows life, no more wrinkles of suicide, almost none of murder; jaw has relaxed, less grinding in sleep; lips softened, the muscle bisecting the lower lip running up from the chin, has receded. Looks all softened, rounded.[69]

More tumultuous was New Year's Eve 1950. The stove broke, the turkey (they feared) was ruined, Isaac's friend Sidney Passin wouldn't stop taking pictures to kiss his wife, Ruth, at midnight, which depressed her immensely. Vasiliki (as usual) flirted with the other man, which made Ruth more depressed. "Then at 4am in the course of getting the turkey out of the oven, I stumble against the heavy wall mirror which has been parked against the dining room door, and it falls over and breaks. . . . All the same, and with all this, a kindly, loving feeling toward Vasiliki, and that night an orgasm for the first time in a long time. . . . Only love shall save ye."[70]

With his move to the Village, the group closest to Rosenfeld was a wildly bohemian circle that included the editor Ray Rosenthal, the beat writer Milton Klonsky, and the Poster brothers, Willy and Herb. The dominant figures were the Poster brothers, an erratic, bookish pair who lived off their parents' property investments and spent most of their time pursuing women. (They kept a special cash fund to pay for abortions.) Willy was brilliant, had a good grasp of philosophy, wrote beautiful pieces for *Commentary* and elsewhere; Rosenfeld would sum him up as "a pagan, anarchist, and a clever dog." His brother Herb was quite mad. In a series of unpublished sketches set in the Village, Rosenfeld described their talk, and especially their mistreatment of those they felt weren't as quick or cynical as they were. Bellow loathed this group; he felt they patronized him, that they looked down on him as too establishment, too bourgeois. Bellow produced a dark portrait of them in "Charm and Death," asserting that they did much to ruin his childhood friend's chance to achieve literary greatness by stoking his contempt for his intelligence. They were—even in Bellow's account—ferociously erudite, sophisticated, by no means merely smooth talkers: "Their relations had no true content, perhaps, but promised a content, signaled a hope of connection, fellowship, friendship. If they could drink the sacrificial bullock's blood, these dwellers in listless Hades . . . could speak the living truth . . . these difficult people, these spooks." The narrator of Markfield's *To an Early Grave* knows he is on the outs with this group—they feel his job is too respectable, his clothes too good, his aspirations too conventional—when, as if by cue, they all begin to tease him about a new suit. They imitate Yiddish-intoned tailors ("*A m'chyah.* . . . Look at the quality. Look at the tailoring. Look how nice it hangs"). None laugh at his jokes. They humiliate him so that he knows he has fallen out of their inner circle: "A look, that was all. But he could not shrug it off. He could not escape the belief that he had been told, once and for all, who he was . . . and where he stood in the world."[71]

Rosenfeld hated these qualities in his friends and wrote despairingly about their pettiness, their humiliation of everyone outside their small, self-important group, and their insistence on hurting one another, too. Some of his final writing is devoted to them, to their clever, unremitting cruelty. Yet he couldn't seem—and perhaps he didn't much try—to separate himself from them.

Rosenfeld admired their comfort with their own bodies; he admired the same quality in Vasiliki, whose own, increasingly vocal, unrestrained criticisms of Rosenfeld's physicality he took to heart. She often now criticized his inability to satisfy her. Rosenfeld felt, too, that she and their Village friends were vastly superior sexually. He wrote in 1948, in the short story "Alpha and Omega," about a dancer who subsists on a couple of glasses of milk and juice daily, and on little else. She spends her time in touch with the rigors of her body, believing that "There is a pattern in everything, the world is without chaos, and even chaos has an order. . . . She has tried, with some success, to integrate the elements of a simple life—the things she sees daily, the daily events, sounds, rhythms, smells, feelings—into an over-all pattern of the most general proportions, which patterns she guards like a treasure and in guarding, seeks to perfect it."[72] To some, this was an idealized portrait of Vasiliki herself.

Rosenfeld fervently wished to be admitted into the inner sanctum of bohemia, but he also appreciated how empty and dangerous it was. Still, he yearned to be drawn into it. He respected the ability to leave one's mind behind and he increasingly depended on Reich's ideas to help him reconcile mind and body. Reich's scientific, daringly nonconformist system could help Rosenfeld remake himself into someone who would react more instinctively to the world.[73] Rosenfeld wrote a long, pained letter to Bellow in the mid-1940s (in it, he complains that he can't finish because he is too drunk):

> I admit that to a degree the village has touched us. Vasiliki for one has been drinking like a school-marm on a furlough from the Pocahontas Township Latin School; and I should not talk either. It's the environment. We live surrounded by "creeps"—people who, without exception, are motivated solely by the desire of knocking themselves out in order to get 4F's. It's a systematic and cynical mass suicide movement. These people I think are the closest approach to and yet the farthest remove from the young Russian intellectuals of the pre-Revolutionary days. A scene I shall never forget: A——, one of our new friends sitting down on the floor with a stick of marijuana intent on hopping himself up. Another: W——, fresh from a saloon brawl, after three nights without sleeping, just folding up, visibly turning yellow and passing out in a room full of people. Charlie himself . . . goes around his face flushed with Alky, swallowing benzedrines. Believe me, my initial reactions are gone: the superiority I might have felt at one time. I see aspects of myself in all of them. . . . All the posing and the pretending and the bohemianism, and the self-destructiveness, the promiscuity— all very desperate and grim—nevertheless impresses me, once I know these people well, as a rare kind of honesty, as

the only kind open to those who are unable to transcend
their experiences. . . . But compassion is inevitable. Christ
himself, if he came to the village, could only . . . sit down
and get drunk with them.

In the same letter he insisted that such bohemians
were superior to the self-important intellectuals that Bellow
and Rosenfeld knew well—indeed, that they were primed to
become. Such men were capable of delusions far worse than
those of the wretched Village bohemians; they managed to believe things both logical and ridiculous. He describes Irving
Janis and Ithiel Pool, both significant scholars and longtime
friends, with whom he spent an evening talking about the war.
Both made the case for a Nazi victory which would eventually
then help bring on socialism. Rosenfeld left, feeling disgust:
"I say that my village friends are more honest, far more honest, and that they have the open hearts of their neuroses and
their miseries and, by the grace of God, they have found in al-
cohol what those . . . snobs have lost in Marx."[74]

By now, he had abandoned Marx and relied diligently
on Freud and Reich. He taught at NYU (one course outline
scribbled in his journal reads, "Swann, Crime & P, Kafka
Trial, Death in Venice, Dubliners") yet was more and more in
despair over his writing life. The manuscript version of "The
Enemy" had grown by the late 1940s into several hundred
handwritten pages, but the protagonist—miserable, lost, in
the midst of war-filled terrain for reasons never specified—
elicited little sympathy or interest even from its author. "The
Enemy," Rosenfeld wrote in 1948, "bores me—how I've ruined it with this nonsense. I want in the Pathfinder a person, not a case-history. A character, by God!" Rosenfeld also
worked long and hard, but without much success, on a
manuscript called "The Empire," an extended version of his

award-winning novella "The Colony," built roughly around
the lives of Gandhi and Nehru. Another manuscript, about
three hundred pages and titled "Mother Russia," was set in
Stalinist Russia. It was intended as an exploration of guilt
and betrayal, but despite his life-long immersion in Russian
culture, Rosenfeld's Russia too much resembled the back-
rooms of Greenwich Village—it was little more than a stage
set for lengthy monologues about shame and sexual emptiness.[75]

He poured his greatest time and energy into the "India" manuscript. He desperately wanted to understand what
had inspired Gandhi's political power, how Gandhi had confronted his own potentially crippling neuroses and turned
them into assets. He began to speak of Gandhi with the same
fervor he had long reserved for Reich. Curiously, there is a
lengthy description of a Nehru-like figure, yet he never came
close in this manuscript to probing Gandhi himself. Rosenfeld spent time in the early 1950s working on the manuscript
at Yaddo, the writers' colony in Saratoga Springs, and described in a letter how he was laboring steadily at least three
or four hours daily. But "the rest of the day's my problem. The
men outnumber the women five to one. I don't like the girls
here anyway, so it's very lonely." He reported that he had finished about one hundred pages of the "India novel," which
was going well, but "I haven't got to Gandhi yet, which will be
the real test." Then he added: "If I were only happy, I could do
prodigious labors with no strain. The problem is loneliness.
But the work must go on anyway. I look back at times in my
life and I think it's damned unfair—because then, when my
capacity was not near so great, I had everything I wanted. And
now when I could do so much. . . . But the image of my grandmother floats up. . . . She would always say it's a sin to complain." He concluded: "You be of good cheer—and if this

letter depressed you, burn it, so at least the flames may dance."[76]

The novel-in-progress most often associated with him by the late 1940s was what friends expected to be his Gogol-like masterpiece about Village life. This is how it was described, and he often read portions of it aloud to the guests at his parties. He completed a small mountain of work on the theme, mostly unpublished stories built loosely around a clutch of mean-spirited, brilliant "boys" who ran with a sallow-faced fellow, slower than the rest, named Joseph Feigenbaum. This was the name Rosenfeld had years earlier given to the rattled, self-destructive narrator of "The Hand That Fed Me." The Village manuscript was made up mostly of tales of bookish, timid souls running with a faster, tougher crowd; reclusive booksellers; meandering, directionless courtships; marriages gone sour. Rosenfeld's ambitions remained immense, and he wrote to Tarcov in the mid-1940s, "Some day soon I hope to start a story about the [V]illage which should say everything I've been thinking and feeling about the village, life in general, people, friends, love, sex, and everything we talked about when you were last in. I think I've come to understand the matter somewhat better now, and if I can clean out the insides of my own head it may do me some good." Nonetheless, he seemed, once again, to be spinning wheels. He would start a work, write a draft but never quite finish it, then type a few pages, often no more than two or three, which he would then abandon to begin something new.[77]

Never did he manage to capture in the manuscript all of "love, sex, and everything." In one unpublished story set in the Village, he came as close as he would in describing his own loss of certainty and direction as a writer. Titled "An Assignment" and written in the late 1940s or early 1950s, it tells of a writer, Toby Nathan, whose girlfriend, Eleanor, persuades him to move to the Village, where he begins to enjoy some success: "He began to publish stories and book reviews in the little magazines, and after two years, he had published a novel which enjoyed a good press." It sells less than a thousand copies, but he is now recognized as a real talent. "Everyone in the Village [knew he had] a certain naïve, fresh quality, it was his best feature." Finally, now that he and Eleanor are in a position to marry, she proposes they live in separate apartments, but insists that this has nothing to do with her feelings for him. Toby begins to have doubts when he learns that she has already rented a new apartment and then discovers that she has taken her diaphragm. He meets her new boyfriend at a party in her apartment and mixes with her guests, all of whom are callow and work mostly in advertising. Toby leaves numb and humiliated, and promptly agrees to take on a job writing pornography.[78]

Reveling in his newfound reputation as a writer, he had presumed that he was celebrated as a minor hero of the Village. But he realizes that Eleanor—willing as she was to break from convention, to sleep with others behind his back, to separate from him at first without admitting that this was what she was doing—is truer to its values. The first pornographic story he writes is based on one that circulated in his grammar school about a boss and his secretary. He remembers his friends passing it around in a "blurry, single-spaced carbon under the desks, from hand to wet hand." A subsequent story is merely mechanical, but then he begins to write a novel with Eleanor as its protagonist, transforming her into frigid, evil Nora, then into a little girl, a dancer, and a housewife who sleeps with repairmen and delivery boys. "She was a negress, then a Chinese girl, and again American working her way through college, until she involved the whole world, and all experience; the whole of existence was a setting in which she made love giving herself with an inexhaustible passion. . . . He wrote only for the sense of life that kept flowing through him, the joy of writing himself out."[79]

Throughout this period, Rosenfeld remained engaged with Reichianism. He pressed friends to embrace it; threw himself into correspondence with devotees, including the radical English educator and founder of the school Summerhill, A. S. Neill; but often admitted that its teachings were unpersuasive, even cranky. "One is left with Reich in a rare moment of poetic insight," he wrote, testily, in 1948.[80] Rosenfeld himself seemed puzzled as to why he leaned on Reich. Often, he poked fun at Reich, ridiculing notions that he himself defended elsewhere with solemnity.

Still, Rosenfeld tried mightily, at times, to free himself, to permit himself to return to what he loved most, which, he admitted, was literature, not character analysis. In 1948, in the immediate wake of a class at NYU, he wrote:

> After last night's class in criticism, I think my career as a psychoanalyst had better come quickly to an end. Vasiliki and Ruthie [Tarcov], who were present, whispered and laughed throughout the two hours and as V. told me later she hears enough Reich, etc. at home. Indeed, I'm beginning to see it myself, I'm obsessed. And last night what a flood of irrelevancies I let loose about characterological analysis, character armor, animal experiments, and so on, well bearing out her point, "You have so many ideas on literature. Why don't you ever talk about that? Why not Dostoevsky's life, for instance?" I agree, I promise to reform. I shall certainly track back to literature. . . . But reform will have to come at a much deeper level, for I have developed a severe case of analysitis. . . . How everything refers to it, turns on it, involves it. Oedipus, complex repression, symbolism, sex, sex, sex, muscular tension, orgasm anxiety, ad

nauseum. . . . Away with this rubbish. I want to find myself. Me! Not a reaction formation, an oral sadistic neurosis, a fixation, by myself! This person I buried somewhere under all this rubbish.[81]

Oddly enough, in a manuscript titled "Halberline"— the closest he came to fictional writing that wasn't abstract and that drew on his own life—he told of a repressive sex colony run by a gruesome, crazed Austrian modeled closely on Reich. Into it stumbles an innocent, childless couple who think they're headed for a hotel. They had learned about the place from a friend and go there on a whim; as soon as they arrive, they're subjected to its strange, eventually awful regimen. At first they seek to cooperate, but soon they find it ridiculously oppressive. Then they rebel and are put on trial. Much of the manuscript deals with the trial, in which Rosenfeld relentlessly parodies Reichian teachings.[82] In his journal, Rosenfeld admitted that the manuscript "got screwed up after p. 75, thereabouts and the next 50 pages are in vain."[83] Still, in its opening pages—it is a 244-page manuscript—it provides a vivid, poignant glimpse of the loving and uneasy banter that Rosenfeld knew so well from home:

> We were already on the train, off on our vacation, but the truth is we were not really sure where we were going. Earlier in the day, when we had set out bright and happy, it had promised to be the very best vacation we had ever had. "Just think," said Ermeline, "by this time at night we'll be there! It's there, wherever it is, waiting for us!" But after we had come to the station and experienced a remarkable difficulty in learning what train we were to take, and after we had waited several hours in the waiting room, hot and hungry with the afternoon already upon us, it no longer seemed such a good idea. "Where exactly is it?" his wife asked pulling down the shade. We had taken a seat which, when

the train pulled out of the station, proved to be on the sunny side, and the car was full.

"I don't know. I told you I don't know."

"The name of the place! How will we know where to get off if you don't know the name?"

"I think the tickets said Halberline."

"You think? Can't you make sure?"

"I've already given up the tickets."

"But that's ridiculous! The conductor hasn't been round!"

"He took the tickets as we were getting on. You went on ahead, and didn't see it."

"Oh, you fool!"

"I remember well enough. The name was Halber-line."

"You'd better remember. You had those tickets in your pocket a whole week."

They are all but pushed off the moving vehicle by a conductor, their bags flung onto the platform, and then are met by an oddly genial man sent to bring them to Halberline. "His smile, when he finally turned to us, was as reassuring as it might be under the circumstances. But his face was hidden under the wide visor of a white cap and a pair of huge, green aviator goggles." Soon enough, they find out that they've come to a nudist colony, which seems to unsettle the man far more than the woman. He notices that, on discovering this, "she was smiling—the sort of light, contemptuous smile which, if you know anything about women at all, tells you that you have something to fear."[84]

The scene is probably meant to be reminiscent of Kafka, of those moments in his writing when the mundane transmutes into the horrific without warning, and without anyone—save the protagonist—noting the difference. The wife draws on Vasiliki; Rosenfeld's portrait of the marriage, strained, sexually unsatisfying, a relationship increasingly between two bickering adults, is much the picture offered in his journal. The man, named Harry, sleeps with other women; his wife knows of his indiscretions. The resentments between them feel impenetrable.

The manuscript soon moves into much the same terrain as the other fictional work he was then writing. Harry finds himself fixed up—as is everyone in the colony, including his wife—with a guide, with whom he has sex. Against all rules, she falls in love with him. Despite her feelings, the relationship seems mechanistic. Rosenfeld doesn't manage to describe sex in a novel largely devoted to sexuality, and it feels as if there is little basis for the guide's affection for Harry. Eventually, he seeks out his wife, they rebel against the deranged leader of the colony and are put on trial, and the Halberline shows itself to be filled with terrors no less repressive than those described in Rosenfeld's Russia novel. This manuscript, too, he left in a drawer.

Reich's ideas, as Rosenfeld at least occasionally appreciated, cramped his fiction, providing it with too much of an excuse for abstract depiction, for a distant analysis of the sort that had long bedeviled his storytelling on the page (but less often, it seems, in person). Ironically, Reichianism provided him as an essayist with a conceptual framework that he put to splendid use. What is perhaps his finest essay, "Gandhi: Self-Realization through Politics," published in August 1950, is enveloped—with great intelligence, empathy, and rigor—by ideas taken directly from Reich's repertoire.

In the essay, Rosenfeld posits Gandhi as a model of probity whose wisdom is the byproduct of neurosis. Rosenfeld loathed hero worship—perhaps because he was so inclined to engage in it—and he gives us the fullest portrait he would ever produce of an ideal man. To be sure, Gandhi was wracked by terrible internal conflict (what honest human being, Rosenfeld might ask, isn't?), but he marshaled his worst instincts to make way for his best ones, which, in turn, helped liberate the lives of countless others. Inspired by Gandhi's autobiography, Rosenfeld described the inner workings of a great man, his capacity to confront his character and move beyond his ego.[85] Gandhi is all the more impressive because he admitted eagerly in his autobiography his worst traits, not out of self-pity but to show how he built on his self-knowledge to confront the English, to build a new state and challenge the foundations of a corroded empire. Here Rosenfeld found just the melding of spirit and politics he had admired since his adolescence. And he identified these qualities in a figure of great achievement whose mark on the world was a byproduct of the good use he made of neuroses that were the hallmark of all but understood by few.

For years, Rosenfeld had seen Gandhi as an "extraordinary paradox," to use Nehru's words, a man of stupendous flaws crucial to his achievements.[86] What Gandhi did for himself—and, ultimately, for the world—was, as Rosenfeld saw it, what all must do:

> He describes himself ironing collars with the same underlying seriousness and attachment to moral significance as when he tells of nursing the sick and the dying. Often one must laugh, our sophistication demands it; to withhold the ridicule this self-confessed quack frequently deserves is to refuse to honor the simpleton in him, the plain nudnik, and to violate his unity. He was all of a piece, the man whose desire was to "wipe away every tear from every Indian eye," the neurotic who regarded sexual intercourse without intent of producing children as a grave crime, the submissive rebel who spent his days confounding authority and meanwhile kept his eye open for a vegetable substitute for cow's milk.[87]

His inner life could well have been crippled by his lusts and repressions but he survived "almost as though he had never led [that life], and more natural than many a man who is pledged to accommodate the instincts." His political ventures were made of much the same stuff as his internal struggles, all part of his effort to achieve "self-realization, to see God face to face," as Gandhi put it. "To understand him," wrote Rosenfeld, "one must understand, as he did, the connections among chastity, self-realization in politics, and the belief that a man's diet should consist only of fruit and nuts."[88]

Gandhi had been a shy boy and married young. His wife was illiterate and he made certain she remained so. He lusted after her intensely, was jealous, and passionately, obsessively preoccupied with her body. He spoke, like an ascetic, of a past defiled, but the event that left a permanent imprint was when, as his father lay on his deathbed, Gandhi left to have intercourse with his pregnant wife. His father died while he was having sex. "Gandhi never forgave himself for this, and all his life remembered that it was sexual desire which prevented him from being at his father's bedside when he died; he assumed also the guilt for the death of his first child, born of this pregnancy." He went abroad, studied in England—a prissy man, already a perfectionist—and then went to South Africa to practice law. Success was accompanied for him by guilt; he learned to detach himself from his ambitions, and his "egotism, which had cut him off from contact with the world, thus diverted, brought him into a growing contact with the world, as he denied himself profit in direct returns. This became the basic operation of his personality."[89]

He came to demand mightily of himself, and he felt it appropriate that he ask much of others, too. He sought power, but could usefully deny that he had any interest in it: "his empire, he could well believe, was not of the world, but of the inner world of his own instincts." Marshaling it, he then brought the greatest empire in the world to its feet.

Gandhi pushed himself, in life, into immortality, and into sainthood; hence, his fasts, hence, the nearer to death he came, the greater the power his people gave him, the fear of parricide that he fueled in them; and he worked hard at achieving these skills, first in South Africa and then back in India. He learned to control his senses; he practiced absolute chastity with sexual intercourse, now wedded in his mind with murder. Joy he found in all this, despite its remaining arduously difficult work: "Having mastered it, he was secure, he had built the last barrier in a system of defenses against the world, which . . . was a defense against his own impulses toward the world, and which was finally to give him command of the world."[90]

The resolution of his struggle meant the elimination of tension between the public and the private ego. Once he knew no temptation, he was ready to go beyond himself and turn to politics. Gandhi became a simpleton, overbearing. He repeated, late in life, adages about self-help, about the need for good handwriting. He put his son at risk. Seriously ill, the boy was prescribed chicken broth by his doctor, but Gandhi refused because of his vegetarianism. The boy's fever rose to 104 degrees, Gandhi gave him baths and orange juice, but he was willing to sacrifice his son's life for the sake of principle. "This is the same brave man, all of a piece, whom the threat of violence never deterred, and who lived by the Sermon of the Mount."[91]

Gandhi's politics were inextricably personal, a byproduct of his own will, his "empire over his instincts," and yet, despite this fierce wrestling with self, he remained impervious to much knowledge about his motives, his inner drives. He

couldn't afford much more self-knowledge. Politicians cannot survive if they are too self-aware and, as Rosenfeld astutely put it, Gandhi covered "through faith a deficiency of
knowledge." He permitted his sexuality to find refuge in his
religious life, and without such a life he could well have
turned into a crank, a mere eccentric. True, he was severe,
and arrogant in his humility, but he was also lighthearted,
childlike, full of charm and grace. His greatness lay in his
ability to perform "a basic operation on life, converting everything natural to the ideal with such success that in his case
one must almost create a special category—this life of artifice
and regulation by the will represents a new species of nature."[92] Never again would Rosenfeld air such a sense of
naked, unadorned awe about a person's capacity to triumph
over his own nature, such admiration for someone who found
himself able, in contrast to most others, to mesh all the various, warring sides of his character: "Can culture really become nature? How does a man go against life and return to it,
distorted but whole, with the satisfactions that failed in the
beginning marvelously restored? . . . This, the living, childlike
smile, so unlike the smile of the Sphinx, and yet of the same
enormous silence, is for me the mystery of Gandhi."[93]

Reich-inspired as the Gandhi essay was, it sheds much
of the quirky scientism that Rosenfeld had long adopted in his
search for an empirical basis for human and societal happiness. Instead, Rosenfeld looked squarely at one truly remarkable man, a man profoundly flawed—as most of us are—but
who found inside himself the capacity to confront these flaws
with rare intelligence, and courage. Gandhi made genius out
of his own stupendous oddness; he never ceased to be odd,
but built on this honestly with clarity of mind to save himself—and then an entire civilization. No one, not even the
Russian classicists Rosenfeld worshiped, had achieved so

much. They had probed the human soul; Gandhi sought to both understand and liberate it.

Rosenfeld found in Gandhi someone who by virtue of character, self-awareness, and willingness to confront human inadequacy was capable of bringing an empire to its feet. What Rosenfeld wanted for himself was, in comparison, really quite modest: the empire he sought was that of literary greatness, the prospect of producing, say, another *Crime and Punishment*. Gandhi's success offered him the assurance that such goals—lavish, to be sure—weren't inconceivable. Gandhi, too, had wrestled with demons similar to his own, and had nearly been leveled by them. He surmounted them, and Rosenfeld sought to learn from him, to construct his own ladder to the heavens so that he might finally accomplish what he had long before set out to do.

CHAPTER THREE

Paradise

But the days went by, the crowds grew, and still the clue was lacking. I was attempting to locate the primal scene within the lifetime of the spectators, and I would long have continued in this mistake, looking for the appropriate infantile memory to account for the fascination of this spectacle, had it not occurred to me that it was not to the childhood of present adults that I must turn, but to the childhood of our people. Now I am prepared to say that this scene had its origin in Paradise.

—Isaac Rosenfeld, "Adam and Eve on Delancey Street"

"BEING A JEW IS LIKE WALKING IN THE WIND OR swimming. You are touched at all points and conscious everywhere," wrote the young Lionel Trilling. The patrician Trilling, doyen of literary studies at Columbia University, winced at such statements. In her memoir, his wife, Diana, admitted that she was forever puzzled by his Jewish autobiographical stories, written in his twenties and published in the *Menorah Journal*. She speculated that the only explanation was that he was pushed into writing them by his mentor at the time, Elliot Cohen, later the founding editor of *Commentary*, whose influence on the young, impressionable Trilling was considerable.[1]

Jewishness was, as we've seen, a sore point in this circle, often the source of obfuscation, embarrassment, awkward distancing. Trilling never "denied his Jewishness," wrote William Phillips, but "one thought less of one's ethnicity than of one's internationalism and concerns for humanity as a whole." The archness of this language—"one thought," "one's internationalism"—suggests something other than cool indifference. Rather, it implies an effort to mark as much distance as possible from a condition feared to be irrevocable. "Abysmal provinciality" was how Phillips described his parents' situation in the Bronx; the term "provinciality" wasn't quite strong enough to express their backwardness. "One of the longest journeys in the world is the journey from Brooklyn to Manhattan" is the first, superbly evocative line in Norman Podhoretz's memoir, *Making It*.[2]

Many intellectuals would later modify this stance. It hadn't been built merely out of denial of Jewish influences; the children of immigrants were frequently taught that theirs was a heritage of backwardness, of ignorance, and were encouraged to grow into something larger, and better. In *Passage from Home*, Rosenfeld captured just this feature of their lives—the lesson communicated by so many immigrant parents that to succeed it was imperative to flee—and although the father of this novel deplores his son's actions, it remains clear that they're inspired by his upbringing. Deracination became an odd, torturous exercise in filial loyalty.

The war robbed these presumptions of at least some of their certainty, rendering terms like "internationalism" a bit hollow, and bringing to the surface feelings of Jewish self-identification previously contained, or seen as tribal, or considered irrelevant. News of Nazi atrocities helped inspire what were, at the outset, at least, mostly inchoate influences prompting some second-generation Jewish intellectuals to see themselves differently, to confront the simple, irrevocable reality of their own bodies. As Irving Howe wrote: "No matter how you might try to shake off your past, it would cling to your speech, gestures, skin, and nose," with the content of it "hard to specify, a blurred complex of habits, beliefs, and feelings. [It] might have no fixed religious or national content, it might be helpless before the assault of believers." Even Jews' taste in literature—for Faulkner, say, over Hemingway or Fitzgerald—was, Howe proposed, born out of their past struggles, their recollection of what it felt like to escape their families stuck in immigrant Jewish enclaves. "Where is the family in Hemingway or Fitzgerald? With Faulkner, despite all the rhetoric about honor, we might feel at home because the clamp of family which chafed at his characters was like the clamp that chafed at us." This new, heightened recognition by Jews of their background and its impact on them was the result of an increased awareness of the European catastrophe, the intrusion of ethnic politics, and, more distantly, the rise of Israel—which most saw as a remote, parched Middle Eastern Catskill, a place packed with too much nationalism and too many tumultuous relations.[3]

Jews stood out as a group—terms like "intellectual vitality" were, and sometimes still are, euphemisms for their presence. Their trademarks included a verbal dexterousness few could match; a willingness to go for broke in discussions that might well morph into arguments; an aggressive intellectuality that some saw as impressive, and others as dreadful, but that was widely viewed as quintessentially Jewish. Jews seemed singularly adept at absorbing the more obscure products of high culture, a quest fueled, perhaps, by their drive to escape anything reminiscent of parochialism. Many would come to recognize that the analytical disdain they employed to distance themselves from Jews was itself a sign of the group's singularity.

From his earliest days as a writer, Rosenfeld insisted that Jewish influences did not cut him off from a larger, more commodious world but rather linked him all the more to it. Growing up Jewish meant that one understood, earlier and more fully, what it meant to live in a state of alienation—which was, for Rosenfeld, the condition in which any thoughtful person now experienced contemporary life. Jews knew, from their long, often grim history that it was inconceivable to feel entirely at home.

Rosenfeld often conflated the fate of Jews and blacks. This is implicit in a 1946 letter of recommendation that he wrote to the Guggenheim Foundation for James Baldwin. He found Baldwin wild and unpredictable, even admitted that he couldn't honestly foresee whether Baldwin would emerge as a great writer or a hoodlum. In the letter, however, he spoke about him solemnly, with no ambivalence, and sought to capture Baldwin's capacity to write about his own without losing his hold on what it meant to write as an American. His sense of Baldwin's qualities reflects some of Rosenfeld's own beliefs of how he sought to write as a Jew:

> He has a sympathy, rare in the rarest men, that can pene-
> trate outward disorder to the inner meaning, where the fact
> that men suffer degradation and the significance for human
> culture of that degradation, are one. This inner, broader
> meaning, the "cultural sense" is not separated from him by
> any area of vagueness, rhetoric or morally self-conscious
> good will; it is an immediate, painful perception. It is this
> which gives his right to say "we," "our," when he speaks both
> for the Negroes and for America; he has instinctively. [sic] I

know of no one with greater authority to speak both the part and the whole.[4]

In one of the most intriguing sections of *Passage from Home*—one of the very few in which the novel follows its protagonist beyond a rather small, claustrophobic cluster of familial rooms—Bernard wanders downtown in search of his aunt Minna. While watching the crowds, he reflects on "Negroes," on what different skin color might mean, and on how his own sense of who he is as a Jew compares: "I had come to know a certain homelessness in the world, and I took it for granted as a part of nature; had seen in the family, and myself acquired, a sense of sadness from which both assurance and violence had forever vanished. We had accepted it unconsciously and without self-pity, as one might accept a sentence that had been passed generations ago, whose terms were still binding though its occasion had long been forgotten. The world is not entirely yours; and our reply is: very well then, not entirely."[5]

For Rosenfeld himself the Jewish condition was, of course, far more than a mere "sentence that had been passed generations ago." His fluency in Yiddish (he spoke and wrote the language as would a native, according to Yiddish writers who knew him), his attachment to religious rituals like those surrounding Passover (which he wrote about often, sometimes passionately), and his emphatic belief that neurosis, and hence Jewishness, helped deepen one's sense of a fractured world—all propelled him to say things about Jewish life that others might have felt were indiscreet, or worse. He drew easily on Jewish sources—far more readily on Yiddish literary texts than on the religious canon neglected by secular Jewish schools of his childhood. When Rosenfeld wrote a letter of

congratulations to Oscar Tarcov on hearing of his engagement to Edith, whom he admitted he found attractive, Rosenfeld alluded to S. An-sky's famous play "The Dybbuk": "I felt
renewed when I cast my eyes on her, and now that she loves
you I feel fulfilled like a Dybbuk." Rosenfeld's writing on Jewish matters possessed a frankness that cut deep, and not only
because of his fabled candor. His relationship to Jewish culture was never that of a careful interloper; rather, he took his
Jewish origins seriously, wrestled with what they meant, and
expected his readers to hear him out. Rosenfeld was one of
the few in his intellectual circle who applauded the creation
of the State of Israel (he also argued this case in letters to his
aunts, who maintained a more stalwart, predictable universalism). He felt the bite of homelessness and believed that
taking Jewishness to heart meant facing squarely the reality
of alienation—"the one international banking system the
Jews actually control."[6]

In his contribution to the symposium "The Situation
of the Jewish Writer" in the 1944 *Contemporary Jewish Record,* he laid out his ideas about his relationship to Jewish life
most fully. The piece, sharp and engagingly eccentric, begins
with general reflections on what it means to be part of a mi-
nority and how such affiliation in contemporary America
might, mistakenly, be thought to constitute a "very simple
state of being," occupying "no more of a man's attention than
any ordinary fact of his history." This, he insisted, cannot be
the case for those minorities who have suffered; a history of
suffering complicates putting one's art first, for how can one
do so while maintaining "the security of a dignified neutral-
ity"? Jewish artists know that at any moment a hostile world
can call on them to account for their Jewishness, and how can
this not influence what they do? "It is therefore clear to me

that whatever contribution Jewish writers may make to American literature will depend on matters beyond their control as writers."[7]

Rosenfeld saw an advantage for Jewish-born artists to retain an intimacy, or at least an affinity, with the immigrant experience and to view society from the distance of a perpetual newcomer. This helps one take in things otherwise hidden: "Since modern life is so complex that no man can possess it in its entirety, the outsider often finds himself as the perfect insider." Moreover, since most Jews now belong to the urban middle class, they are inundated by influences richer and more varied than experienced by most Americans. (Rosenfeld was now, as always, an uncompromisingly urban writer who linked culture with city life.) He also argued, probably playfully, that as people mostly coming from semi-urban, even rural, settings in Europe, Jews continue to benefit "through subliminal orientation to more primitive surroundings" from an access to rural society that might deepen their appreciation for the rural American past. More important is that they know insecurity more intimately than others do, and this sense of dislocation, of persistent alienation, can put them in closer touch, at one and the same time, with their own people and the universal condition of humankind. To be Jewish helps in appreciating a condition now increasingly normative: "Today nearly all sensibility—thought, creation, perception—is in exile, alienated from the society in which it barely managed to stay alive."[8]

Jewish artists who are part of a community of sufferers and infused with an acute sense of justice are likely to feel all the more deeply the need for social change, Rosenfeld believed. Those who have experienced the worst have the capacity to treat the world the best. "Out of their recent sufferings one may expect Jewish writers to make certain inevitable moral discoveries. These discoveries, enough to indict the world, may also be crucial to its salvation." The piece ends by evoking Bellow: "[I]n every society, in every group, there are what Saul Bellow has called 'colonies of the spirit.' Artists create their colonies. Some day these may become empires."[9] It's striking that in a symposium highlighting America's leading Jewish writers—in which Bellow himself wasn't invited to participate—Rosenfeld drew him in, and concluded the essay by conflating his own vision with that of his friend.

One such artists' empire might resemble the once perilously fragile, now obliterated Jewish world of Eastern Europe, whose greatest bard was the Yiddish writer Sholem Aleichem (the pen name of Sholem Jacob Rabinowitch), who lived from 1859 to 1916. Rosenfeld wrote often about Sholem Aleichem, whom he first encountered at home or as a student at his afternoon Yiddish school, but his fullest essay on him was a 1943 review of Maurice Samuel's book *The World of Sholem Aleichem,* the first to introduce him widely to an English-reading audience. Rosenfeld shows himself as someone inside, intimate with this literary and cultural tradition, and he goes as far as to propose that Sholem Aleichem's attitudes toward Jews, culture, and even God are virtually identical to his own.

Best known today as the (actually, rather remote) inspiration behind *Fiddler on the Roof,* Sholem Aleichem was, as Rosenfeld understood, a writer of great sophistication who used a comic savagery to probe the Jewish condition, to interrogate the continued validity of Jewish theology, to understand the wages of family, fate, and politics. He was quite independent in his politics (eschewing, for example, the socialism popular among his Yiddish-reading public), adopted a conversational style of writing distinctly his own, and devoted immense energy to consolidating Yiddish literature as a force in Jewish life with some of the more innovative and well-funded publishing ventures in the history of the language. Rosenfeld described Sholem Aleichem as someone without faith but attuned to the issues at the core of religion. Speaking of the Jews of Eastern Europe, Rosenfeld proposed that "Their religion affected their most familiar and intimate emotions—the perpetual insecurity, fear, and nostalgia of the homeless—fortified them with parables, and provided a metaphysics of sentiment as well as an immediate guide to the conduct of life . . . it was fundamentally a secular religion, for it provided the only available basis for culture." Rosenfeld viewed Sholem Aleichem as a singularly intuitive student of alienation, as someone torn between the outdated religious mores of his people and the allure of a Russian cultural world that, on the whole, loathed Jews. His work is suffused with a preoccupation with salvation, with deliverance that wasn't the stuff of either traditional Jewish messianism or Russian radicalism. "Their revolution would first have to be historical: the history of the Diaspora would have to be brought to a close. Until then they had not even chains to lose."[10]

Sholem Aleichem has been superficially compared to Dickens. But a realist like Dickens is free to write in ways unavailable to a folk artist like Sholem Aleichem, for whom society must be "less the object than the source of his sentiment, and thus love." Writers like Sholem Aleichem cannot write simply as individuals; they remain attached, always, to their intimate and complex relationships with their own beleaguered community. Sholem Aleichem may have been "capable of greater individual expression than the one he achieved. But folk artists lose nothing by their sacrifices. . . . It was his love, not only his uncertainty, which made him cling to Jews, to a faith he had abandoned, and to celebrate with as great a joy and tenderness as possible, the impoverished world within which they built, and later lost their lives."[11] As in "The Situation of the Jewish Writer," Rosenfeld, despite his desire to be celebrated as a major world writer, here claimed that he understood—perhaps even saw himself as emulating—artists like Sholem Aleichem who, by casting their fate with their own people, sacrificed a measure of fame for the sake of integrity.

Still more autobiographical were Rosenfeld's reflections on the Yiddish writer Isaac Leib Peretz, who lived from 1852 to 1915. In a brilliant essay published in 1949, prompted by the appearance of another book by Maurice Samuel, *Prince of the Ghetto,* Rosenfeld lauded Peretz's (loosely defined, humanistic) socialism as well as his engagement with Hasidism, and confirmed that he felt a greater kinship with him than with any other Yiddish writer. His portrait of Peretz was cast against the backdrop of a milieu where the "life-energy" of Jews was being freed from religion, where writers like Peretz were engaged in forging a new, pragmatic Jewry. Rosenfeld considered pragmatism "an uncommon philosophy for Jews, whose practical sense had always been hitched to a religion." Peretz envisioned a Jewish culture that was more "renewal" than "revolution." He sought its secularization, which would preserve the spirit of Jewish tradition; its symbolism would remain but its content would be revamped. Peretz loathed soulless assimilators; shunned those willing to dump Judaism in the name of Spencer, or statistics, or baptism; and built much of his work around Hasidism's exuberant love of life, its communalism. He believed that these features could be meshed with the best of European culture to produce a splendidly new, culturally integrated Judaism. Peretz was, of course, too optimistic, too enraptured with lib-

eralism and its belief in the power of love, its inability to recognize the force of pure, brute power.[12] Rosenfeld wrote:

> This was of course a serious mistake, but the blame lies
> more on generosity than myopia. . . . Under this new dis-
> pensation the Jews from all over Europe were to form a com-
> munity within a community of nations in close and harmo-
> nious contact with one another; this influence was to
> radiate from Poland, which in turn had it from Peretz in the
> image of the balanced complexity of his own nature.[13]

Certainly a part of what Rosenfeld envied in folk artists like Sholem Aleichem and Peretz was the prospect of an
ongoing relationship with community. He hated isolation,
craving connection, not metaphorical but concrete; and these
predilections grew more acute as news of the Nazi catastrophe was disseminated. He read widely about these horrors,
and had strong views of their mostly inadequate treatment in
history or memoir. He made an emphatic case for the European Jewish catastrophe as the central marker distinguishing
prewar culture from that of the postwar world—moorless,
decultured, with all illusions shattered by the Nazis. Rosenfeld deplored all effort to maintain distance, to conduct oneself coolly, something all the more loathsome in the face of
such horror.

His journal in 1949 records how exasperated he was
with the statements on tyranny made by a widely read, anti-
Bolshevik Russian philosopher who sought to confront a now
murderous Marxism with spiritual arguments. As Rosenfeld
wrote, "Berdyaev: 'A tyrant never speaks with power. The man
who exerts force is absolutely powerless over those upon
whom he exerts it . . . ' Absolutely powerless!—no less! Concentration camps, death camps, furnaces running on sched-

ule, 6,000,000 Jews exterminated—the tyrant is powerless. This is idealism in the disgraceful sense."[14]

Early in 1948, he captured in a series of sketches he composed in English, then translated into Yiddish (first published in the socialist magazine *Tsukunft*), how a folk artist might write about the Jewish wartime catastrophe. The most compelling of these, "The Tailor," tells of a poor worker whose troubles grow out of his inability to stop thinking about the killing of the Jews of Europe. "With every stitch of the needle it seemed to him that he was stabbing a Jew. Another stitch, another life, another stitch, another life. And no one cared." He runs through the streets, crying, "Jews, ratevet"—"Jews are being murdered"; he shows newspapers to passersby; sends telegrams, letters; meets with the influential, but no one seems to care.[15]

One night he pulls the handle on the fire alarm box in his building. Immediately firemen appear, and once they arrive he explains about the "real fire blazing, the one seeking to burn the entire world." He shows them the newspapers, and he is, of course, taken away as a madman, strapped to a bed: "the nails against the tender skin . . . he falls into nightmarish sleep full of wild dreams."[16]

Rosenfeld appreciated that musings about catastrophe couldn't sustain a culture that saw itself as an heir to the beauty and wisdom of Sholem Aleichem or Peretz. He thought sporadically about what might be absorbed from the classical Jewish sources of the past and built into a new, transmuted Judaism. In *Passage from Home* he has Bernard reflect on the biblical tale of David and Bath-Sheba as an entry into a richly life-affirming Jewish culture. (Rosenfeld's friend Paul Goodman spoke often of the pertinence of King David as a model.) Rosenfeld built the same biblical allusions into an unpublished short story, "David and Bath-Sheba," that tells of Eisenstein, an inept Yiddish afternoon schoolteacher, taunted by students, blighted by narrow-minded school administrators, flattened by petty concerns. Stepping out of the toilet—where his students had locked him during recess—he faces his class as he takes a volume of Bible stories off the shelf and begins to read about Bath-Sheba: "He could feel, as he read, a quickening response from the children. He glanced up and he saw a flush mounting on their faces as they sat forward on their desks . . . all the children were intently watching the naked woman at her bath. . . . 'And she came in unto him, and he lay with her; for she was purified from her uncleanness.' And Eisenstein read on, feeling the children drawing closer and restored to him, clinging to his words, while he revealed a mystery to them, and with a lightening heart he joined them, he, too, listening intently to the story of David and Bath-Sheba."[17]

The prospect of nurturing communal bonds didn't, of course, figure prominently into Rosenfeld's agenda. He was an iconoclast, and he could be quite combative, even recklessly so. It is not impossible that sometimes he trumpeted his Jewish interests because he knew how uncomfortable they made those around him. But these interests of his remained fertile, and serious. Rosenfeld was one of the least likely of all the young, brash intellectuals then writing about Jewish matters in *Commentary* and elsewhere on the New York literary scene to be accused of disloyalty to the Jews.

Yet for a few explosive months—from late 1949 until early 1950—Rosenfeld was the enfant terrible of American Judaism.[18] In his October 1949 *Commentary* article "Adam and Eve on Delancey Street," Rosenfeld aired—comically, wildly, and with an earnest intelligence that gave the article its cocky, subversive power—matters then rarely made fun of by Jews, at least not within earshot of non-Jews. He called for the abolition of all Jewish dietary laws. He linked them to sexual repression, proposed that both were indelible features of the Jewish psyche, and declared that for Jews to more than merely survive they'd have to abandon both.

The article offended many—especially since it appeared in a Jewish magazine—and led to an effort to censure *Commentary,* even close it down. The denunciations galvanized the magazine's (then mostly liberal) readership, who deplored the pressure leveled on them. Letters for and against Rosenfeld poured into the offices of *Commentary* and its sponsor, the American Jewish Committee. Rosenfeld was shocked to find himself at the center of an explosive communal battle, and one with significant intellectual ramifications. Much, it then seemed, was at stake: Who was in the best position to speak about Jewish life—insiders or outsiders, old or young, pious or impious, the most learned or the most independent, and daring? How freely might one feel as a Jew in talking in a free society about embarrassing Jewish matters? Was there a risk in speaking openly about such things? Was the risk of not speaking about them still greater?

"The space between his large teeth gave his smile an ingenuous charm," wrote Bellow of Rosenfeld. "He had a belly laugh. It came on him abruptly and often doubled him up. His smiles, however, kindled slowly. He liked to look with avuncular owlishness over the tops of his specs. His wisecracks were often preceded by the pale blue glance. He began, he paused, a sort of mild slyness formed about his lips, and then he said something devastating. More seriously, developing an argument, he gestured like a Russian-Jewish intellectual, a cigarette between his fingers."[19] Rosenfeld could be very funny. His jokes were often tinged with angst; he tended to joke about misery or discomfort, which was, of course, one reason he so admired Sholem Aleichem. He could be as uninhibited as a little boy, and was probably more playful as an adult than he was as a boy. He built this humor—sharp, generous, and, as the years passed, not infrequently bitter—into his essays, less often into his fiction.

Reviewing an especially awful piece on Kafka, he wrote that it "attains a level of idiocy that surpasses even the demands of Stalinism." If, he proposed after reading the splendidly flaccid best-selling novel *Marjorie Morningstar,* he were pressed to summarize it: "The only continuous action or principle of suspense in this 565-page work is will she—or won't she? This goes on for 417 pages to become the longest tease in the modern novel until Marjorie is spoiled of her treasure during a total eclipse of the moon." In its original draft, his review of *Marjorie Morningstar* may well have been much funnier. Soon after his death, one of his friends wrote: "The only recent thing of [Isaac's] that I have, besides some letters, is the Herman Wouk review. And I have the rough draft he wrote of it before *Partisan Review* edited out the really nasty parts. It was truly funny, but they wouldn't print it." He was a brilliant mimic. "He imitated steam irons, clocks, airplanes, tugboats, big-game hunters, Russian commissars, Village poets, and their girl friends," recalled Bellow. He loved jokes, said Irving Howe, "even more than arguments . . . I would beg him to do his Yiddish version of Prufrock . . . or his devilish skit about Rahv and Phillips now deflated to Weber and Fields, spatting over who should go downstairs to buy stamps." He could revel in silliness: Monroe Engel remembered walking with him on a hot day in the Upper West Side when they spotted a boy masturbating near an open window; Rosenfeld called out to him, gesticulating wildly, happily. At parties Bellow and Rosenfeld would often compete with one another as to which of the two was funnier.[20]

The most comically savage of Rosenfeld's short stories is "The Party"—the piece of fiction that had so rattled Howe when he read it as a Trotskyist activist. Related in the staccato prose of an activist, with solemn references to "Great Days" and "Noble Ancestors," it is also peppered with swipes at Trotsky himself. "I cannot accept their interpretation of the character and personality of the young members, an altogether shortsighted approach which, for example, attributes Comrade Mexican's querulousness to the fact that he suffers from acne. It cannot be denied that his trouble is severe; but to limit his whole being to his pimples is to betray one's own limitations." It describes the sectlike workings of a marginal group that relishes its own invisibility. It works for a revolution that, in fact, it would never really want to experience because, quite simply, it wouldn't know what to do if the world were really in its hands: "But what a fortune—the whole world. You understand what is meant by the embarrassment of riches. Think—some day the world may actually fall into our hands! Then where would we run?"[21]

The party has some younger members, but they are restive, unhappy with this aimlessness, while the older members remain stalwart, immune to criticism. Finally, a protest is waged from within by a secret cell that calls itself the Ennui Club, and to call attention to the group's hopeless dullness, they engage in the politically corrosive, disruptive act of sustained, highly audible yawning. A leader of the Ennui Club is named, as it happens, Comrade Board: "Here, he yawned again. Some of the younger comrades yawned in return. The yawning spread to the other members and I, too, succumbed to it. Long drawn-out 'ho-hums' were heard, peculiar animal noises. Then, to everyone's astonishment, Board quit the platform in the middle of a sentence—something he had never been known to do. He shuffled to his seat and threw himself down, as one might throw himself onto a couch to sleep."[22]

Rosenfeld found virtually every institution he encountered constricting, hypocritical, silly, or worse, and bohemia was not spared. Henry Miller, he wrote, "falls so readily into the American stride, the tricky, self-advertising gait, that he becomes merely a conscious citizen, disgusted by his society, but by no means disassociated from it. Miller, the decultured man, can thrive only on the ruins of ancient cultures." Rosenfeld was certain that his friends who worked for *Commentary* had grown prematurely old, fat, and staid. He poked fun at the pompously provincial editor of *The New Leader,* Sol Levitas, who cobbled together a job for him as editor of the magazine's literary section. Rosenfeld was indiscreet, loved gossip ("gossip is a form of social history," he quipped), and fought battles (for Reich, especially) that he knew were doomed. "He loved to argue unpopular subjects and causes," remarked Phillips.[23] He had long been thinking about Orthodox Judaism, and months before the appearance of "Adam and Eve on Delancey Street" in *Commentary,* he had written a mocking riff that the magazine had decided not to run. He felt some admiration for Orthodoxy, especially its unpretentious tenacity, and the adults with the greatest integrity in *Passage from Home* are the Hasidim of Bernard's grandfather's tiny West Side synagogue. But ultimately Rosenfeld found Orthodoxy of any sort constraining (including, in time, Orthodox Reichianism). He tended to throw ideas around, testing them, poking at them, seeing which might float, or sink, or inspire better ones. "He was dogmatic, but he wore his dogmas out," observed Bellow.[24]

The writing of "Adam and Eve on Delancey Street" troubled Rosenfeld, and he pondered it long and hard, as described in his journal. He felt certain that he had hit upon something crucial; proof was that the mere thought of these matters made him uneasy, more so than anything he had written in years. He was convinced the piece spoke to some of his earliest, most disturbing influences. In November 1948, he published a sort of trial balloon, a piece titled "Kreplach," which appeared in *Commentary* as a review of Nathan Ausubel's *Treasury of Jewish Folklore*. It prompted no letters at all, not a whimper of protest. Yet its arguments were quite similar to those he made the next year in "Adam and Eve on Delancey Street." In "Kreplach," he explained the psychic backdrop to folkloristic preoccupations with kreplach, a food that figures in many popular Jewish tales: "The kr and ch sounds in Yiddish are deeply guttural, produced with a sound of phlegm, and the whole word . . . is plainly faecal in character. So also is the chopped meat, particularly when the kreplach is done. Now feces, as any child knows, is devil's food."[25] Preparing the essay, Rosenfeld discussed with Vasiliki how food was "a security symbolism" for Jews, with "Jewish mothers stuffing their children and fretting over food, as a way of giving them security against the outer world." He wrote extensively about it in his journal:

> I could never form any connection between Jews and sex; and the family was sexless. There was not even any dirty words in our speech . . . I don't recall any outright sexual repression; but then it wasn't necessary. Even before families got to it, it was licked.
>
> But then the milchigs-fleishigs taboo may be the sexual repressant. Milchigs, obviously, is female, fleishigs, male (but why is fish pareve?). Their union in one meal, in one vessel, on one plate is forbidden—the sex act! If this is so, one may expect to find that the contamination of a milchig vessel by fleishigs is less lightly regarded than vice versa—

investigate. Also look up the codes of conduct in it in
Deuteronomy or Exodus?

"Sticky love" seemed to take complete precedence
over contact love, driving it out. The life-image is familial
rather than sexual. . . .

My difficulty, even today, is reconciling sex-talk with
Jews, etc. Dirty jokes.[26]

"Adam and Eve on Delancey Street" was inspired, as
Rosenfeld described in the essay's beginning, by the window
of the new Lower East Side Kosher Beef Fry, where crowds,
mostly Jews, stood "oblivious to the burden of parcels, of er-
rands, and of business and in silence, not to interfere with
one another's contemplation" while they watched the making
of kosher bacon. Rosenfeld admitted that he too stood on the
spot longer than he could have imagined, mesmerized for reasons that were, at first, unclear: "The days went by, the crowds
grew, and still the clue was lacking. I was attempting to locate
the primal scene within the lifetime of the spectators, and I
would long have continued in this mistake, looking for the appropriate infantile memory to account for the fascination of
this spectacle, had it not occurred to me that it was not to the
childhood of present adults that I must turn, but to the childhood of our people. Now I am prepared to say that this scene
had its origin in Paradise."[27]

The window, as Rosenfeld saw it, provided an opportunity to spy on forbidden sexuality (at least the simulation of
it), lent special significance because it was highlighted by a
fictional overturning of the most obvious of all Jewish taboos,
the taboo of food. Rosenfeld proposed that even the food restrictions meted out to Adam and Eve were prompted by the
desire to regulate sexual conduct. This preoccupation with
sexual restriction permeates the Jewish consciousness, and

the maintenance and multiplication of dietary restrictions in Judaism through the ages is infused with a never-articulated sexual repressiveness. Especially since such repression is never linked explicitly with dietary laws, the lesson is all the more baffling, and potent. This is why onlookers are so fascinated by the window of Kosher Beef Fry, where Jewish bacon traduces a mental universe of unspoken, terrifying distinctions—treyf and kosher, milk and meat, female and male, shikes and shkotsim, Jews and the unrestrained. "My own Orthodox grandparents would tremble, as though some catastrophe had occurred, if milchigs and fleishigs ever came into contact with one another, and with good reason. This is the sexual taboo not only of exogamy, but of the sexuality of the tribe itself. It is the taboo of sex as such."[28]

Rosenfeld's argument isn't bolstered by much Jewish learning, as noted by his critics, and many criticized him on just these grounds. It was meant to be audacious, to shock a complacent culture, to force it to absorb belatedly some of the basic presumptions of modernity since Freud. Judaism has been ill-served by ignoring its own neurotic foundations—such foundations are at the basis of all cultures and Judaism would be far richer, and healthier, if it opened itself to other classical Jewish texts: "It is sad evidence of the sexual displacement in Jewish living that the sexual forms in the popular Jewish conception should derive not from the Song of Songs or any indigenous source within a rich and close-textured contact with life Judaism maintains, but from a forbidden exogamy, symbolized in food taboos." Only Hasidim should be permitted to keep kosher, he wrote. When Judaism quashes natural enthusiasm elsewhere, the kosher home becomes "an insidious ruin of life. The food taboos are all that is needed."[29]

The crowd finally, reluctantly, leaves the window: "Still

possessed, they tear themselves away, and recovering practical consciousness, rush down the street—to stop again at the corner, where they are lured . . . in the form of an egg cream. There is time for a quickie, to try once more to satisfy this hunger which is not hunger, to drown this anxiety in the bottom of a paper cup."[30]

None of this (or so was claimed in furious letter after letter) enraged his critics as a joke—the same joke that he admitted in his journal he was loath to tell—about the tenacity of Jewish food taboos. It spoke to the terror of mixing milk and meat because their mixture was a reenactment of the sex act itself. The piece tells of a man diagnosed with cancer whose doctor instructs him to soak his penis in hot water. His wife finds him, and she is outraged: "Cancer, shmancer, Dos iz a milchig teppel!" (Cancer, shmancer, that is a milk pot).[31]

That Rosenfeld attacked something as basic to Jewish culture as its dietary restrictions in America's leading Jewish monthly and, worst of all, used a (mildly) dirty joke to do so, stunned readers. The response was an immediate torrent of shock, and recrimination. "So indecent that no other reputable magazine would have tolerated it," M. L. Isaacs, dean of Yeshiva University, wrote to the Anti-Defamation League. Rabbi Samuel Kramer, president of the New York Board of Rabbis, spoke of his organization's "grief and shame" about the "scandalous piece." He warned that the "The crude vulgarity of 'Adam and Eve on Delancey Street' makes a change in editorial policy imperative." It was denounced in much of the Yiddish and Hebrew press: *Hadoar*, the Hebrew weekly based in New York, spoke of it as the product of an author whose literary talent is "mediocre at best," one of the many new *Commentary* writers who were "Johnny-come-latelies . . . [and] . . . have rediscovered the fold of righteousness." They were no better than "self-hating penitents," it insisted.[32]

The most comprehensive and influential attack—by a figure of intellectual stature in Jewish life and, to an extent, beyond—was leveled by the rabbi of the prestigious Park Avenue Synagogue, Milton Steinberg. He was a widely published writer who had appeared in the *Atlantic Monthly* and elsewhere, held a philosophy degree from Columbia, and was one of the leading thinkers of the new, burgeoning, and professedly liberal Reconstructionist Movement headed by Mordecai Kaplan. He had written several books, including the popular guide *Basic Judaism* and an intriguing novel set in ancient Judea. The novel, *As a Driven Leaf*, published a decade before the Rosenfeld affair, was devoted, as it happens, to the theme of heresy. Its protagonist was the well-known ancient rabbinic rebel Elisha ben Abuyah, who in Steinberg's book is a brilliant, intellectually ambitious man who pursues radical ideas to their most extreme and dies friendless, bitterly aware of his folly. The line separating (what Steinberg saw as) legitimate from destructive debate had long preoccupied him, and he viewed himself at the cusp of Jewish liberal thinking in America. Rosenfeld's piece—and more so, *Commentary*'s approach to Jewish life—defined its outer limits. The magazine was misguided; Steinberg loathed its editorial policy with its jaundiced treatment of Jewish communal and ritual life, its cool attitude toward Zionism, its skittish stance toward recognized Jewish leaders who were seldom invited to write for it. His last two books had been shabbily reviewed in *Commentary*, which probably had not endeared him to the publication.[33]

Prompted by the Rosenfeld essay, Steinberg waged something of a one-man campaign against the magazine. He gave a sermon on *Commentary* at the Park Avenue Synagogue and circulated it to all members of the American Jewish Committee, *Commentary*'s sponsor, which had more or less maintained a hand's-off policy with regard to its content. He also collated—in the form of a lengthy memo—the many, mostly enthusiastic responses he received in the wake of his attack on *Commentary* and forwarded this document to the leadership of the AJC. He wrote to at least one member of *Commentary*'s publication committee (which nominally oversaw the monthly): "from the point of view of both religious and elemental decency . . . ['Adam and Eve on Delancey Street'] is one of the nastiest flights of imagination that has come my way in a long time." He added that it was "straight pornography, to boot." In his widely distributed sermon, he insisted that *Commentary* had succeeded in "making enemies of its natural friends." "I fear," he appended, that "it is engaged in nothing less than undermining its own status, perhaps its existence."[34]

Steinberg coordinated his efforts with the pugnacious Jewish journalist Carl Alpert, who also contacted the entire AJC membership: "If you approve of pornography and anti-Semitism peddled under the imprint of the American Jewish Committee, you may not be interested in the rest of this letter. . . . Please re-read the Rosenfeld article. It is not only smut, but actually anti-Semitism worthy of the best efforts of Streicher and Goebbels." Alpert—and Steinberg—asked how the committee could justify spending money (they claimed $295,746 annually) on *Commentary,* especially since, as Alpert put it, this "is not a solitary instance, but is typical of an editorial policy . . . which I plan to continue probing publicly."[35]

Given the ferocity of these attacks, it is surprising that there is so little historical residue. Retrospective assessments of the two most public Jewish intellectual controversies of the 1950s and '60s—Philip Roth's fiery entry as an author in the late 1950s and the explosion over Hannah Arendt's 1963 book *Eichmann in Jerusalem*—make no mention of the Rosenfeld affair. Yet it was the immediate precursor, especially in the prominence it gave the question as to whether there was a cost for Jews living in a free society when one of their own made outrageous claims about their people. The obscurity of the Rosenfeld episode remains puzzling, a reminder of the fickleness and the oddity of historical memory, how it records some matters indelibly, sometimes obsessively, and blithely blots out others.

Calling it an "explosion" that was "positively medieval," Philip Rahv wrote, "I cannot remember such a furor in the pages of a magazine not primarily addressed to a Jewish public."[36] It quickly turned into a fight over the editorial independence of *Commentary* and, more broadly, the role of intellectuals in American Jewish life. In the November issue, Elliot Cohen apologized for the piece; "certainly there was one anecdote that was in very bad taste," he noted in a statement in the magazine. In December, the American Jewish Committee president Jacob Blaustein stated in a letter to the editor: "During the four years that the American Jewish Committee has sponsored *Commentary*, it has, as you know, never attempted to exercise control over its contents. . . . The publication in your October issue, on the other hand, of an article entitled 'Adam and Eve on Delancey Street,' which besides offending the religious sensibilities of a large number of our coreligionists, violated every canon of good taste was, in the opinion of our officers and Administrative Committee, an abuse of the editorial freedom accorded you." He added that he was pleased that he received assurances from the magazine's editor and its publication committee that "steps will be taken to ensure against a similar occurrence in the future."[37]

Letters now poured in from leading intellectuals like Dwight MacDonald, Irving Howe, Mary McCarthy, Oscar Handlin, Harold Rosenberg, and many others. (Oddly, Bellow, away in Paris, doesn't seem to have weighed in.)[38] Rosenfeld's piece was, said McCarthy, "a buoyant fantasy, amiable, mildly ribald, full of good feeling." Any objection to it "quite takes one's breath away."[39] Referring, perhaps, to Steinberg, Howe accused those who attacked the Rosenfeld article of being "mediocre enemies" motivated by "professional jealousy."[40] In response to an attack on Rosenfeld in the *Congress Weekly*, an organ of the American Jewish Congress that denounced the shameful article written by a "certain Isaac Rosenfeld," the novelist and critic Harvey Swados retorted that he was "one of this country's leading literary critics" and the author of a first-rate and sympathetic novel about Jewish life.[41] Included among Rosenfeld's few defenders in the Yiddish press was the iconoclastic cultural critic S. Niger, who had long admired the intellectual stamina of the young intellectuals writing for *Commentary*. He admonished his colleagues in his column in *Der Tog (The Day)*: "When one of them, through lack of knowledge, makes jokes and errs, they want to exterminate him as in the case of Isaac Rosenfeld. . . . They want to exterminate not only him, but every one who does not write as we would want him to. We completely lose control of ourselves, all in the name of Jewishness."[42]

For a month or two until the furor died down, the magazine's editorial freedom felt at risk. Rosenfeld wrote to Elliot Cohen: "What would a man in Mr. Blaustein's position do about this? Demand the burning of Freud's books, the excommunication of anyone who dares to suggest that the Jewish religion, like any other, has a latent sexual content? Insult the magazine of which he should recognize that he has the greatest reason to be proud? And perhaps my article was right—doesn't the irrational response to it demonstrate that many deep taboos are present in our religion?"[43] *Commentary* had, since it started in 1945, been a mainstay of Rosenfeld's writing life; it was the only magazine that excerpted *Passage from Home* and he depended on it for his income (the magazine paid well). The treatment he received felt galling, and he couldn't appear in its pages for a year and a half.

Commentary was, indeed, an odd beast. Funded by one of the most staid and respectable Jewish organizations (and one strongly committed to serious, original research on Jewish life), the magazine sought to give visibility to the fullest range of contemporary culture, including those with only distant pertinence to obvious Jewish concerns. It presumed, as Cohen stated in its first issue, that for Jewish life to flourish in a liberal society meant that Jews' concerns needed to be drastically expanded: "There will be new patterns of living, new modes of thought, which will harmonize heritage and country into a new sense of at-home-ness in the modern world. Surely, we who have survived catastrophe can survive freedom, too."[44] Elliot Cohen felt, as Steinberg and others rightly suspected, a disdain for most involved Jewish communal life. Yet his contacts were numerous—for years he had been a successful Jewish community fundraiser and he knew how to flatter as well as bludgeon. He was more a brilliant impresario of ideas than an original intellectual, and his writing style was wooden. As an editor, he had impeccable taste, although he was known to revise the work of the magazine's best writers too extensively. He tended to vacillate in his relationships at *Commentary* between paternal and abusive behavior, and while he could be nurturing (and often was, especially to young writers), he could also be hectoring and relentless.[45]

The battle over Rosenfeld's essay was familial and thus all the more angrily fought. "Well you probably know all about the fuss my article created," he wrote to his aunts, Dora and Rae, in early December.

I hope you were on my side, but I suppose you thought I
went too far. It's just about blown over by now, and I can
come out of hiding. It was really a shock for me that there
should have been such a crazy reaction—after all, Freud
and hundreds of others had said the same thing for years,
even if they didn't apply it directly to Jewish life. But why
must Jewish life be the exception? I suppose I would have
written it differently—though I would have said the same
thing. I mean in a different tone—had I suspected it would
produce such a mad response, and the editors, you can be
sure, were also flabbergasted. But any way, don't let any one
brow beat you about it. It was not anti-Semitic, not terrible,
not a disgrace. It tried to say something about a subject
that's been a taboo for centuries. I was glad to see that Pa
[Rosenfeld's father] stuck up for me.[46]

For most of Rosenfeld's defenders, the issue was simple and clear: freedom of expression, not censorship. But, as
Commentary's critics argued, the magazine was an avowedly
Jewish publication, sponsored by a Jewish organization: did
this not imply certain allegiances and, no less pertinent, also
limitations? The issues highlighted in Commentary mattered
urgently to the magazine's writers and readers precisely because they cut deep, as indicated by both the quantity and the
intensity of the letters written in reply. The letters made clear
that the Rosenfeld piece reminded many who weighed in (on
Rosenfeld's side, at least) of adolescent battles waged, mostly
inconclusively, at parents' homes. Rosenfeld appreciated—he
recorded in his journal while writing the piece—that he had
touched a nerve that unsettled him, too; at stake was far more
than the origins—irrevocably obscure, no doubt—of Judaism's dietary laws. At stake were relations between the intellectuals and community in Jewish life. Did the two have
anything useful to say to one another? What did it mean for

Steinberg to write off someone like Rosenfeld? What was lost as a result?

Historian Oscar Handlin, at the start of what would be a distinguished career at Harvard, wrote in support of Rosenfeld: "We can't have it both ways. The reason why people I could name to you respect *Commentary* is because it is a medium through which the Jewish community shows it can tolerate free enquiry on its own life. To limit, or even to arouse the suspicion of limiting, that freedom would undermine the basis of that respect." *Commentary* emerged from what Handlin described as a Jewish cultural desert, one where all the other existing Jewish literary efforts, like the Jewish Publication Society, were faulted for their inwardness, their parochialism. To thwart *Commentary* was, insisted Handlin, to shut down the one significant conduit between the Jewish communal world and the Jewish intelligentsia.[47]

Handlin's argument assumed aridity, lack of any real independence beyond the avant-garde at *Partisan Review* or *Commentary,* whose Jewish sensibility, according to Howe, was their "quickness, skepticism, questioning."[48] What unsettled so many in the Jewish community about *Commentary* was, as Podhoretz put it, "the general tone of detachment in which things Jewish were discussed . . . with the same disinterestedness, the same candor, the same range of references, and the same resonance as any serious subject."[49] Many of the magazine's writers were, indeed, detached from much. Many, like Rosenfeld, were the first to define themselves in America through something other than their relationship to the immigrant experience, the first to be neither nostalgic nor hostile toward the immediate past. What excited them about it—and brought them to *Commentary*—was, as Howe noted, "precisely the idea of discarding the past, breaking away from families, traditions and memories."[50] How to embrace, albeit uneasily, a culture that you also felt free to savage? Indeed, how to make such critical engagement the primary, even singular, way in which you were involved in Jewish life? Rosenfeld's essay gave sudden, widespread prominence to these dilemmas.

Harold Rosenberg (then an uncommonly loquacious East Village intellectual who eventually became the influential art critic for *The New Yorker*) wrote a letter reacting to the AJC president's proposal that editorial freedom could exist with implicit constraints: "Mr. Blaustein cannot have it both ways; he cannot grant freedom to an editor and at the same time retain it for himself. Nor is [*sic*] the fact that there is a wide area of editorial choice that would arouse no objection from Mr. Blaustein reduce the degree to which editorial freedom is violated. Freedom exists precisely on the borderline where one man's choice does conflict with another's."[51] Blaustein's approach to this problem, which he sought to resolve by administrative fiat, conceals something crucial:

> The issue here is that the Rosenfeld article did, as Blaustein declares, offend religious sensibilities and certain orders of taste. Yet the editor of *Commentary* did not find the piece offensive. Nor did many of the readers among whom . . . I unhesitatingly include myself. That some Jews should be deeply outraged by a thing, while other Jews are not even aware of the offense, and even find pleasure in it, what could be more serious?
>
> The cleavage among thoughtful Jews which Rosenfeld's piece surprisingly exposed seems to me one of the most significant facts of Jewish life in America. If the publication of the article was a mistake, it was one of those mistakes which open a shaft into the darkness, and of which the intelligence should always stand ready to profit. The writers in the Jewish press who pounced on Rosenfeld as an example of the separation of certain Jewish intellectuals from the

moods, views and values of the Jewish "mass" and its cultural representatives had a very strong point. . . . Instead of
covering up this cleavage in the Jewish world with administrative edicts and editorial apologies—a cleavage which can
hardly fail to extend into a youth which is, after all, much
more taken with Freud, and Reich, D. H. Lawrence and
Joyce, than with the Shulchan Aruch [Code of Jewish
Law]—should not *Commentary* regard it as a major function
to discuss it fully, with the courageous resolve to face whatever the discussion may reveal?[52]

Recalling the period, Howe wrote about how rabbis
and other communal leaders would now often beseech young
intellectuals like him to "come home," to return to synagogue,
and to the bosom of institutional life. Few were drawn in, said
Howe, because for them things Jewish pinched, offering risk,
not certainty.[53] But attracted they were—as is clear from
richly probing, sometimes brilliant articles produced for
Commentary, and elsewhere. They were drawn in by the war,
the resilience of antisemitism, the discovery of Kafka (to a
lesser extent, Isaac Babel), their sense of kinship, or at least
fate. Some months later, Harold Rosenberg sought to clarify
what it meant to build a Jewish culture around risk rather
than security, in another *Commentary* essay—"Jewish Identity in a Free Society." He did so referring to the Rosenfeld affair. Beginning the text with Kafka's allusive "What have I in
common with Jews? I have hardly anything in common with
myself," Rosenberg acknowledged that while few Jews of his
day look, dress, or speak like their grandparents, and while
one's background, or physical build, or the kinkiness of one's
hair no longer determines fate, it is impossible to presume
that one exists in an anonymous world without history. It
seems clear to many of us, noted Rosenberg, that who we are
is influenced by our ancestors, but "that something is not all

there is to us." Freedom is a contemporary fate, and being Jewish doesn't free one from its burdens. "We are anonymous enough to have to make ourselves; yet we *are*, too, and cannot make ourselves in utter freedom."[54] The prospect that some form of Orthodoxy might be embraced—much as T. S. Eliot adopted Anglicanism because (as he put it) "I do not hope to turn again"—cannot solve this dilemma for most. For most intellectuals there is only the prospect of living with uncertainty, yet despite their being outsiders, their opinions ought to be solicited. Hearkening back to Steinberg, Rosenberg wrote:

> One eminent rabbi summed up the case by pointing out that while criticism of Jewish life and tradition is always welcome, such criticism ought to be constructive criticism—but that constructive criticism could not come from the detached individual since he is "rootless" and without commitment to "the Jewish enterprise."[55]

But if "rootless" intellectuals are uninterested in the Yiddish press or rabbis, is it because they are destructive or defeatist? Is it possible that they're disinterested because neither is interesting? There is no longer a Jewish community that commands allegiance or presumes that anything less is unacceptable. In this new moral universe, "is it always known what will be constructive and what destructive?" Rosenberg responded to this question with a Hasidic tale: "There is the story of the Hasidic rabbi who said to another Hasid, 'I have more learning than you and more righteousness—how is it that so many come to you and so few to me?' Said the other, 'Perhaps they come to me because I am surprised that they come, and they don't come to you because you are surprised that they don't come.'"[56]

To define is to exclude, and those who seek strict de-marcations on the boundaries of Judaism may well alienate many who might otherwise come inside. And it may well be precisely such outsiders that might help best determine the most creative future for Jewish life: "For instance, few Ortho-dox Jews of two generations ago would have expected that the ideas of the 'goy' Herzl would become a center of Jewish feel-ing." Rosenberg ended the essay with an extraordinary asser-tion, a prediction of cultural primacy:

> The Jew whom the Jewish past has ceased to stir, whom every collective anguish or battle for salvation passes by, may tomorrow find himself in the very center of the movement toward the future. Like the reputation of the zaddik, a com-munity is often built by surprise. Perhaps it is just those Jews who arrive from nowhere who will come to resemble most closely their remotest and most venerable grandfa-thers.[57]

In a liberal age, argued Rosenberg, Steinberg was the anachronism, his presumptions—essentially conservative de-spite his vigorously asserted theological progressivism—out of kilter. Freedom meant that identity was made of disparate pieces that didn't easily fit. Rosenfeld understood this far bet-ter than his critics, and intellectuals like him might well offer a more authentic, vibrant vision of Jewish life.

In the end, little changed. Steinberg justly felt that his criticisms weren't taken to heart; more than a month after he lodged his complaints, *Commentary*'s editors had sent no more than a formal acknowledgment. Elliot Cohen dismissed him in a memo to the American Jewish Committee as a garru-lous partisan; Cohen's friendships with donors to the AJC helped him withstand the onslaught. Steinberg died soon af-terward. *Commentary* wasn't checked in its editorial policy, but Rosenfeld was kept out of it for some time. When he wrote for it again, journalist Carl Alpert sought to stir up new protests (against his Gandhi piece) but failed.[58] Just how Rosenfeld reacted to the firestorm remains unclear. His letter home about it to his aunts, Rae and Dora, was coy. He told them in early December that the situation had basically blown over and that he was distressed by his estrangement from *Commentary*. He confided to friends how angry he was about the loss of money at a time of mounting financial difficulty (he had given up his job at *The New Leader*); his marriage was frayed and he could ill-afford the strain. Friends later remembered him as intensely depressed by it all.[59]

Still, when he began publishing again in *Commentary*, one of his first essays was a lengthy analysis of Abraham Cahan's *The Rise of David Levinsky*, widely considered an unassailable fixture in the Jewish literary canon, and Rosenfeld used in it arguments basically identical to those that had ignited the 1949 storm. Times had changed and Steinberg was dead, but Rosenfeld was still furious about what had transpired and he continued to lean (more critically by then) on Reich's teachings. On rereading Cahan's book, Rosenfeld discovered, much to his surprise, an acutely perceptive portrait of the modern Jewish condition, with ample evidence of the destructive yearnings he had highlighted in "Adam and Eve on Delancey Street." Once again, he insisted in the pages of *Commentary* that these must be purged if Jews were to become healthy, fully realized human beings. This time he used the venerable Cahan, a mainstay of America's Jewish cultural arsenal, to bolster his case.

In his essay, "David Levinsky: The Jew as American Millionaire," Rosenfeld described his discovery that a novel he had long "imagined . . . was a badly written account of immigrants and sweatshops in a genre which . . . was intolerably stale by now" was, in fact, an illuminating study of the "Jewish character." He called this portrait—of a millionaire adrift, engulfed by longing that money and power cannot assuage—"one of the best fictional studies" of its kind. "Nothing in a man's life could be more purely Jewish [than] his constant longing," Rosenfeld claimed. The story of the millionaire who finds his life meaningless is a staple of American literature, but what Cahan understood especially well was the interplay between tensions uniquely American and Jewish. Born in the novel to a poor family in Lithuanian Russia, Levinsky, an excellent student, distinguishes himself in Jewish learning, but when his mother dies violently (he had been fatherless since the age of three), he begins a life of yearning: "Levinsky's character was formed by hunger," noted Rosenfeld. "The individual experiences of his life—poverty, squalor, orphanage, years of religious study, and sexual restraint, the self-sacrificing of his mother and her violent death—all these experiences contain, as their common element, a core of permanent dissatisfaction."[60]

No doubt Rosenfeld's discovery that Levinsky's hunger is inspired by a quest—doomed and hence all the more encompassing—for his dead mother drew him still closer to the novel, which seemed to mirror his own, anguished search. Levinsky's quick disposal of women, his distrust of those interested in him, his sense that somewhere out there is a woman utterly pure and that only she can redeem him—all this spoke deeply to Rosenfeld.

Everything that brings others pleasure feels stale, hollow, for Levinsky. Entering business feels like a compromise, an escape from the scholarly life he considers most important although, in the end, wanting. In his personal life, he is condemned to loneliness and the belief that the only reason people like him is his money. "No matter how many transformations [his life] undergoes, his hunger remains constant. He longs for his wretched boyhood (which appeals to him 'as a sick child does to its mother') from which, were he able to reenter it, he would again be driven in an endless yearning after yearning."[61] Such feelings were insatiable, especially since they were so primal that they clouted Judaism's heart— with its injunctions to yearn for Jerusalem, and the anguish concretized (as Rosenfeld understood it) in "the obdurate and seemingly ridiculous prohibition of shaving the beard." All this built into the heart of a culture to sustain a hunger preserved at all cost and with no prospect of ever ending.[62] America has added a new, perverse twist with its lesson that riches bring no happiness, that the chief joy is in getting there, not being there. Judaism seems a powerful expression of what Tolstoy described as the "desire for desire." The "congruity" linking Jews and Americans on this score is one reason, Rosenfeld suggested, for the "almost flawless Americanization" that Jews have experienced.[63]

Cahan's style, Rosenfeld admitted, is often clumsy. But his understanding of Jews—and human nature—is sharp. Rosenfeld saw Cahan's book as a brilliant analysis of what it felt like to be lost in a search that consumes all and obstructs the best in life. Levinsky sacrifices his enjoyment of his wealth and stature and loses all capacity for love. In Levinsky's story, Rosenfeld read the same message as at the window of Kosher Beef Fry, where Jews—and, of course, he too— stood in a state of perverse glee, watching the traducing of taboos whose obliteration is essential for Jews to partake in any future joy.

By the early 1950s, Rosenfeld's life once again felt as if it was unraveling. His second novel sat unfinished, together with other uncompleted manuscripts on his cluttered desk.

He had no money, little joy at home. If Howe's characterization of Rosenfeld in a state of "lonely sloth" is accurate, it probably refers to the early 1950s. After years of indiscretions, he decided to leave Vasiliki. He insisted she had never looked better: "I still admire her, and she's still the best girl I know, but whether I still love her I don't know." He longed for the children, who took the separation badly, especially George. Monroe Engel recalled that when, in the late 1940s, Rosenfeld first announced to him that he and Vasiliki were splitting up, the couple couldn't take their hands off one another. They separated, came back together, and repeated much the same pattern until they divorced shortly before Rosenfeld's death.[64]

His relationship with Bellow, too, had worsened, and now in ways that neither could ignore. Bellow was already a well-known writer with a name that mustered admiration far beyond the confines of New York intellectuals. Even if his second novel, *The Victim*, published in 1947, sold modestly, it consolidated his international standing. In London in the late 1940s, he was feted as a literary celebrity. He returned to New York from his Guggenheim-funded stay in Europe stiffer, a bit pompous, slipping the odd French phrase (mispronounced, or so said critics) into casual conversation. Bellow found the bohemian scene at Rosenfeld's apartment pathetic, sordid. They saw one another less and less outside NYU, where both taught, and although they continued to joke in public both knew the friendship had soured: "I see Saul once in awhile— in fact, quite often—but still don't get along too well with him," Rosenfeld wrote to Tarcov. "I'm jealous of him and I think he is of me; I'm ready to admit it, but I don't think he is. . . . He's poured everything into his work, which seems to be all he lives for. He's really very sad and the 'literary figure' and the self consciousness don't hide it." Rosenfeld understood that an unrelenting jealousy was at the heart of his painful relationship: "Jealousy is a twitch at the nostril, the muscle at the side of the nose contracting and raising the upper lip, accompanied by queasy sensations in the diaphragm and a disturbance of the regular rhythm of breathing," he wrote in his journal. Bellow remained convinced that Rosenfeld didn't take his talent seriously, that he wasted too much time on random sentiment, on friendships, on sex, on the sort of things that were, as Bellow saw them, best done once the writing day was over.[65]

Desperate for a regular salary, Rosenfeld in 1952 followed Ralph Ross, a loyal friend, to the University of Minnesota to teach in the humanities program Ross now headed. A powerful presence at the time as an academic administrator, Ross was invited to launch a humanities program built largely around the teaching of Western culture by writers, not scholars, and threw himself into this work. (Robert Penn Warren, Allen Tate, John Berryman, and Bellow were among those Ross brought to Minnesota.) "Enough sickness, misery, pain, tears, and agony; I say this for myself, too. Now let there be peace and recovery, God grant it," Rosenfeld wrote to Tarcov. Rosenfeld was warmly received in Minnesota and managed to dispense "with the arbitrary distance customarily placed between students and teachers." He urged that they call him Isaac and was often surrounded by a cluster of students as he walked the campus. "He sat on the table like a tailor in his Johnson Hall classroom," wrote Doris Hedlund, a former student, in a eulogy in the student newspaper, the *Minnesota Ivory Tower,* "and borrowed cigarettes from all the students (or did he borrow? I guess he just asked for them). He was always in need of matches, flipping the used ones on the floor somewhere near the corner wastebasket." His teaching style was informal, but his commitment to learning was

fierce: "He liked argument and discussion, the hotter the better," said Hedlund. "He became visibly depressed when his
class was not stirred to do battle over Voltaire. . . . Isaac, who
was colorful enough when expounding philosophical ideas or
political theory, was doubly so when his subjects were poetry,
drama, or fiction."[66]

Soon after his death, another of his students, Joanne
Joseph, later a poet and actress, wrote this reminiscence of
his teaching:

> see you damning and
> Justifying and personifying
> The privilege of living and
> Literature
> In that canoe saying what a
> Faker is Hemingway and
> Across the coffee table with
> Coffee and lines of Hopkins, and
> Sitting on the professor's table
> Swaying your short round legs
> Languidly
> Telling profundities to your
> University infants
> Who took them like pop from you . . . [67]

She ended the poem with these words scrawled at the
bottom of the page: "I think of a dream once with you walking
up and embracing and smiling. And then you again come . . .
no greeting, and you clasp a pocket red-covered copy of The
God That Failed against your cherub chest."[68] The imagery
feels romantic, and the emotional pull she described was the
product of Rosenfeld's intellectual charisma, the ability to
make learning feel indispensable.

As always, he lived in the midst of impossible clutter;

William Phillips, who sublet his Minneapolis apartment, was volubly appalled by it. (Phillips discovered a beehive nestled in the wall.) Rosenfeld had separated from Vasiliki before leaving for Minnesota, but they sought to reconcile and she and the children joined him for several months in Minneapolis. "I'd like to try leading a regular middle class life with a garden . . . to play ping-pong. Seriously, the next year or so should be more crucial for our marriage than even the separation was and I'd like to give it a real hard try," he wrote to Oscar. Vasiliki charmed many who met her in Minnesota. They were entranced by how she threw back her head when she laughed and by her liveliness at faculty parties. Her candor and sisterly warmth drew people to her. She tried hard to hold onto Rosenfeld; they talked about his taking a job teaching writing in Oregon; and she sought to contain her volatility, to hold back her temper, and to flirt less. But she seemed frantic, desperate. He continued to seek out other women, she sought out other men, and the reconciliation failed.[69]

Rosenfeld admitted to his new friends that never had he managed to satisfy Vasiliki sexually and she openly acknowledged that this was the case. By their time together in Minnesota in 1952, they had strayed too far, and stretched the boundaries of their married life recklessly: "I was naughty with Saul," she confessed, coyly, to a Minnesota friend.[70]

Once Bellow's *The Adventures of Augie March* appeared in 1953, Rosenfeld spoke openly, obsessively, to friends in Minnesota about his jealousy. He couldn't seem to stop talking about Bellow, the novel's countless faults, how overrated it was. He acknowledged these feelings even to his aunts, Dora and Rae; typically he edited the most unsettling aspects of his life out of letters to them. Rosenfeld praised Bellow's new novel in his letters to him, but even there he couldn't resist a note of equivocation: "I have not been able to

Sidney Passin with Eleni and George.
Photograph courtesy of Daniel Rosenfeld.

get along with you in recent years, but I got along famously with Augie. I loved it, immensely, most every bit of it, & even the parts that I didn't like I liked. It's an ocean-full of everything you've been & and not been & and dreamed & wanted, a tremendous spouting proclamation of someone struggling up from the depths." He admitted to Tarcov that "my friendship with Saul . . . [is] . . . almost no friendship at all. I was terribly jealous of him, mistrustful and hostile . . . I'd like to change it, though this is also something I'd rather do in person." Rosenfeld described himself to Tarcov as "fat, gassed, depressed and on the verge of tears." His depressions grew more acute. He felt burdened by Bellow's sense of him as having failed literature; he spoke of Bellow with anger and disappointment, something akin to the hurt of a bruised lover. Bellow recognized this, and it ate at him. "I still resent his not too well hidden hope that I fall on my face," he wrote to Tarcov in 1953. "If we're ever to be friends again, that's got to stop."[71]

Perhaps prompted by jealousy over Bellow's great breakthrough and, no doubt, because of the financial burden of supporting two households, Rosenfeld threw himself into an odd array of publishing commitments. He agreed to write a book on the Chicago fire; biographical information about him in several of his last published essays describes him as working on the book. A rather pedestrian draft with the working title "A Hot Time in the Old Town: The Great Chicago Fire, 1871" was found among his papers at the time of his death. He agreed to write a book on Tolstoy for New Directions. (Vasiliki indicated that Rosenfeld liked to give the impression that he knew the Russian language, which he did not.) No more than a chapter of it was completed. And, in 1954, having failed to persuade major publishers to take it on, he published a collection, *King Solomon and Other Stories,* with a new, untested Minneapolis press, McCosh and Sherman. Launched by a bookseller, McCosh, and a nervy literary hanger-on—later a speechwriter for Herbert Humphrey—Norman Sherman, the venture may well have published only this one book. (The only library copy I've been able to locate is in Special Collections at the University of Alberta.) Rosenfeld's decision to publish with them seemed a particularly desperate one. "What a life!" he wrote to Tarcov in April 1953. "I remember the dreams, plans, ambitions, and energies I used to have—and they make me feel insignificant now. I hope you're not such a middle-aged shmuck like me." Curiously, at much the same time, he agreed to serve as an editor working with the poet Eliezer Greenberg on an English-language anthology of Yiddish literature—but then resigned. Once published, in 1954, *A Treasury of Yiddish Stories* edited by Greenberg and Irving Howe became the most widely read, influential book of its kind. Rosenfeld continued to appear often in *Commentary* and elsewhere, and traveled to the Salzburg Seminar in Austria, in March 1954 to teach (together with the preeminent literary critic of the day, Edmund Wilson) at a nine-day seminar on American philosophy in relation to literature. Hannah Arendt, an admirer, may have helped firm up the invitation. Rosenfeld left a vague, indeterminate impression on Wilson, who merely noted disparagingly in his diary that there was a philosopher on the faculty named Rosenfeld who drew his lectures from class notes prepared for students back in the United States. There, at least as Wilson saw him, Rosenfeld wasn't much of a teacher, and Wilson seemed unaware that Rosenfeld wrote fiction and literary criticism.[72]

In the summer of 1954, Rosenfeld left Minnesota—much to the surprise of his closest friends there—to teach at the basic humanities program at the University of Chicago. Classes were downtown, far from the spirals, intellectual intensity, splendid libraries, and literary dives of the main Hyde

Park campus, and the program had little of the university's prestige. Rosenfeld continued to feel at odds with himself and admitted that he was eager to return to New York to be close to his children and the center of the literary world. He hated his dependence on a university salary, but knew of no other to way to survive. He mused about returning to Vasiliki. He was rejected for a second Guggenheim Fellowship. He wrote to Bard College and was either turned down or (as at least one friend recalled) refused to pay for transportation to his interview. He seemed more and more easily bruised, increasingly desperate. Rosenfeld tried hard, again without success, to get an invitation to teach at Brandeis, and urged Tarcov, who worked for the Anti-Defamation League, to find a job for him with a New York Jewish organization. He planned to be in the city later that week: "I'm perfectly serious," he wrote in October 1955, "I've had enough of living in exile in rooming houses, I want to be back where my life is. If there's anyone I could see about a job this Friday (I should be there around 10:45 AM) please let me know." He asked for the address of "Wally Markfield," who worked for the American Jewish Committee.[73]

To some, he seemed more tranquil, happier, in his last months. Hyman Slate, a friend from adolescence who saw him a week before his death, felt he looked "at least outwardly, reasonably contented." Yet only a few weeks earlier, Slate had spotted him in downtown Chicago and feared from his appearance that Rosenfeld was in the midst of a "panic attack." Earlier the same year, Rosenfeld had told Slate in despair: "All I want is a wife and children, but then again that's what I have." Late in 1955, Rosenfeld wrote in his journal: "I live in an eggshell [sic] precariousness, in fear that I will crack."[74]

At Minneapolis and during his first months in Chi-

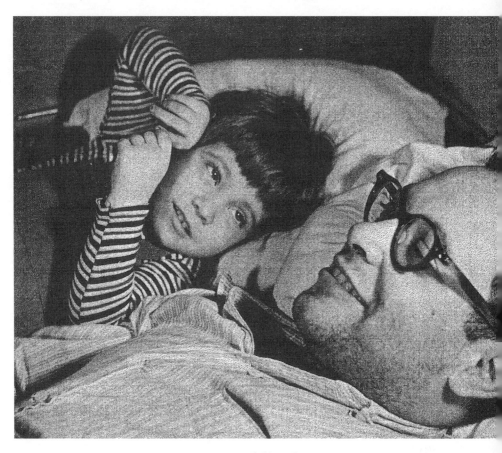

Isaac Rosenfeld with George.
Photograph courtesy of Nathan Tarcov.

cago, he fell into several sexual relationships, including an especially intense one with a student, Sheila Stern, in her mid-twenties. Sheila had come to Minneapolis as a faculty spouse but soon left her husband. She was a strikingly attractive, tempestuous music student, raised in the Caribbean, and she wore her exotic background seductively. Sheila followed Rosenfeld to Chicago. (When describing her to me, a Minnesota friend of Rosenfeld, the political scientist Philip Seigelman, lit up, walked to a delicate figurine of a southeast-

ern goddess in his Berkeley, California, living room, and remarked: "She had a body much like this.") Sheila insisted that
they marry but Rosenfeld refused, perhaps because he continued to consider returning to Vasiliki.

In April 1955, Sheila announced: "I have no energy left
to worry or brood, live for food, sleep, and sex and love it." In
August, their love remained heated. "Being with Isaac these
last few days has been wonderful," she wrote, "so busy are we
devouring each other to make up for lost time. How long this
honeymoon will last is a matter of conjecture." Sheila added:
"The weather is beautiful now and Isaac and I would be de-
lighted to see you. I don't know how long I'll be here—maybe
for good."[75] By Thanksgiving, she had slept with her psychoanalyst, whom she soon married (Rosenfeld recorded this "ag-
onized discovery" and "betrayal" in his journal and was devastated by it). Sheila and her new husband were soon living on
East 67th Street "with a dishwasher, 2 bathrooms, and 2 bedrooms."[76] Her relationship with Rosenfeld had been explosive, both marvelous and, as she now insisted, awful ("We had
fun together but I think it's all over but the shouting," she
wrote). He did all that he could to subvert it: "I adore him, of
course, but I'm tired of the regular crises that seem to attend
this relationship and I do not intend to contact him anymore.
He doesn't know this yet but I rather think he won't care until
one day he wakes up and realizes that something warm and
comforting he once owned is no longer in his life . . . I loved
him more than is likely he will ever be loved again."[77]

Sheila was sensuous, uncommonly beautiful, and reckless. (Years later, after her premature death from cancer,
friends described her as a woman of rare self-possession and
integrity, an accomplished, admired piano instructor, and the
happy wife of a mild, gentle American historian—still another
husband—at NYU.) One might feel that her descriptions at

the time of the breakup with Rosenfeld shouldn't be trusted, but they are—especially in their depiction of Rosenfeld's intense, sometimes rapid interplay of warmth and anger—consistent with his own assessments of himself. Her letters about Rosenfeld may be the most revealing account of what it felt like to live with him. (Vasiliki wrote little, and later in life tended to repeat many of the same details about his womanizing.) Sheila abandoned him while still much in love with him, but felt it was impossible to continue to live with him. He seemed to her too haunted by explosive forces, by intermittent bitterness, and, perhaps most devastatingly, by an inability to believe that she truly loved him. She had good reason to feel defensive (having left behind a faculty spouse, and Rosenfeld, and then wed her psychoanalyst, all within the span of no more than two years), but her picture of life with Rosenfeld seems credible.

Sheila's betrayal haunted him. He still brooded about it in the last months of his life, and he pondered the explosiveness of their sexual relationship, which, he claimed in retrospect, might well have obscured their incompatibility. "So destructive, so utterly devoted—to the point of impersonality . . . amorous jelly dripping and clinging all over one," he described in his journal. And then, quite accidentally, Freda reentered his life. She learned from a friend, the owner of the building that Rosenfeld had moved into, that he had moved back to Chicago. She was now divorced with two small boys, he had only recently lost Sheila, but quickly they fell into a relationship. Freda felt certain that she had rediscovered her first, true love, while he speculated one day that they might marry and the next day that they might well break up. His letters to her lacked the spark of his youthful ones but, then again, he wrote to Freda infrequently, mostly during trips to New York. He had moved into an airy, one-bedroom apartment on East Huron, near downtown, and purchased an old but sporty car, perhaps with money from book advances (he had driven a beaten-up Buick in Minneapolis). He wrote to Eleni and George in New York to reassure them that he had moved out of the awful, basement apartment where he had first lived in Chicago. He also courted other women—Rene, Muriel, perhaps others. His orgone box was folded up in a corner of his flat, but he continued to play with Reichian concepts. In the summer of 1955, he offered to send Bellow the guidelines for an "improvised . . . orgone blanket" that could be put together in no more than two or three hours "at a total cost of $5."[78] Whether Bellow continued to flirt with Reich or whether this was but another of Rosenfeld's attempts to shake up a friend he considered to be too conventional remains unclear.

Bellow's achievements continued to obsess Rosenfeld, even flatten him; he felt all the more cut off from his friend in Chicago and from the prospect of literary success, but he did much to take in the city. Working on his Chicago book—or so he told himself and his publisher—he wrote a brilliantly perceptive essay on the city that had nothing at all to do with the fire. This was his one significant reflection on the interplay between urban space and culture, one of his more persistent interests, and in it Rosenfeld described the city as a place for revelry, playfulness, and creation. He built into "Life in Chicago" (published posthumously in *Commentary*) a marvelously suggestive theory about what it is that makes for the best city culture. The piece is especially poignant because it is crafted around America's most workaday metropolises:

> Not until stairways, benches, and walks sprout among the still unplanted trees and gardens at the river banks, will Chicago become a proper place for loafing and dreaming as

are the Seine and the Tiber. . . . Not until then will water become a property of the city as a whole. . . . As I see it, [the]
principle is very simple (but then I am a lumftmensch: with
a thirst for water). It is to give the city something to lose.
And this can be done by producing without manufacturing,
consuming without eating . . . and finding the everlasting in
the ephemeral things: not in iron, stone, brick, concrete,
steel, and chrome, but in paper, ink, pigment, sound, voice,
gesture, and graceful leaping, for it is of such things that the
ultimate realities of the mind and the heart are made.[79]

Despite his sense of estrangement in Chicago, he
sought out new friends beyond the confines of academia or
literature. Perhaps through Sidney Passin—then acting in
the Chicago troupe The Last Stage—Rosenfeld fell in with
Mike Nichols, Elaine May, and Shelly Berman at the just-
formed, Hyde Park–based Compass Players. (This was the
kernel of what would become the well-known comedy group
Second City that then inspired *Saturday Night Live.*) He
wrote a skit for them and performed with them onstage.
Rosenfeld's skit was called "The Liars," and Mike Nichols optioned it for television. Daniel Rosenfeld remembered watching his cousin perform a routine onstage where silently, intently, and searching all the while for mysteries, he unwrapped
the skins of an onion to find nothing. Rosenfeld was a popular
figure in Hyde Park. Arthur Geffen, then studying at the University of Chicago, recalled sitting at the University Tavern
when Rosenfeld—about whom he had heard a great deal—
walked in accompanied by a striking-looking "West Indian
woman." (Perhaps this was the dark-complexioned Sheila?)
People immediately got up from their seats, called to him,
and greeted him like a celebrity.[80]

This certainly isn't how he described himself. In Chicago, Rosenfeld once again started keeping a journal. He had

stopped for a few years but now almost daily jotted down his thoughts:

> It has been a long time since I faced myself by means of a journal, and perhaps by the time I had put down my last entry in the last journal, confession and notation had become a way of evading myself. Today (11/20/55, Sunday), while out on a walk, I thought that the true way of facing oneself may be only through feeling—not by pushing it into words—for the style stands ready with all its deceptions, it a decent, clever, well-cut garment to cover each naked feeling. Best of all may be merely to feel the disquiet and the uneasiness that leads writers to keep journals. But my disquiet has gone for such a long time and is such a nasty and unsettling one—the rat in the rib cage—I must do what I can to get rid of it.
>
> All my troubles are with women. . . . Principally Sheila, now Freda, and then again (still!) Vasiliki. And anyone else whom I may meet right now would only be additional anxiety. Let me have the brains to discover and the courage to do what is right.[81]

He pined for Vasiliki ("Love her and God bless her. . . . Would that I could love her!"). He spent his last Thanksgiving and a "lovely Saturday afternoon" with yet another girlfriend, Muriel: "How she has changed, so much livelier in bed and a voluntary fellation." The problem, all along, he now concluded, had been guilt. "Was I guilty because I didn't love Vasiliki, or did I fail to love her because I was guilty to begin with? It seems to me the latter—for surely I started out with love. What I would feel at the sight of her sweet, radiant face—at the very beginning, before we slept together." He slept with Freda, recalling their first time, in Humboldt Park, and then awakened: "I began to feel damp, depressed, tight-chested guilt. I was thinking, I must get out of this, how will I get out . . . ?" He suffered from nightmares, dreamed of suicide, and overheard friends speaking "about something in the near future [and] realize that I will already be dead."[82] He remained torn between women: Freda, someone named Caroline (a "younger girl"), Rene, Muriel, even Vasiliki. "This mess, this Augean stable, this horse-shit love, I must clear out." Still, he spoke of sex in Reichian terms:

> But the only question is, can I make it with Freda in the absence of a binding, drawing passion? How much do I really fear involvement with a woman with two kids? Am I just using her, temporizing—and isn't this the source of the guilt I feel? Yet what holds me in this weak sexual connection—she hasn't nearly the bodily heat that poured so fiercely out of Sheila, and the skin-contact is so much weaker—what holds me is the promise of more—the "swell of promise" about her—and the hope of giving her what she has never had. Then, presumably, I will feel justified in leaving.[83]

Sometimes, he admitted, the old, splendid feelings of great love returned when he was with Freda: "The other night, holding her in my arms, clutching her white gowned body, I felt I was running over a meadow. All the images of vegetation she stirs in me." He had nightmares of a detached penis; he dreamed of Vasiliki, and of Sheila, whose head he caressed while saying: "this is the brain of a Dostoevsky."

The journal's last entry, undated but written shortly before his fatal heart attack, reads:

> This is what I have forgotten about the creative process and am only now beginning to remember—that time spent is time fixed. One creates a work to outlive one (only art does this), and the source of creativity is the desire to reach over our own death. Maybe now, if I want to create again, I want once more to live; and before I wanted, I suppose, to die.[84]

Death seemed a frequent companion. He wrote in his journal about suicide, and it is startling that the very last words there were about dying. The evening before his fatal heart attack he complained to Freda at a concert of terrible stomach cramps. In "Ruth," an unfinished story written just before he died, Rosenfeld's protagonist Appleman, a depressive, states now that his wife has left him and he has borrowed from everyone, he feels that he could be on the verge of "an early grave." (Rosenfeld likely showed the draft to Markfield, who called his novel about the day of Rosenfeld's funeral by the same title.) David Ray, a student of Rosenfeld in Chicago who would go on to become a poet, recalled standing with him one night "in a hallway in the Downtown College. He taught a class there, up about the tenth floor. And we were chatting while waiting for an elevator and when those bronze doors opened Isaac turned, though still looking our way, still talking, and stepped off toward a black abyss. I think but will not swear I was the one who grabbed him. In any case, he gasped, jumped back just in time."[85]

Rosenfeld revisited, time and again, moments of un-realized inspiration. "But when I was younger," he wrote in an unpublished autobiographical fragment, "how different everything was. I was surer, I had life. I felt a holiness and beauty in the world. I understood everything, and my own existence as well. I was called upon to be great."[86] In his fullest exploration of this theme, the short story "The World of the Ceiling," which appeared in *Midstream* in early 1956, he remembered a childhood where he was capable of feats of imagination, now gone: "When I was a child, I spent my days playing on the ceiling, and it was all my family could do to get me down for dinner. As I grew older and it became time, as they would tell me at home, to take life seriously, I established permanent residence on high."[87]

His father would insist that he ground himself, that he must prepare to make money, to live a practical life: "I would cut him short and the phrases, which I had prepared beforehand for just such occasions, would come smoking out of me. Spinoza, I let him have it, died a pauper, Socrates went around in rags, Diogenes lived in a barrel, and when Alexander the Great asked him, 'What can I do for you, my good man?' he replied, 'Move over a bit. You're standing in my sun.'" Of course, he also knew that Plato was an aristocrat, that Descartes and Voltaire and Henri Bergson carried on with royalty, or wore spats, but he didn't bother to share this data with his father.[88]

On the ceiling, he imagined himself in Russia: "I step out of the house in summer and walk right into a drift of snow in nineteenth-century Russia." There he encounters a youthful Lev Davidovitch, or Trotsky; there, too, he meets the "violently beautiful," dark-eyed terrorist Yevgenia Borisovna, who is loved by all men and who herself knows only love for terror, for reckless action. He travels, in much the same way, the world over: "from London to Zagreb to Istanbul, with a stopover at Baghdad." He can blot out the world, but can also heal it. "I can call down from the sky an influence to enlighten the people, lead them to conduct their intercourse in love and in the reverence which is owing to everyone who has been formed in the image of man."[89]

And then little by little, he aged, and changed: "I grew up, married, raised children, ran after them wiping their noses, and thus sank deeper and deeper into reality and, as my father had predicted, into poverty. I haven't had much time to spend on the ceiling. When I step out of the house I see no more troikas, aristocrats, and revolutionaries. The ugly, narrow, crowded street in which we live, full of smoke and noise, is an ugly, narrow, crowded street—goodbye Nevsky Prospekt, goodbye Istanbul forever."[90]

He takes a stab at revisiting these early, transcendent moments. At the Chinese laundry, he asks for the name of a truly grand Chinese dish, not the sort of Americanized fare typically eaten in such places. The owner of the laundry writes its name on a slip of paper, and the text itself seems enticingly mysterious: "I see little houses decked out in flags, with a stream of carpet tacks tumbling from the window." The next time he sits with his wife and friends at a Chinese restaurant, each of them having ordered chop suey or chow mein, he takes the paper from his pocket, and hands it "with great dignity" to the waiter, "one mandarin to another." He imagines "roast spaniel, ten-thousand-year-old eggs, nightingales dipped in honey and fried in their own feathers." He feels his old powers returning; the restaurant takes on a glow, suddenly seeming filled with "audible music of ancient instruments and vanished generations." He feels warmed, newly alive, but all this collapses when the waiter brings "lokschen!" "Nothing but noodles, boiling hot, without even a pat of butter, without cheese, without meat. Plain, slippery, starchy noodles." His friends laugh, his wife and others offer him portions of their own food, but he refuses, "swallowing, scarfing and slurping without pausing for breath. I want to get done as fast as I can, pay up and beat it, blow this baronial hall."[91]

If only Rosenfeld had been grabbed—as David Ray seems to have done at that elevator shaft—before he fell into the abyss, somehow been given the assurance to reclaim those early, stunning powers, this book wouldn't now move, as it must, toward his death. I linger here wishing for the story to be different, especially because it is clear to me from reading him carefully how desperately Rosenfeld himself sought, in the last year or so of his life, to alter his downward trajectory. I know such thoughts are useless; Rosenfeld died of a fatal heart attack, not writer's block. And thoughts like mine take Rosenfeld and his admirers too much at their word. They risk taking for granted that Rosenfeld's youthful promise would have blossomed into literary brilliance, when one knows too well how often promise, however stunning, rots, how easily self-assurance or elegance or even an initial moment or two of apparent genius can be mistaken in literary life for lasting talent.

Yet, in his journal—and still more strikingly, in work after work written late in his life—Rosenfeld faced these very issues directly. Just before his sudden death, he completed a series of remarkable stories and essays—among his very best—confronting the impact of his mother's death, the cost of being a writer in an age of conformity, and—perhaps his finest story of all—an elegiac reckoning with Bellow.

"Wolfie," published posthumously, is the darkest and perhaps the most transparently revealing of Rosenfeld's fictional works, even more probing than *Passage from Home*. It portrays a grown intellectual in the dead of night, with intimations of the author's bleakest sense of himself. It is also explores Rosenfeld's sense—now clearer than before—of what it is that had most stunted, and haunted, him. Although the story ends with its protagonist's oblivion, it also hints at his ability for self-discovery.

Wolfie is "one of the most miserable creatures in the Village, without a friend, everywhere ridiculed, scorned and despised, and utterly poor." Born somewhere in the Midwest, "he managed to maintain a vaguely literary air, mostly by gossiping about writers . . . a big macher, with his air of fantastic enterprise . . . he kept the Village informed of activities in the

intellectual world. . . . Politics, literature, swindles of all
sorts, the very hottest and the latest; wherever there was con-
niving, cheating, grifting, horning, or plain adultery, Wolfie
had it, steaming bucketful right from the horse's behind." His
appearance is pathetic: "The kinky filaments that grew sparse
and woebegone on his head . . . , the battered, tufted, boxer's
eyebrows, the cunning, pale, fearful eyes, the broad nose . . .
and the pitted face." His sexual life is furtive, mostly joyless.
Once, he fell in love with a lovely, guileless newcomer to the
Village named Myra, but he ruined this relationship and now
spends much of his time watching a suave émigré neighbor
successfully seduce woman after woman. For reasons he cannot explain to himself, Wolfie gives the neighbor the phone
numbers of women from his own address book, and, finally, in
an act that he knows to be irredeemably shameful and impossible to resist, he gives Myra's phone number, too. Wolfie then
listens, in anguish, for noises in the nearby bedroom:

> He lay spent, shivering, and feverish. If only he could sleep!
> . . . He sobbed and wept, calling [Myra's] name, and at last,
> it seemed to him, she came and stood beside his bed, not the
> Myra from across the hall, but, as it were, one who had been
> long dead, come to intercede for him: one of the mothers, in
> a white-gown. She laid a cool hand on his fever. . . . Now
> lights of many colors, in the distance, began to blink and
> draw nearer.[92]

Rosenfeld had come full circle, revisiting more explicitly than he had for years much the same terrain as he had in
Yiddish at the age of fourteen. There, too, was the mother—
white, wordless, the true object of all love, the only source of
solace. "Wolfie" concludes with this image transmuted, undermined as it deteriorates into that of a clown, but having
confronted it, the protagonist watches as "the orange and

green lights blinked out, one by one, and there was darkness and he slept." Whether this is intended as a peaceful or a fatal sleep, redemption or oblivion, is left unsaid. Wolfie does acknowledge openly, with a sense of gratitude that he has managed to recognize this truth, that his quest for women has been utterly wasteful: "He had thrown his life away on them." The story may have felt dreadful to write, and there is evidence that Rosenfeld withheld it from publication. But in the story there is ample evidence of his relief that he had confronted, as directly as he ever would, the source of his obsessions.[93]

On the act of writing itself, Rosenfeld now produced his most sharply crafted statement, which remains probably the most cited of his works. Delivered as a talk, "On the Role of the Writer and the Little Magazine" grew out of a long conversation in a popular Hyde Park bar with a new friend, the poet Reuel Denney, then at the University of Chicago. The two had argued about whether writers ought to see themselves as having a societal role. (Denney's widow, Ruth, described similar discussions to me in a letter: "I recall evenings we spent at Jimmy's Bar when a dozen or so people sat together and during the course of the evening one after the other would get up and make outrageous, hilarious political speeches. These were full of wonderful literary allusions and historical comparisons . . . I doubt that such great extemporaneous speech-making was being made in many other places at that time.")[94]

In the text of Rosenfeld's talk—which the *Chicago Review* transcribed and published soon after his death—he sounds fresh, smart, and also starkly angry. He employs a voice Rosenfeld rarely permitted himself to use in print but, of course, it is published in the form of an essentially unedited transcript: "I don't think there is really such a thing as a social role. I am not sure that there ought to be. There is only something the writer does do and should do." He explained that he was speaking only about the real writer, the serious and conscious one, "the one who regards his writing as an art." The pressure on such artists is now especially intense because of the "shrinkage of extremes," the fact that in a conservative age, one where pressures to conform are so profound, writers are increasingly co-opted, bought off, hired for advertising or cheap journalism, which means that the writer who takes work seriously can only assume an "anti-role," precisely because the outside world is so artificial.[95]

Rosenfeld argued that the avant-garde, too, has been co-opted by paperback book publishers that have undermined the little magazines that were once the purveyors of the newest, most experimental ideas. With the intrusion of commerce into the world of art and literature, the "distance between extremes disappears and it becomes harder and harder to recognize differences which at the time were significant and were essential." In the past, an avant-garde existed precisely because writers had nowhere else to go: "[B]ut as William Phillips . . . put it, it is so difficult to stay in the garret [today]. It is so hard because there are so many temptations to come out."[96] These include the temptations of academia but, above all, the allure of Madison Avenue, a world that seeks to persuade that it alone is real, and meaningful. In fact, "It has nothing to do with the realities that he, as a writer, deals with and which he must live in all the time. I should say that to the extent that there is a role for the writer today, the writer is better off without it."[97]

The text of the talk is full of preoccupation with money. Rosenfeld equates poverty with his thirty-five-hundred-dollar salary. (In letters to friends, he mentions this as what he earned at the University of Chicago, and this was more or less what he made at Minnesota.) With the depletion of bohemia, what remains is little more than the emptiness of a jazz culture, a cool culture of aimless people who pepper their conversations with terms like "crazy" or "gone" or "gas." "There is no communication and yet there is a hell of a lot of noise . . . once your eyes get used to the gloom, you can see that there is an appearance, perhaps it's an affectation, of a certain poverty, certain roughness, rudeness, crudeness."[98]

This was as close as Rosenfeld would ever come to declaiming a literary credo. But he went further still, and provided a powerfully candid view of what he felt like, deep in the night, in the grip of the sort of terror that must afflict a writer if they're serious about what they're doing: The writer must be seen as the only "living man, the one left alone at three o'clock in the morning, when it's always the dark night of the soul; to be the man whom one encounters when there is no longer any uniform to wear . . . the man who is naked, who is alone, and the man who pretty much of the time is afraid: the man who sees himself as he really is in this flesh and in these bones and in these feelings, in these impulses, in these emotions; the man who confronts himself in his dreams and his reveries."[99]

Reality for the writer is fundamentally different from how the term tends to be commonly utilized and this distinction must be maintained if writing is to survive. His insistence on parsing the meaning of "real" and "unreal" is crucial because it helps clarify the values that any honest writer must adapt, or resist. The values of the marketplace, or Madison Avenue, must be rejected "in the name of reality . . . because that world, when you really look, is the unreal world; and it is different from the world that the living man with the acuteness, the trained and the born acuteness, the artist's acuteness, enters into and leads us always into a deeper understanding of. The world of art, for me, is the real world and the writer's real role is his natural occupation within that real world."[100]

In his fiction, too, Rosenfeld ultimately showed himself surer, and more pronouncedly Jewish. In contrast, Bellow's great breakthrough novel, *The Adventures of Augie March*—a work without a cerebral narrator, without the brooding grimness of Bellow's earlier novels, and with its famous declaration of being nothing less than "American born"—was his least expressly Jewish work. Later, Bellow would mourn the Holocaust, he would report from Israel, and he would evoke the "old system" with longing as he described the norms of his parents' immigrant milieu. But first he wrote a great novel that wasn't, as he well knew, explicitly Jewish in any way. "The American-Jewish novel," wrote Leslie Fiedler, "is essentially an act of assimilation." Fiedler probably overstates, but the characterization is certainly true with regard to Bellow's first masterpiece.[101]

In what would be his last significant work of fiction, Rosenfeld made the opposite move: he wrote his most explicitly Jewish story, a biblical takeoff inspired by Sol Bellow, with whom his dearest childhood friend sought to make peace. Their last meeting in Chicago had been warm; Rosenfeld admitted to Bellow that he had been a bit mad, not merely angry or jealous but perhaps slightly insane, for the last decade or so. He hoped to confide in his friend, to convey that he saw himself emerging from a long, rough, fallow period. Bellow found Rosenfeld's living conditions horrible (he visited before Rosenfeld moved to his last apartment on Huron) but came away from the meeting with the impression that his emotional—and intellectual—life had improved.

"King Solomon" is something of a reflection on the Augean stable, the odd medley of women in Rosenfeld's—and also Bellow's—life at the time. It is an affectionate, probing look at an aging monarch, a man not unlike the now kingly Bellow, someone who has published book after book but whose wisdom, as described in the story, is fading. (In this respect, much of the competitiveness that was a vital part of their relationship remains.) Descriptions of the two commingle: the story is, in some measure, a composite portrait of two, interlinked men whose emotional and intellectual lives, as Rosenfeld seemed now to understand, could only be comprehended in relation to one another. It is also a study of the slippage of youth, the sadness and perceptiveness that come from accumulated, mostly disappointing experience. And, oddly, it is also a tale of a man preparing to die.

It begins with a statement that could well describe Rosenfeld's own life, or Bellow's, and it resonates with the life of the biblical Solomon: "Every year, a certain number of girls. They come to him, lie down beside him, place their hands on his breast, and offer to become his slaves."[102]

Here, in a tale that speaks of the physical intermingling of men and women, there is no sex. The presence of women, their lying in one's bed, is deemed important, but no one—neither Solomon nor his slaves—seems to engage in, or, for that matter, take pleasure in, a sexual life. The king takes these women and their offers as expressions of what the world provides him, but with little relish. "Every few years he publishes a collection of his sayings, most of which he has never said, but the sayings have little to do with the case, and their melancholy tone is held to be an affectation."[103] This is meant as an evocation of Ecclesiastes—whose author, according to Jewish tradition, was King Solomon—but it is probably also intended as a comment, flattering and somewhat disparaging, on Bellow's own cascade of works—*Dangling Man*, *The Victim*, and *Augie March*. The emotional depth and sincerity of these works is said to be less impressive than their sheer quantity. Still, whatever wisdom Solomon could once dispense, his intellectual resources are now depleted and probably permanently so.

The story is preoccupied less with Solomon's waning wisdom than with his inability to feel. No one seems to feel great passion in this story about love; neither Solomon nor his women are drawn to one another. The king is capable of remorse, not affection. Rosenfeld describes a Jerusalem that is also something of a Lower East Side: King Solomon's women shop for him, haggle over prices, seek to live economically, and he lives like an elderly man on a pension. His residence is both a palace and an apartment with mice in its walls, and there are strange sounds in the night such as one might hear in a rooming house. The king is slovenly and careless; the following description is probably meant to evoke Rosenfeld, not the more fastidious Bellow, now concerned more than ever with his ungainliness:

> None has seen the King's nakedness; yet all have seen him in shirt sleeves or suspenders, paunchy, loose-jowled, in need of a trim. Often in the heat of the day he appears bareheaded, and all have looked upon his baldness, sometimes he comes forth in his bare feet, and the men have observed bunions and corns. When he appears in this fashion with, say, a cigar in his mouth and circles under his eyes; his armpits showing yellowish and hairy over the arm holes of his undershirt; his wrinkles deep and his skin slack . . . he does show himself in human nakedness after all. . . . And sometimes, unexpectedly, he summons the cabinet to a game of pinochle.[104]

He enjoys children—they pull at him, they smudge his glasses, he tells stories to them—but they're usually pointless and dull, and they scatter when they see him. He seeks to play with them, but they see him both as a king and as an aging man in decline. With the children, too, there is an unbridgeable distance. He'd like to satisfy the desires of his people, especially their hunger for revelation, but he has little more to say and, indeed, "all his wisdom lies scattered from his hand."[105]

Lately, his aesthetic standards have begun to slide; he takes women to his bed that he would earlier have rejected. It is in just this way that he accepts the Queen of Sheba, who arrives in a royal entourage with archers and trumpeters. She is black, with kinky hair, her lips thick and breasts that emanate a "sense of tremendous power and authenticity. . . . Some thought she was beautiful, others not. No one knows what the King thought."[106]

They eat together, she asks for seconds, but the visit deteriorates, perhaps because she demands that he teach his wisdom. "Nor was Sheba so slender as her autographed picture may have led one to believe. When she set her feet down, the table shook, and the carafes of wine and sweetened water swayed and threatened to topple." She begins to dance for him, to entertain; she sings, and cries, and whoops, and, finally, falls beside him right on the table where his meal has been.[107] For several days, they spend time together, play chess, listen to the radio, play croquet, talk politics. And then she leaves him. "Yours is the wisdom of love," she tells him, but "your love is love only of yourself; yet you share it with others by letting them love you—and this is next to the highest." He mourns her leaving, watches the camels as they disappear into the distance. "He stood till evening fell, and the rump of the last plodding animal had twitched out of sight beyond the sand hills. Then he averted his face and wept silently, for it is a terrible thing for the people to see their King's tears."[108] It seems unlikely, out of character, that

Solomon is weeping because of her: the relationship is described as compatible, never passionate. Indeed, he is so wasted emotionally that he cannot even fall in love with the Queen of Sheba. And this is precisely why her departure so moves him: the king is left in mourning over his inability to feel truly close to anyone. He is shattered not so much by her departure, but by her final, parting words, which aren't answered by the king because they're meant to be taken for the truth.

More and more often now, Solomon goes to bed not with a slave but with a hot water bottle. And the tale comes to a sober, poignant conclusion. It is haunting, simply inexplicable, that these are among the last words of fiction that Rosenfeld would write:

> The [water] bottle has grown cold. Shall he ring for another? He shifts the bottle, kneads it between his knees. "And be thou like a young hart upon the mountain of spices." Look, forward, look back, to darkness, at the light, both ways blind. He raises the bottle to his breast; it does not warm him. He gropes for the cord, and while his hand reaches, he thinks, as he has thought so many times, there is a time and a season for everything, a time to be born and a time to die. Is it time now? They will lay him out, washed, anointed, shrouded. They will fold his arms across his chest, with the palms turned in, completing the figure. Now his own hands will lie pressed to his breast, and he will sleep with his fathers.[109]

Postscript

Our best hitter, who once led the League at .389—he stands there, working his jaws and wagging the bat, waiting to strike out, and I can feel all the power in his shoulders and forearms and wrists, his muscles straining to connect. I see his eyes squint as the ball sails toward him, and there is that last, pinched strain of energy in his face as he begins his wild swing—and I think, God damn it, all that power and that glory gone to waste.

—Isaac Rosenfeld, "The Misfortune of the Flapjacks"

ROSENFELD PUBLISHED THE STORY "THE MISFORtune of the Flapjacks" in 1947, a slapdash tale, brief and hilarious—in the way a Yiddish joke about piles and heaps of misfortune is hilarious—about a hapless baseball farm team. The Flapjacks' manager is crazy, the players can't win a single game (even a pickup game against a small-town high school team), and they haven't the money to finish out the season. But they possess a grace, a poignant nobility, that misfortune can't erase. Their once splendid hitter, Eglantine, steps up to the plate: He "draws back his shoulders and sticks out his left leg as he used to do in the old days, when he was knocking down the fence. He wags his bat, a slow, menacing motion, his elbows are cocked, his teeth are clenched in the tobacco plug, he is stocky and muscular, over the middle, and Eglantine twists all the way around on a murderous swing, but a mile wide, he can't connect any more."[1]

Freda Davis discovered Isaac Rosenfeld's body. Her brother had accompanied her to his apartment, and it was he who saw Rosenfeld first, slumped over his writing desk. Rosenfeld was buried in Chicago next to his mother. Rumors circulated for years that it was a suicide. Sheila Stern wrote to a friend about how difficult it was for her to believe that he was truly gone: "I needn't describe to you [the] pain I experienced after reading about it in a newspaper of all places. But now, the idea has somewhat settled in my head and I no longer regard it as a complete unreality which my initial numbness had me believing for the first week."[2]

Many of his friends commented on the unbelievable news; despite his ill health, he seemed so robust, so large, as healthy, some said, as a Russian peasant.[3] His death seemed unimaginable to many and I, too, have envisioned him in other, altogether different scenarios: marrying Freda and returning with her to Minnesota, or leaving Freda for a job at the American Jewish Committee. Or, he might have continued on his downward spiral, accumulating more and more unpublished manuscripts, living off fellowships, friends, or past glory. He might have become like his writer-friends whom I interviewed for this book—aging badly, seeking to hide their envy without success, remaining ever aware of the better fortunes of others, including Roth, certainly, but also Allegra Goodman and, for that matter, quite nearly anyone with a respectable publisher, tenure, or a closet with more than one or two good suits.

Sitting across from writers like these, in bars with tabs covered by my research fund, I've shifted uneasily in my chair, thinking that looking straight at me, speaking into my tape recorder, could have been an old, crafty, now immeasurably sadder Rosenfeld feeding me tall tales of life back on Barrow Street.

Time and again while writing this book, I was reminded how fragile, and ephemeral, literary fame can be. Novelist and short story writer Wallace Markfield, author of *To an Early Grave,* was in the mid-1960s a "comer." When Bernard Malamud in 1966 listed the seven most prominent writers in America on Jewish themes, Roth, Bellow, Salinger, and Markfield were among them. I interviewed Markfield many years later. A quirky and amusing fellow, just retired from a job as a speechwriter for the Bnai Brith's Anti-Defamation League, he regaled me with imitations of Howard Stern, whom he greatly admired. He told me how Evelyn Shefner ran into him soon after the appearance of *To an Early Grave,* in 1964, and said to him, testily, "Well, you've now certainly made it." Markfield grinned painfully at the recollection, and then turned the conversation back to Howard Stern.[4]

But there might have been an altogether different fate for Rosenfeld, far from the offices of the American Jewish Committee or the ADL—where he most probably would have wilted—or the increasingly frayed, joyless environs of literary bohemia. A few short years after his death, the literary world would burst wide open with underground voices previously deemed irrelevant, pressing up against the literary center of American life: Allen Ginsberg's *Howl* appeared in 1956, Jack Kerouac's *On the Road* in 1957. In 1961 James Baldwin exploded onto the American public scene with *The Fire Next Time,* a collection of essays powerfully and intuitively smart, deeply personal, and ethnically as well as sexually self-aware in just the ways Rosenfeld treasured. At more or less the same time, Norman Podhoretz devoted the better part of three consecutive issues of *Commentary,* which he now edited, to his friend Paul Goodman's partly Reich-inspired rambling ode to adolescent freedom, *Growing Up Absurd*. Rosenfeld had heard Goodman rehearse many of these ideas a decade or so earlier. Suddenly the once unrivaled literary arbiters Mark Van Doren and Lionel Trilling looked—at least in some influential cultural circles, and already in the early 1960s—like august figures from the past.

Rosenfeld could well have emerged, as did Goodman, an elder sage of this movement. Though critical of its irrationalism, he would have understood better than most the vulgarity of contemporary life and letters, both mainstream and countercultural. He might also have been embraced as a precursor to the fiction—battered, built of nightmares, the underside of realism—produced by Thomas Pynchon, whose first book, *V,* appeared in 1961. Rosenfeld's voice might have resonated better, more coherently, in this new, more experimental literary environment. He was, of course, writing superbly at the end of his life: His last short story, "King Solomon," was bought by *Harper's,* his skit "The Liars" had been optioned by Mike Nichols, and his sense of certainty and confidence as a writer of both fiction and essays was, if anything, growing deeper.[5] Rereading Goodman now can make one wince, and leave one puzzled about the literary enthusiasms of one's youth. This is by no means true for the best of Rosenfeld's work. When Ted Solotaroff released his collection of Rosenfeld's essays, *An Age of Enormity,* in 1962, he believed the times had become more conducive to Rosenfeld's edgy temperament: "In the 1940s, with its sense of 'crisis,' Rosenfeld was thus a deeply representative figure; during the 1950s he seemed to many of his friends quixotic and dated, an 'underground man' in an open and practical and not unpleasant society. Today, as the complacent bets of those years are going off the board and we find ourselves at an even more fearful extreme; as we experience once again, coolly or in panic, the modern dilemmas of contactlessness, the inability to grasp the life around us, the numbness and uncertainty toward terror and vulgarity that it embodies—Rosenfeld's consciousness of contemporary mind and feelings is once again pertinent."[6]

My own copy of *An Age of Enormity,* picked up at a secondhand bookstore in San Francisco, has inscribed on its front inside cover "A. Davis, 1971." I studied with Angela Davis around that time as an undergraduate at UCLA and I have imagined her reading Rosenfeld, nodding in agreement or perturbed when encountering views inconsistent with her starkly dogmatic sense of what was politically feasible, but adding him, nonetheless, to a list of writers she deemed essential to read on contemporary America.

"Every life has a theme," wrote Rosenfeld in his essay on Gandhi.[7] The posthumous theme attached to his life was failure. To an extent, this was a byproduct of his lifelong preoccupation with failure, which he explored in the lives of his fictional antiheroes; those close to him read these as more than fleetingly autobiographical. And then there was his own slow, ponderous, and imperfect literary output, which Rosenfeld couldn't help but compare with Bellow's, especially since his friend's success came so soon after his own emergence as a promising writer. Then again, as William Phillips observed, the best work of writers and intellectuals like Robert Lowell, Irving Howe, and Richard Chase—who first appeared in *Partisan Review* in the 1940s—was, in fact, produced only in the 1950s, when Rosenfeld, too, wrote at his best and then, suddenly, was dead. Failure was a primary literary theme of his and he did slip into a long, torturous, gray period in his last few years, but at the same time, the web of stories surrounding him, many of them tales of waste and dissipation, also had much to do with his own unrestrained candor. Rosenfeld talked far too openly about his enthusiasms, spoke freely, even recklessly, about his fears, and experimented with life all too publicly. He then fell from grace quickly. Many of the embarrassing moments in Markfield's novel, *To an Early Grave,* can only have been learned directly from Rosenfeld.

Rosenfeld paid a price for these indiscretions in the form of grim posthumous accounts of his life. "All this time that I have been in New York I have had acquaintances, but no friends," he wrote to Tarcov soon after his move to the city. "People to talk to—but when I talk to them I do not tell them the whole truth. . . . The whole truth! To think that you and I used to and still can tell each other that."[8]

Rosenfeld's reputation was, it seems to me, solidified by Bellow's treatment, especially in his obituary in *Partisan Review,* whose editors, as Bellow acknowledged, "were the first to recognize his great talents."[9] Bellow loved Rosenfeld, but he was also a man of complex jealousies, deep, unremitting hurts, bruises decades old that hurt as if they were yesterday's. Bellow could turn on someone in a moment; as a result of one perceived insult, he could cut off lifelong friends. He lost many of these friends because of stray comments he took to be insults, or something even more elusive. Still, his deep concern for Rosenfeld never ended. He helped Vasiliki financially, intermittently, until the end of her life, and he spoke of her with great affection. He continued to write about Rosenfeld often, and brilliantly.[10]

Bellow's friendships with his closest male friends were intense; he luxuriated in these relationships that often singed him but also sustained him throughout his life. "Those boys loved one another more than they loved any of us," one of

their ex-wives told me. Appended to a letter Bellow wrote to
Tarcov in the summer of 1950 was a "Spring Ode" describing a
visit with his old Chicago friend:

> My bathrobe sleeves are stiff with yolks,
> Speckled with crumbs of my winters eating;
> Bottles and eggshells on the floor
> Lie between us at our meeting.
> He falls into my arms, we kiss,
> We cry like reunited brothers.
> He tells me how he searched for me
> Among the others.
>
> My cheeks are fat, my eyes are wet,
> His hand rests sadly on my shoulder;
> We cannot help but see how much
> Each has grown older.[11]

Not in the *Partisan Review* obituary (whose writing, he
admitted, made him suffer "through several kinds of hell")
but in an essay written not long afterward, Bellow stated, "I
am among his friends perhaps not the best qualified to speak
of him. I loved him, but we were rivals, and I was peculiarly
touchy, vulnerable, hard to deal with—at times, as I can see
now, insufferable, and not always a constant friend."[12] Soon
after hearing the news of his friend's end, Bellow rewrote the
last pages of *Seize the Day*. It may well have been recast with
the tragedy in mind. Wilhelm, the book's protagonist, who is
now quite nearly ruined—abandoned by his father; betrayed
by a cynical, calculating confidant; faced with divorce and the
loss of his job—enters the funeral parlor:

> Standing a little apart, Wilhelm began to cry. He cried at
> first softly, and from sentiment, but soon from deeper feel-

ing. He sobbed loudly and his face grew distorted and hot, and the tears stung his skin. . . .

"It must be somebody real close to carry on so."

"Oh my, oh my! To be mourned like that," said one man and looked at Wilhelm's heavy, shaken shoulders, his clutched face and whitened, fair hair, with wide, glinting, jealous eyes.

"The man's brother, maybe?"

"Oh, I doubt that very much," said another bystander, "They're not alike at all. Night and day."[13]

Rosenfeld's death while Bellow was readying the last pages of *Seize the Day* for publication as a book (it appeared earlier, in a slightly different version, in *Partisan Review*) likely inspired these pages. Daniel and Pearl Bell, quite close to Bellow at the time, recalled this as having been the case. Bellow readily admitted that Rosenfeld is pictured throughout the ribald *Henderson the Rain King*, published in 1959, where he permitted himself his wildest, most fanciful reconstruction of his childhood friend. "All the while I was writing Dahfu I had the ghost of Rosenfeld near at hand, my initiator into the Reichian mysteries." There was in Bellow's description of the African Dahfu ample evidence of the mad, brilliant Reich, but Rosenfeld, too, was packed into the dizzying portrait: "You must try to make more of a lion of yourself," the King Dahfu insists. "Your roaring still is choked. Of course it is natural, as you have such a lot to purge." The narrator admits his love for him: "I was grateful to him. I was his friend then. In fact, at this moment, I loved the guy." Dahfu's biography, despite the African setting, does resemble Rosenfeld's: "[H]e had been a zealous student and great reader [*sic*] he had held down the job of janitor in his school library." Above all is the way he talks: "We talked and talked and talked, and I can't pretend that I completely understood him. I can only say I suspended judgment, listening carefully and bearing in mind how he had warned me that the truth might come in forms for which I was unprepared." In the end, Dahfu dies, and the narrator wallows in the simple, irrefutable fact that he "never took another death so hard."[14]

While writing this book, I often found it impossible to picture Rosenfeld without thinking of Bellow's Rosenfeld. Time after time, Bellow wrote about him with an unrivaled authority not only because he knew Rosenfeld so well and loved him but because Bellow's greatest gift as a writer—and he possessed many—was his capacity to link physicality and character, to see how the soul imprinted itself on the body, to sketch in meticulous detail pictures of character. His biographical as well as semifictional portraits remain unforgettable and carry with them an unequaled persuasiveness, even when inaccurate or misleading. "Only the unshavable pucker in his father's chin was a sign of pathos" is Bellow's description of Sam Rosenfeld in "Charm and Death," and I find it difficult to think of Rosenfeld's father without imagining this chin.[15]

Exactly what Rosenfeld represented for Bellow as the years passed and the two grew apart, as one became increasingly famous and the other obscure and resentful, and then all came crashing down with Rosenfeld's sudden death is impossible to know. For years Bellow boasted about Rosenfeld as one might boast about a beloved, brilliant brother—someone smarter than anyone else who would almost certainly have the world at his feet. Bellow remained insecure about his philosophical knowledge, turning obsequious, sometimes irate, when others—like a University of Chicago colleague, the sociologist Edward Shils, who read and criticized *Mr. Sammler's Planet*—pointed out his failings. As an essayist of ideas, Rosenfeld came of age much earlier than Bellow and, arguably, Bellow would never write essays as clear-eyed and powerful as those his friend wrote, week after week, in his early twenties. Both Bellow and Rosenfeld viewed their passages through life as intertwined; Monroe Engel remembered sitting with Rosenfeld, in the early 1950s, leafing through a glossy women's magazine that featured a story about Truman Capote, replete with pictures of his attractive apartment. Rosenfeld responded: "No matter, someday Saul or I will win the Nobel Prize."[16]

The belief that philosophical and fictional ability were made of the same stuff—a touchingly naive notion born, perhaps, of the classical Russian literary influences that enveloped Rosenfeld and Bellow early and for much of their lives—meant that both believed that it would be Rosenfeld who would, despite Bellow's ample gifts, rise to the very top. Bellow admitted to friends his fear that had Rosenfeld survived, he might have become prominent in the more disreputable currents of the 1960s—a hippie, a figure of the New Left.[17] That Bellow triumphed, that he summed up his achievements by leaving an unavoidable imprint on how his dear friend and rival was remembered, became, of course, a crucial part of Rosenfeld's story. ("I have to write for the both of us now," he told friends.) Even in the 1960s, when Marilyn Mann married Sam Freifeld, one of the Division Street Movement and by then a prominent lawyer, she would hear that the most talented of those in the Chicago circle had been Rosenfeld.[18]

In the end, it was Rosenfeld's death that came to be far better remembered than anything he achieved in his lifetime. The section of Bellow's *Partisan Review* obituary that influenced Rosenfeld's legacy most powerfully, it would seem, addresses the solitariness, the tawdriness, of Rosenfeld's death:

He endured boredom and deadlines, despair, even madness. This is the truth about the reign of the fat gods. It is not merely dull and harmless. It destroys, and consumes everything, it covers the human image with deadly films, it undermines all quality with its secret rage, it subverts everything good and exalts lies, and on its rotten head it wears a crown of normalcy. Most do not fight but make peace with it. Isaac fought.

He won. He changed himself. He enlarged his power to love. Many loved him. He was an extraordinary and significant man.

He died in a seedy, furnished room on Walton Street, alone—a bitter death to his children, his wife, his lovers, his father.[19]

Did Bellow mean madness? And, if so, was this a madness so different from what Bellow himself seems to have experienced? In *Herzog,* he provided acutely observed, thinly disguised details about himself, the men and women, the wives and ex-wives, and the lovers who pollinated his turbulent, maddening life. In *Seize the Day,* too, there were ample intimations of his own prolonged flirtation with Reich, and his own descent into a sort of madness. Was Rosenfeld's engagement with these teachings more unbalanced than Bellow's, even if it lasted longer? Both had orgone boxes, both used them for a long time, and both eventually ceased to believe in the boxes' efficacy. Rosenfeld admitted to Bellow, in one of their very last conversations, that he had experienced long periods characterized by (what he called) "madness," but Rosenfeld was known to speak in excessively self-lacerating terms; he was as lavishly candid about his inadequacies as Bellow was guarded about his own.

True, Bellow insisted that Rosenfeld was a "significant" man, but where he succeeded was in spheres—never delineated, and that remain unclear—beyond literature. Bellow then added that Rosenfeld died "alone" in a "seedy, furnished room." The word "alone" carried powerful connotations in the milieu in which both were raised—it meant existing beyond the care of family and loved ones, beyond all that made life bearable. But wasn't this, in effect, how Bellow and many writers close to both him and Rosenfeld lived? Despite their serial marriages, despite the cramped living conditions of academic or literary bohemia, they spent their lives apart, fundamentally self-involved, and essentially alone. Bellow would often complain about his own unremitting loneliness even while married or surrounded by children, friends, and lovers.

These were men with few safety nets, with no family money, and if they fell they could fall fast, hard, and—so they feared—forever. (Bellow himself remained financially insecure, and not only because of divorce, well into the 1960s.) "Even his dying would be a . . . failure," wrote Kazin of Rosenfeld, a cruel, patently absurd statement that, in its own way, revealed immeasurably more about Kazin's own terrors.[20] Rosenfeld was the first to visibly falter, the first to fail, and after much initial fanfare. Then, suddenly, he was dead. Many of those nearest to him, whose lives resembled his—and more so than they themselves might have been willing to admit— may well have lived with the fear that they, too, would fall prey to similar demons, to a comparable fate. No one captured such fears better than Bellow, in his novel *The Victim*, published in 1947: "He said occasionally to [his wife] May, revealing his deepest feelings, 'I was lucky, I got away with it.' He meant that this bad start, his mistakes, the things that might have wrecked him, had somehow combined to establish him. He had almost fallen in with that part of humanity of which he was frequently mindful (he never forgot that hotel on lower Broadway), the part that did not get away with it—the lost, the outcast, the overcome, the effaced, the ruined."[21]

Bellow would eulogize Rosenfeld in strikingly similar terms. The words stuck, and immediately became the way Rosenfeld was eulogized by others. *The New Republic* ran a full-page poem in its September 3, 1956, issue titled "Isaac Rosenfeld: For a Friend Who Died Alone," written by a friend from the University of Minnesota, the writer and critic Morgan Blum. It captures him vividly:

> Isaac, the Age of Reason came of age
> That day you stiffened, suffered, died alone:
> Its capsules, hypos and its cradled phone
> Then failed your heart, how whet our frustrate rage.[22]

John Berryman, who taught with Bellow at Minnesota and who knew Rosenfeld only distantly, built a similar set of images into the ending of a poem he wrote at the time. He inscribed it "For George Rosenfeld, for his father":

> I have to glare into a room where, half-through, he crampt dead
> where all his lovers, seeking his cry, drown
> and solo I reel in a word dispelled.[23]

Markfield, too, picked up this same theme in *To an Early Grave*, where one of his characters exclaims: "All alone—that's what I can't get over. A guy who could call up six people when he wanted to take in a movie." In 1971 James Atlas published "Isaac Rosenfeld Thinks about His Life" in the journal *Poetry*. It opens with Rosenfeld contemplating:

> I'm in a single room again.
> Always it's the same

a cellar crammed
With papers, ashtrays, books . . . [24]

In Alfred Kazin's 1978 autobiography *New York Jew,* Rosenfeld is linked with some of Kazin's own worst years—the suffocation of a marriage, the most awful of his uncertainties as a writer. He speaks of these years as having had the "intimations of shipwreck."[25] Rosenfeld is introduced by Kazin after a series of breathless, effusive portraits of Bellow, Paul Goodman, and others; later in the book, Kazin offers the same of Edmund Wilson, Hannah Arendt, and Ignazio Silone. There is, overall, a dour, grim tenor to the book, but Kazin's friends are depicted, on the whole, warmly, often rapturously. Yet when Kazin describes pristine, memorable moments in which Rosenfeld is known to have participated, the other is excised: "I was to meet Marc Chagall wandering about Fifty-seventh Street one Yom Kippur not sure whether it was altogether fitting for him to look in at Pierre Matisse's gallery."[26] And when he does refer to Rosenfeld, it is in terms that border on the vicious: "Isaac as his own subject eventually drove himself wild. Stuck between his demand for perfect love and his desire to be a writer, he missed out on both. As even the Village desperados noticed, Isaac was a 'failure.' Precocious in everything and understandably worn out, he died at thirty-eight. Even his dying would be a kind of failure."

Fear of failure was, Kazin admits, what frightened him most and never more acutely than when he was closest with Rosenfeld, in the mid-1940s. Kazin sublet the Barrow Street apartment after he had impulsively left his wife and was at a crossroads, painfully uncertain as to what to write now that he had finished his first, much acclaimed book, *On Native Grounds.* As Kazin tells it, Rosenfeld was insinuated into his life in various ways during this anxious, uncertain period.

(Not only did Kazin live for a while after his separation in Rosenfeld's apartment; he also carried on an affair with a woman he met at Rosenfeld's house.) At first, Rosenfeld represented the prospect of artistic, even human transcendence: "Going down the steps from that Barrow Street tenement and back home from eccentric winding streets of the Village, the sound of Isaac's impeccable phrasing still in my ears, I felt that some promised beauty in my life waited for me . . . I always felt redirected, and in Barrow Street had a new instinct." Eventually Kazin would link Rosenfeld with bleak wildness, abandon, and a potentially lethal irresponsibility. According to Kazin, Rosenfeld "smelled of death." In this section of his autobiography, he depicts Rosenfeld as having fallen prey to seductions that quite nearly devastated Kazin, too: "and everything came back to Isaac the prisoner in his cell the orgone box. He never broke out."[27]

Yet as Kazin himself admitted in the privacy of his journal, Rosenfeld was by no means alone in his orgone box, which was widely used by many of Kazin's closest friends, perhaps by himself as well. "Everybody of my generation had his orgone box . . . his search for fulfillment. There was, God knows, no break with convention, there was just a freeing of oneself from all those parental attachments and thou shalt nots."[28]

Soon after I decided to write this book, I spoke with Kazin and he tried to dissuade me from doing so. "He fucked, he fucked, and then he died," is how he summed up Rosenfeld's life. Then, much as in my meeting with Lionel Abel, he spoke at length about himself. Of the nearly two hours I recorded him, barely a few minutes were devoted to Rosenfeld, and those were full of rancor. At the time, this seemed not only unkind but also a gratuitously bleak assessment of a man who had been a dear friend and a writer Kazin had once, quite vocally, admired. Later, as I pondered Kazin's reactions to Rosenfeld—and those of others once close to him who had survived and surpassed him—their disdain felt too emphatic, too fierce, and self-referential.

His sudden death, his oblivion as a literary presence, suggested to at least some of these men that theirs might well be the same fate. Some felt that they, too, were skidding on ice, barely avoiding perilous falls, and there was Rosenfeld testing the fates, playing the odds. No one is more explicit about this than Kazin in *New York Jew*; few of Rosenfeld's former friends with whom I spoke were more dismissive than Kazin with regard to Rosenfeld and his achievements. It wasn't, as I came to see it, only the unevenness of Rosenfeld's literary output, or his death at a young age, or the inevitable changes that occur in literary fashion, for that matter, that contributed toward his diminishment. Some who were once good, even intimate friends contributed significantly to it as well. No doubt they did so carelessly, on the whole with little malice, for reasons often complex and little understood, probably even by themselves. They did so out of self-protection and overidentification, and they did so because they sensed that if someone so promising, so full of life, had his life cut short, it could happen to any of them, too.

Eventually, the linkage between Rosenfeld and a sordid, anonymous room that itself represents a literary fate of no exit became so resilient that in Brian Morton's novel of New York literary life, *Starting Out in the Evening*, published in 1998 and made into a film, the mere mention of Rosenfeld's name inspires reference to such a room. The book's protagonist, an erudite, out-of-print novelist named Schiller, explains to his young, eager, would-be biographer his ambivalent relationship in the 1940s and '50s with the work of D. H. Lawrence. He tells her that what particularly upset him about

Lawrence at the time was his impact on the likes of Norman Mailer and Isaac Rosenfeld—Jewish intellectuals like himself whose attraction to the "wisdom of the blood" he deplored:

> She wasn't happy about this answer. She had never heard of Isaac Rosenfeld, and Mailer had never meant much to her. . . . But it wasn't that she wasn't interested in these people. It unsettled her to hear Schiller putting himself in this context. When she thought of Schiller as a writer, she liked to imagine him in the "one big room" that E. M. Forster speaks of in *Aspects of the Novel*—the room in which all novelists, past and present, are writing side by side. In her mind Schiller's place was somewhere in eternity, next to Lawrence or Melville, not in the 1950s, next to Isaac Rosenfeld.[29]

As described by Morton, there is this stark juxtaposition, a set of profoundly different fates for the novelist. There is Forster's room, a place of grand achievement, even immortality. And many, many floors below, quite literally in the cellar, is Rosenfeld's room, a grim place, a mid-twentieth-century metaphor for Grub Street, where the unread (like Rosenfeld) or the overrated (like Mailer) go to die.

In fact, Rosenfeld didn't die in the room described by Bellow, who had last seen his friend in the bleak place he rented on Walton Place. He had moved months before his death to an airy, two-room apartment on East Huron near Chicago's Loop, not far from where he taught at the University of Chicago's downtown campus. Rosenfeld wrote to Freda Davis about a conversation he had had with his son about his new flat: "[George] knew I was sad. I assured him my life was much better now. I'm no longer in that basement.

Isaac Rosenfeld's tombstone.
Photograph taken by author.

I have a nice room, new clothes, a car. I have lots of friends."
The previous room was too dank and dark, it had depressed
the children when they visited, and he left it. His new apartment was, as always, packed with books; it wasn't terribly
clean, and the bathroom was down the hall, but as Sheila
wrote in a letter soon after his death: "He . . . appeared, at
least outwardly, reasonably contented. He was in analysis. He
was writing. And he was for the first time in years reaching an
economic level that might have been considered at least mod-
erately satisfactory." He bought himself a red convertible—a
dubious purchase, to be sure, for life in Chicago. Nowhere in
the published accounts of his death is there mention of the
sporty car. And his life was far from isolated: Freda planned to

see him that day (they planned to drive to visit her son's summer camp); another woman, Erica Aronson, a student at the basic program at the University of Chicago, was set to meet him for dinner. His romantic life remained full, hectic, perhaps obsessively so.[30] The assertion that he died alone seems off-kilter.

Freda recounted a phone call from him the morning of his death. He sounded excited, even elated, and announced that he had finally made the great breakthrough on his novel; which one remains unclear. This was the last she heard from him, and he must have died soon afterward in the writing chair where she and her brother found him later that day. She remained convinced that they would have wed, and although she remarried, she never reconciled herself to the immense loss.[31]

His children, George and Eleni, remembered incorrectly his having died at night. George recalled waking up that night, sobbing after a terrible nightmare in which Isaac had died. He was convinced that it was at that moment that his father's death had occurred; he also recalled that his parents were on the verge of reconciliation. Eleni remembered picking up the family photo album that same night—for reasons unclear to her at the time—studying pictures of her father at the very moment when, as she later believed, he dropped dead. Coincidences—odd, grim, almost impossible to imagine—stalked those closest to him: Vasiliki forbade the children to attend the funeral, but those in the procession related that as they drove through Chicago on the way to bury him, they happened to pass Eleni and George standing outside, staring at the cars; some in the procession called out their names.[32]

Vasiliki was flattened by the death. Not surprisingly, she found it difficult to support two little children as a single mother in her early forties, and Rosenfeld's family was unwilling to help. He had left behind no money, of course, and a collection was mounted by Bellow and others to help pay for the children's education. The story circulated that Vasiliki went out looking for jobs in an old fur coat held together by a diaper pin. She was hired as a publicist for publishing houses. Furious with Rosenfeld's father, Vasiliki changed their name to Sarant and shortly afterward had the children converted so that they could attend tuition-free a good Episcopalian private school, St. Luke's, just across from the Barrow Street apartment. She refused to allow the children to visit Rosenfeld's family, but they saw each other secretly with the help of Vasiliki's parents while vacationing in Chicago. As the years went by, she grew more and more eccentric; afraid of sleeping in the dark she kept the lights burning in her room throughout the night. She tended to disparage Rosenfeld's memory when she spoke of him to the children, describing him mostly as a womanizer. She continued to hold court—it was now a frayed, rapidly emptying court—and in the last, increasingly desperate years of his life, Delmore Schwartz found solace in her company. They probably slept together; Eleni remembered him reading poetry to her mother on the living room couch.

Vasiliki eventually married John White; he worked in publishing in New York and sporadically as an actor. He was brought to Hollywood to play the school principal on the television series *Welcome Back, Kotter*, which ran for four years. Vasiliki never adjusted to California. Although flushed for the first time, she pined for New York. Her marriage to White was tumultuous: both drank a great deal. White's son, David, described him as an alcoholic who fought fiercely and reconciled warmly with Vasiliki, whom the son recalled as moody, darkly beautiful, and hard to get to know. She spent most of her time locked away in her room reading or buying goods on the shopping channel. The Whites bought a large home with a pool in Sherman Oaks and later retired to Waikiki. There, following a stroke and White's death, Vasiliki went through their small fortune, wasting it on merchandise purchased on TV.

In the eyes of her children, she appeared grasping, self-justifying, and shallow. Still, many of her friends, especially those dating back to her first years in New York, in the early 1940s, and later in Minnesota, continued to see her as among the most electrifying women they had ever encountered.[33]

Where Rosenfeld was headed is impossible to say. It remains unclear whether he was in the midst of a comeback at the time of his death or sinking deeper and deeper into a morass. The basic program for which he then taught at Chicago was almost entirely staffed by men and women in their twenties. He was certainly among the oldest, and while he served as a seasoned intellectual guide to them, he also played the clown, often falling into an avuncular routine from which he couldn't manage to extricate himself. Bellow once observed: "His power to attract people might have made more difference to him than it did." At a retreat for faculty of the University of Chicago basic program held at the beginning of the academic year, he recited his Prufrock translation with consummate charm. But this college spoof (albeit brilliant) had become all too predictable a way to ingratiate. Yet he never lost his "affective magic," as Philip Seigelman put it. Rosenfeld hung out with his young colleagues; he befriended Allan Bloom, then at work on his master's degree and teaching at the basic program, and they frequented bars together. The novelist Herbert Gold, who met him around this time—

Vasiliki Rosenfeld.
Photograph courtesy of Nathan Tarcov.

having been told by Bellow that they would like one another—found Rosenfeld to be uneasy with himself, incapable of saying much of interest. All that Gold recalled years later about their encounter was Rosenfeld's insistence that they smoke marijuana, which, Rosenfeld boasted, he grew himself.[34]

His funeral was a traditional affair—officiated by an Orthodox rabbi who didn't seem to know Rosenfeld at all. It drew a large crowd. Friends later related that there were odd disputes with an especially crass funeral attendant. Freda recalled having been accosted by Rosenfeld's uncle and asked whether she had not misjudged that he was dead at the time she discovered his body. Vasiliki was inconsolable, wailing. Some noted that this might well be the way Greeks bury their dead. The fictionalized funeral in Wallace Markfield's *To an Early Grave* bore no resemblance at all to the actual event. Shortly afterward, a memorial service was held in a classroom at the downtown campus. It was Vasiliki who contacted Victor Gourevitch, head of the basic program and a man who knew Rosenfeld rather distantly, to deliver an oration. Gourevitch found Vasiliki very much in charge that day. She thanked him by giving him a wooden serving dish, a dime-store item that the courtly man treasured. Gourevitch recalled a small crowd, and no other speakers. Bellow had begged off, and attended neither the funeral nor the memorial service. (He was known to try his best to avoid the funerals of friends, and the excuse he gave for not coming to Rosenfeld's—his pregnant wife was apparently unwell—wasn't persuasive.) This poorly patched together send-off—sparse, with few who knew him well in attendance, despite the fact that it was held in a city where he had fervent admirers and dear friends—was, no doubt, related to the shock that his sudden death had left on Vasiliki and the rest of his family.[35]

An awareness of the vast, mostly unbridgeable discrepancy between what one imagines life to be and what it is, figures as one of the many lessons distinguishing adulthood from the years before it. Rosenfeld wrestled long, painfully, and, as a writer, quite fruitfully with this tension. He understood the difference between childhood dreams and adult reality. In his daily life, he sought to collapse their boundaries. In his writing, he explored the impossibility of doing just this.

"Isaac would have been a wonderful sixty year old," his friend Sidney Passin—who had many years earlier built Rosenfeld's orgone box—once told me.[36] I see Rosenfeld now, in a book-filled study, old, and wise, and calm—finally; his own books crowded onto shelves beside those of Philip Roth, and Henry Roth, and Joseph Roth, a singularly humane, intellectually mature, and justly celebrated body of work that appeared steadily, book after book, and combined love, comedy, dark, terrified broodings, and an astute sense of his own people: their obsessions, their limitations, their capacity for astonishment, and transcendence. There are also countless essays, stunning and astute reflections on books, their intersection with life, ruminations on their ability to stretch and diminish and wreak havoc, essays ranked alongside those of Cynthia Ozick or John Updike as monuments of mind and heart, testaments to the ways in which critics reared in the "age of criticism" transcended its strictures, its scientism. But Rosenfeld cared, above all, about his literature. Eventually he grew to become a master of tales free from dogma but filled with political stirrings, unerringly Jewish and thus all-encompassing; tales about home and escape; and tales that include moments of recognition that no matter how far one flees, if one is honest, flight is rarely achieved, or, for that matter, desired. It is work that no longer seeks to imitate Babel or Kafka, or to lacerate Hemingway, or to deny its author's own brilliant ability to re-create the complex, confounding voices around him. It is a body of literature at home with itself, with a voice as intelligent as Bellow's—indeed, not dissimilar from his in some respects—but, perhaps, still more intimately attuned to what it feels like to seek, hard and honestly and uncompromisingly, to be a truly good person and a truly good artist. It is fiction that draws on a singularly capacious mind, but critically, ruefully. Bellow and Rosenfeld continue to be paired together; reading both, book after book, side by side, one hears them, watches them, as they take their steps through life, as they try to make the whole damn thing a bit more recognizable, more wondrous to one another and to the rest of us, too.

Notes

Introduction

1. See Theodore Solotaroff's introduction to *An Age of Enormity: Life and Writing in the Forties and Fifties,* by Isaac Rosenfeld, edited and introduced by Theodore Solotaroff, foreword by Saul Bellow (Cleveland, 1962), 17; also Solotaroff, "The Spirit of Isaac Rosenfeld," in *The Red Hot Vacuum* (New York, 1970), 3–21.

2. Biographical treatments: Solotaroff's introduction to *An Age of Enormity,* 15–40; Mark Shechner's introduction to *Preserving the Hunger: An Isaac Rosenfeld Reader,* edited and introduced by Mark Shechner (Detroit, 1988), 21–27; James Atlas, *Bellow: A Biography* (New York, 2000); and Atlas, "Golden Boy," *New York Review of Books,* June 29, 1989; Steven J. Zipperstein, "The First Loves of Isaac Rosenfeld," *Jewish Social Studies* 5, nos. 1–2 (Fall 1998–Winter 1999): 3–24; and Zipperstein, "Isaac Rosenfeld's Dybbuk and Rethinking Literary Biography," *Partisan Review* 69, no. 1 (Winter 2002): 102–17. Bellow's eulogy was published in *Partisan Review* 23, no. 4 (Fall 1956): 565–67; the quotation I cite can be found on page 565. Shechner's volume—a work of scholarship and devotion—contains a reasonably comprehensive bibliography of Rosenfeld's published writings. A characteristic assessment of Rosenfeld at the time of his death may be found in "Between Issues," *The New Leader* (July 23, 1956), 2; the editor states in this column that "Never was he so shocked" by any news as by word of Rosenfeld's sudden death. Also see George Dennison, "Artist in His Skin," *Commentary* (November 1966): 102; on Bellow's reaction to the Nobel Prize: David Peltz interview with author, March 4, 1998.

3. Irving Howe, *A Margin of Hope: An Intellectual Autobiography* (San Diego, 1982), 133.

4. The only published part of "Charm and Death" is titled "Zetland: By a Character Witness," in Bellow's *Collected Stories,* edited by Saul Bellow and Janis Freedman Bellow, introduction by James Wood (New York, 2001), 240–54. Howe, *A Margin of Hope,* 133; Alfred Kazin, *New York Jew* (New York, 1978), 52; Wallace Markfield, *To an Early Grave* (New York, 1964), 51–52.

5. Howe, *A Margin of Hope,* 134; Eliezer Greenberg, "In Memoriam—Isaac Rosenfeld (1918–1956)," Box D, Saul Bellow Papers, Special Collections, Regenstein Library, University of Chicago; Diana Trilling, *Reviewing the Forties* (New York, 1978), 167–69.

6. See Andrew Delbanco, *Melville: His World and Work* (New York, 2005).

7. Bellow's foreword to *An Age of Enormity,* 13.

8. George Sarant letter to James Atlas, undated, copy in author's possession.

9. A. S. Byatt, *A Biographer's Tale* (London, 2000), 23.

10. Ted Solotaroff, *First Loves: A Memoir* (New York, 2003), 218.

11. Isaac Rosenfeld, "On the Role of the Writer and the Little Magazine," *Chicago Review* 11, no. 2 (Summer 1957): 14.

12. Bellow's foreword to *An Age of Enormity,* 14.

13. Isaac Rosenfeld Notebook no. 2, typed, approximately 1948–50, private collection, 82–83; Rosenfeld Notebook no. 1, typed, approximately 1948–50, private collection, 93–94.

Chapter One. Home

Epigraph. Isaac Rosenfeld letter to Oscar Tarcov, undated, probably 1945, Oscar Tarcov Papers, private collection.

1. For information on Rosenfeld's family I relied primarily on interviews with relatives and friends, including his widow, Vasiliki (Sarant) White; his daughter, Eleni Rosenfeld; his cousin Daniel Rosenfeld; his half sister Annette Hoffman; and his childhood friends Saul Bellow, Freda (Davis) Segel, and Lester Seligman.

2. Isaac Rosenfeld Notebook no. 1, typed, approximately 1948–50, private collection, 74; Oscar George email to author, April 20, 2008.

3. "A reikhn yingels atabiografiye," 27. I thank Daniel Rosenfeld for a copy of this text.

4. "A reikhn yingels atabiografiye," 29.

5. "A reikhn yingels atabiografiye," 28.

6. Isaac Rosenfeld, *Passage from Home* (New York, 1946), 126; Saul Bellow, "Zetland: By a Character Witness," in *Collected Stories,* edited by Saul Bellow and Janis Freedman Bellow, introduction by James Wood (New York, 2001), 243.

7. Isaac Rosenfeld letter to his aunts, Box 5.1, Isaac Rosenfeld Papers, Special Collections, Regenstein Library, University of Chicago.

8. Untitled manuscript, begins "For the thirteenth year," Box 1.7, Rosenfeld Papers.

9. Untitled manuscript, begins "My grandfather was a famous Talmudist," Box 4.1, Rosenfeld Papers, 13.

10. Mead Composition Notebook, Box 4.2, Rosenfeld Papers.

11. Irving Howe, "Strangers," in *Selected Writings, 1950–1990* (San Diego, 1990), 330; Bellow, "Zetland," 241.

12. Isaac Rosenfeld Notebook no. 2, typed, approximately 1948–50, private collection, 61; *Tuley Review,* November 21, 1934; Isaac Rosenfeld, "The World of the Ceiling," in *Preserving the Hunger: An Isaac Rosenfeld Reader,* edited and introduced by Mark Shechner (Detroit, 1988), 367; Freda (Davis) Segel interview with author, March 19, 1998; David Peltz interview with author, March 4, 1998.

13. Herbert and Sidney Passin interview with author, February 14, 1998; Saul Bellow interview with author, February 12, 1998.

14. Bellow, "Zetland," 240.

15. James Atlas, *Bellow: A Biography* (New York, 2000), 30; Rudolph Lapp interview with author, February 25, 1998; Saul Bellow interviews with author, January 5, 1996, and February 12, 1998; Herbert and Sidney Passin interview with author, February 14, 1998; Freda (Davis) Segel interview with author, March 19, 1998; *Tuley Review,* November 1, 1933, and April 18, 1934; Rosenfeld Notebook no. 1, typed, 103.

16. Bellow letter to Tarcov, undated, probably 1941, Tarcov Papers.

17. Bellow, "Zetland," 245.

18. Rosenfeld letters to Tarcov, January 19, 1938, and undated, probably 1939 or 1940, Tarcov Papers.

19. Hyman Slate interview with author, March 2, 1996; Saul Bellow, *Dangling Man* (New York, 1944), 39; Isaac Rosenfeld, "The Situation of the Jewish Writer," in *An Age of Enormity: Life and Writing in the Forties and Fifties,* edited and introduced by Theodore Solotaroff, foreword by Saul Bellow (Cleveland, 1962), 69.

20. Bellow letter to Tarcov, October 13, 1937, Saul Bellow Papers, Special Collections, Regenstein Library, University of Chicago.

21. Hermione Lee, *Virginia Woolf* (London, 1996), 269.

22. Albert Glotzer interview with author, October 30, 1997; Alan M. Wald, *The New York Intellectuals: The Rise and Decline of the Anti-Stalinist Left from the 1930s to the 1980s* (Chapel Hill, 1987), 91–163; Rosenfeld letter to Tarcov, October 7, 1937, Tarcov Papers; Rosenfeld Notebook no. 2, typed, 5; Albert Glotzer letter to Alan Wald, July 7, 1984. I thank Alan Wald for a copy of the letter.

23. Rosenfeld letters to Tarcov, September 19, probably 1938, and undated, probably fall 1938, Tarcov Papers.

24. Rosenfeld letter to Tarcov, April 28, 1941, Tarcov Papers.

25. Rosenfeld, "Life in Chicago," in *An Age of Enormity,* 332; Albert Glotzer

interview with author, October 30, 1997; Rosenfeld letter to Tarcov, undated, probably fall 1939, Tarcov Papers.

26. Isaac Rosenfeld, "The Party," in *Alpha and Omega* (New York, 1966), 125; the story first appeared in the *Kenyon Review* 9, no. 3 (1947). Rosenfeld, "Journal of a Generation," in *An Age of Enormity*, 46; the review appeared in *The New Republic*, January 11, 1943. Also see Richard M. Cook, *Alfred Kazin: A Biography* (New Haven, 2007), 79.

27. Rosenfeld letters to Tarcov, April 28, 1937, and undated, probably fall 1937, Tarcov Papers; Rosenfeld letters to his aunts, Box 5.1, Rosenfeld Papers.

28. Bellow letter to Tarcov, September 29, 1937, and October 2, 1937, Bellow Papers; Bellow, "Zetland," 246; Rosenfeld letter to Tarcov, September 25, 1937, Tarcov Papers; Isaac Rosenfeld, "The Precocious Student at the University of Chicago," *The Beacon*, April 1937, 19.

29. Alfred Kazin, *New York Jew* (New York, 1978), 48.

30. Saul Bellow, "Isaac Rosenfeld," *Partisan Review* 23, no. 4 (Fall 1956): 566.

31. Ruth Wisse, *The Modern Jewish Canon* (New York, 2000), 289.

32. Rosenfeld letters to Tarcov, March 18, 1938, and April 28, 1939, Tarcov Papers; Bellow, "Isaac Rosenfeld," 566; Rosenfeld, "The Precocious Student at the University of Chicago," 19.

33. Francis X. Clines, "Laureate's Mission Is to Give Voice to a Nation of Poets," *New York Times*, March 17, 1998, National News section.

34. Quoted in Ruth Wisse, "Language as Fate: Reflections on Jewish Literature in America," *Studies in Contemporary Jewry* 12 (1996): 129.

35. David Peltz interview with author, March 4, 1998; Journal, Box 4.6, and Rosenfeld, "Paper Dolls," Box 3.2, Rosenfeld Papers; Freda (Davis) Segel interview with author, March 19, 1998.

36. Rosenfeld letters to Freda (Davis) Segel, probably 1933 or 1934, Freda Davis Papers, private collection.

37. Rosenfeld described the end of the relationship in a letter to Tarcov, January 1, 1940, Tarcov Papers; Rosenfeld letter to Davis, undated, probably 1933 or 1934, Davis Papers.

38. Mead Composition Notebook, Box 4.2, Rosenfeld Papers, 224–25; Rosenfeld letter to Tarcov, undated, probably fall 1939, Tarcov Papers; Bellow letter to Tarcov, December 5, 1939, Bellow Papers; James Atlas, "Starting Out in Chicago," *Granta* 41 (1992): 40.

39. Bellow letter to Tarcov, undated, probably October 1939, Bellow Papers; Rosenfeld letter to Tarcov, undated, probably fall 1939, Tarcov Papers; Abe Kaufman letters to Tarcov, November 17, 1939, and December 22, 1939, Tarcov Papers; Rosenfeld letters to Tarcov, December 5, 1939, and undated, probably early 1940, Tarcov Papers; Bellow letter to Tarcov, undated, probably 1939, Tarcov Papers.

40. Rosenfeld letters to Tarcov, December 5, 1939, and undated, probably January 1941, Tarcov Papers.

41. Bellow, "Zetland," 247; William Phillips, *A Partisan View: Five Decades of the Literary Life* (New York, 1983), 183; Rosenfeld letter to Tarcov, undated, probably January 1941, Tarcov Papers.

42. Rosenfeld Notebook no. 1, typed, 67; "A Season of Earth: The John Billings Fiske Prize Poems (1937)," Box 5.6, Rosenfeld Papers.

43. Rosenfeld letter to George Herman, May 2, 1938, Tarcov Papers; Kaufman letter to Tarcov, May 25, 1941, Tarcov Papers.

44. Vasiliki (Sarantakis) Rosenfeld letter to Edith Tarcov, undated, probably spring 1945, Tarcov Papers.

45. Rosenfeld letter to Oscar Tarcov, April 6, 1941, Tarcov Papers.

46. Master's thesis, Box 2.43, Rosenfeld Papers.

47. George Herman letter to Tarcov, March 22, 1941, Tarcov Papers; Rosenfeld letter to Tarcov, July 26, probably 1942, Tarcov Papers; Rosenfeld letter to Tarcov, undated, probably 1943, Tarcov Papers.

48. Bellow, "Zetland," 250.

49. Saul Bellow, "Charm and Death," Bellow Papers.

50. Rosenfeld letter to Tarcov, September 12, 1941, Tarcov Papers.

51. Rosenfeld letter to Tarcov, November 13, 1941, Tarcov Papers; Atlas, *Bellow*, 113; Bellow, "Isaac Rosenfeld," 566; David T. Bazelon, *Nothing But a Fine Tooth Comb: Essays in Social Criticism, 1944–1969* (New York, 1970), 18.

52. Rosenfeld letter to Tarcov, undated, 1941 or 1942, Tarcov Papers.

53. Rosenfeld letters to Tarcov, undated; February 1943; July 26, probably 1942; and probably 1941, Tarcov Papers.

54. Bazelon, *Nothing But a Fine Tooth Comb*, 18; Phillips, *A Partisan View*, 217; Howe, "The New York Intellectuals," in *Selected Writings, 1950–1990*, 245.

55. William Barrett, *The Truants: Adventures among the Intellectuals* (Garden City, N.Y., 1982); Alexander Bloom, *Prodigal Sons: The New York Intellectuals and Their World* (New York, 1986); Phillips, *A Partisan View*; Howe, *A Margin of Hope*; Norman Podhoretz, *Making It* (New York, 1967); Mary McCarthy, *The Oasis* (New York, 1949), 16.

56. Bloom, *Prodigal Sons*, 7; Podhoretz, *Making It*, 109–76; Atlas, *Bellow*, 112.

57. Podhoretz, *Making It*, 165; Barrett, *The Truants*, 112; Cook, *Alfred Kazin*, 66; Elizabeth Pollet, ed., *Portrait of Delmore: Journals and Notes of Delmore Schwartz, 1939–1959* (New York, 1986), 441; Atlas, *Bellow*, 182.

58. Phillips, *A Partisan View*, 55. See the alternately adoring and terrifying portrait of Rahv in Barrett, *The Truants*, 1–159, for example: "Though he could,

on occasions that called for it, go through the gestures of a grand gentleman to the manner born, he was also one of the rudest men I've ever known" (39).

59. Phillips, *A Partisan View*, 48; Barrett, *The Truants*, 12–13.

60. McCarthy, *The Oasis*, 23, 35.

61. Phillips, *A Partisan View*, 55.

62. Barrett, *The Truants*, 76, 112; Bloom, *Prodigal Sons*, 296.

63. Rosenfeld letter to Tarcov, November 13, 1941, Tarcov Papers.

64. Rosenfeld, "Joe the Janitor," in *Alpha and Omega*, 27, 31–34.

65. Rosenfeld, "Joe the Janitor," 34.

66. Rosenfeld, "My Landlady," in *Alpha and Omega*, 25–26.

67. Solotaroff's introduction to *An Age of Enormity*, 27.

68. Rosenfeld, "The Hand That Fed Me," in *Alpha and Omega*, 7.

69. Rosenfeld, "The Hand That Fed Me," 14.

70. Rosenfeld letter to Tarcov, October 4, 1941, Tarcov Papers; Bellow, "Zetland," 252; Bazelon letter to Bellow, November 15, 1944, Bellow Papers.

71. Saul Bellow, "Isaac Rosenfeld," in *It All Adds Up* (New York, 1994), 264.

72. Sidney Hook, "The New Failure of Nerve," *Partisan Review* 10, no. 1 (January–February 1943): 3–23. Rosenfeld published his reply, "Philosophical Naturalism: The Failure of Verve," in *The New Republic*, July 19, 1943.

73. Rosenfeld, "Philosophical Naturalism: The Failure of Verve," in *An Age of Enormity*, 60–62.

74. Rosenfeld, "Philosophical Naturalism: The Failure of Verve," 61–62.

75. Rosenfeld letters to Tarcov, undated, probably late 1943, Tarcov Papers; Mitzi McCloskey interview with author, January 18, 2006; Rosenfeld, "The Two Gides," in *An Age of Enormity*, 181; Rosenfeld, "Poor Nitza," Box 2.9, Rosenfeld Papers; Pollet, ed., *Portrait of Delmore*, 296.

76. Rosenfeld letter to Oscar and Edith Tarcov, undated, probably 1943, Tarcov Papers.

77. Rosenfeld letter to Tarcov, undated, probably 1945, Tarcov Papers.

78. Rosenfeld letter to Tarcov, undated, probably 1946, Tarcov Papers.

79. Rosenfeld letter to Tarcov, undated, probably 1945, Tarcov Papers.

80. Rosenfeld, *Passage from Home*, 19.

81. Rosenfeld, *Passage from Home*, 3–4.

82. Rosenfeld, *Passage from Home*, 152–53.

83. Rosenfeld, *Passage from Home*, 23.

84. Rosenfeld, *Passage from Home*, 27.

85. Rosenfeld, *Passage from Home*, 123.

86. Rosenfeld, *Passage from Home*, 72–73.

87. Rosenfeld, *Passage from Home*, 76.

88. Rosenfeld, *Passage from Home*, 280.

89. I'm grateful to Ruth Wisse for this insight.

90. Rosenfeld letter to Tarcov, undated, probably 1945, Tarcov Papers; Rosenfeld, "Poor Nitza," Box 2.9, Rosenfeld Papers; Sidney Passin interview with author, October 28, 1997. I thank Daniel Rosenfeld for a tape of the radio program.

91. Diana Trilling, *Reviewing the Forties* (New York, 1978), 169; Daniel Bell, "A Parable of Alienation," *Jewish Frontier* 13, no. 11 (November 1946), republished in *Jewish Frontier Anthology, 1945–1967* (New York, 1967), 52; Irving Howe, "Of Fathers and Sons," *Commentary* (August 1946): 192.

92. Howe, *A Margin of Hope*, 110.

93. Howe, "Of Fathers and Sons," 190.

94. Howe, "Of Fathers and Sons," 190–92.

95. Howe, *A Margin of Hope*, 112.

96. Howe, *A Margin of Hope*, 113; Howe, "The Lost Young Intellectual," *Commentary* (October 1946): 361–62.

97. Howe, *A Margin of Hope*, 113.

98. Bell, "A Parable of Alienation," 53.

99. Trilling, *Reviewing the Forties*, 167–68.

100. Trilling, *Reviewing the Forties*, 169.

101. Howe, *A Margin of Hope*, 133–34.

102. Rosenfeld letter to Tarcov, undated, probably 1943, Tarcov Papers.

103. Barrett, *The Truants*, 112; Wallace Markfield interview with author, October 30, 1997.

104. Bellow, "Zetland," 246; Ralph Ross interview with author, November 3, 1998; Phillips, *A Partisan View*, 216–17; Sidney Passin interview with author, October 28, 1997; Rosenfeld Notebook no. 2, typed, 3, 66–67; Mead Composition Notebook, Box 4.2, Rosenfeld Papers.

105. Monroe Engel interview with author, December 4, 2007.

106. Wallace Markfield, *To an Early Grave* (New York, 1964), 191.

107. Mead Composition Notebook, Box 4.2, Rosenfeld Papers; Howe, "Of Fathers and Sons," 190; Rosenfeld Notebook no. 1, typed, 1–2; Kazin, *New York Jew*, 52.

108. Alfred Kazin letter to Rosenfeld, May 22, 1946, Box 5.2, Rosenfeld Papers; Kazin, *New York Jew*, 52.

Chapter Two. Terrors

Epigraph. James Atlas, *Bellow: A Biography* (New York, 2000), 98.

1. Isaac Rosenfeld Notebook no. 2, typed, approximately 1948–50, private collection, 76.

2. Saul Bellow, foreword to *An Age of Enormity: Life and Writing in the Forties and Fifties,* by Isaac Rosenfeld, edited and introduced by Theodore Solotaroff (Cleveland, 1962), 11–12.

3. Rosenfeld, "A Barge Captain's Log," Box 1.39/40, Isaac Rosenfeld Papers, Special Collections, Regenstein Library, University of Chicago, 2.

4. Rosenfeld, "A Barge Captain's Log," 2.

5. Isaac Rosenfeld letter to Oscar and Edith Tarcov, undated, Oscar Tarcov Papers, private collection; Rosenfeld, "A Barge Captain's Log," 1.

6. Rosenfeld, "A Barge Captain's Log," 3.

7. Rosenfeld, "A Barge Captain's Log," 6.

8. Rosenfeld, "A Barge Captain's Log," 7.

9. Rosenfeld, "A Barge Captain's Log," 13–14.

10. Rosenfeld, "A Barge Captain's Log," 42–43.

11. Rosenfeld, "A Barge Captain's Log," 43.

12. Rosenfeld, "A Barge Captain's Log," 16.

13. Rosenfeld, "A Barge Captain's Log," 27–29; Rosenfeld Notebook no. 2, typed, 17.

14. Rosenfeld, "A Barge Captain's Log," 31.

15. Rosenfeld, "A Barge Captain's Log," 32.

16. Rosenfeld, "A Barge Captain's Log," 34.

17. Rosenfeld, "A Barge Captain's Log," 77–78.

18. Rosenfeld, "A Barge Captain's Log," 80–82.

19. Rosenfeld, "A Barge Captain's Log," 82–87.

20. Rosenfeld, "A Barge Captains Log," 87–95.

21. Rosenfeld, "A Barge Captain's Log," 96.

22. Rosenfeld, "A Barge Captain's Log," 98–100.

23. Rosenfeld, "A Barge Captain's Log," 101.

24. Mead Composition Notebook, Box 4.2, Rosenfeld Papers, 252–54, 272–75; Isaac Rosenfeld Notebook no. 1, typed, approximately 1948–50, private collection, 8–9, 52.

25. Rosenfeld letter to Tarcov, undated, probably 1945, Tarcov Papers.

26. William Phillips, *A Partisan View: Five Decades of the Literary Life* (New York, 1983), 63.

27. Mary McCarthy, *The Oasis* (New York, 1949), 24.

28. Isaac Rosenfeld, "It Is Hard to Be a Jew" (reviews of Ben Hecht, *A Guide for the Bedeviled,* and Ludwig Lewisohn, *Breathe Upon These*), *The New Republic,* April 10, 1944.

29. Alfred Kazin, *New York Jew* (New York, 1978), 51.

30. James Baldwin, "The New Lost Generation," in *Collected Essays,* edited by Toni Morrison (New York, 1998), 662–63; original essay published in *Esquire* (July 1961).

31. See Eli Zaretsky, *Secrets of the Soul: A Social and Cultural History of Psychoanalysis* (New York, 2004), 219–25.

32. Sidney Passin interview with author, October 28, 1997; Saul Bellow, "Charm and Death," Saul Bellow Papers, Special Collections, Regenstein Library, University of Chicago, 95–97. David Peltz also recalls having built an orgone box for Bellow; Peltz interview with author, March 4, 1998.

33. Bellow's foreword to *An Age of Enormity,* 11.

34. Phillips, *A Partisan View,* 216–17.

35. Laura Perls, "A Peg to Hang My Hat On (Requiem for Isaac Rosenfeld)," Box 5.18, Rosenfeld Papers.

36. George Sarant letter to James Atlas, undated, copy in author's possession.

37. Lionel Abel interview with author, October 29, 1998.

38. Solotaroff's introduction to *An Age of Enormity,* 38–39.

39. Rosenfeld Notebook no. 1, typed, 58–59.

40. Rosenfeld, "Terror beyond Evil," in *An Age of Enormity,* 197–98.

41. Rosenfeld, "Terror beyond Evil," 198–99.

42. Rosenfeld, "Terror beyond Evil," 199.

43. Rosenfeld, "The Meaning of Terror," in *An Age of Enormity,* 206.

44. Rosenfeld, "The Meaning of Terror," 207.

45. Rosenfeld, "The Meaning of Terror," 207.

46. Rosenfeld, "The Meaning of Terror," 209.

47. Rosenfeld, "Approaches to Kafka," in *An Age of Enormity,* 170–71.

48. Rosenfeld, "Approaches to Kafka," 174.

49. Eleni Rosenfeld interview with author, February 26, 1996; Claire Sarant interview with author, September 5, 1995.

50. Eleni Rosenfeld interview with author, February 26, 1996.

51. Janet Richards, *Common Soldiers: A Self-Portrait and Other Portraits* (San Francisco, 1970), 108–10.

52. Wallace Markfield, *To an Early Grave* (New York, 1964), 12, 19, 46.

53. Markfield, *To an Early Grave*, 31–32.

54. Markfield, *To an Early Grave*, 31.

55. Markfield, *To an Early Grave*, 50–51.

56. Evelyn Shefner, "Monday Morning," *Hudson Review* 7, no. 4 (Winter 1955): 557–69.

57. Shefner, "Monday Morning," 557.

58. Shefner, "Monday Morning," 559–60.

59. Shefner, "Monday Morning," 561.

60. Shefner, "Monday Morning," 564.

61. Shefner, "Monday Morning," 564.

62. Shefner, "Monday Morning," 567.

63. Shefner, "Monday Morning," 567–69.

64. Shefner, "Monday Morning," 569.

65. Cynthia Ozick, *The Din in the Head: Essays* (Boston, 2006), 111; Mead Composition Notebook, Box 4.2, Rosenfeld Papers, 88–90, 195, 234; Rosenfeld, "The Two Gides," in *An Age of Enormity*, 181.

66. Rosenfeld Notebook no. 1, typed, 7–10.

67. Mead Composition Notebook, Box 4.2, Rosenfeld Papers, 194–201, 213–15; Rosenfeld Notebook no. 1, typed, 60–61, 74, 81; Rosenfeld Notebook no. 2, typed, 23, 27–29, 34.

68. Mead Composition Notebook, Box 4.2, Rosenfeld Papers, 88–94.

69. Mead Composition Notebook, Box 4.2, Rosenfeld Papers, 89.

70. Mead Composition Notebook, Box 4.2, Rosenfeld Papers, 89.

71. Rosenfeld letter to Tarcov, undated, probably 1945, Tarcov Papers; Bellow, "Charm and Death," 26; Markfield, *To an Early Grave*, 16.

72. Isaac Rosenfeld, "Alpha and Omega," in *Alpha and Omega* (New York, 1966), 195.

73. Mead Composition Notebook, Box 4.2, Rosenfeld Papers, 218–21.

74. Rosenfeld letter to Bellow, December 25, perhaps 1942 or 1943, Tarcov Papers.

75. Rosenfeld Notebook no. 2, typed, 82; Rosenfeld, "Mother Russia," Box 2.1–4, Rosenfeld Papers.

76. Rosenfeld letter to Tarcov, undated, probably late 1946, Tarcov Papers.

77. David T. Bazelon, *Nothing But a Fine Tooth Comb: Essays in Social Criticism, 1944–1969* (New York, 1970), 18; Rosenfeld letter to Tarcov, undated, Tarcov Papers.

78. Rosenfeld, "An Assignment," Box 1.3, Rosenfeld Papers, 6, 17–23.

79. Rosenfeld, "An Assignment," Box 1.3, Rosenfeld Papers, 33–34.

80. Rosenfeld Notebook no. 2, typed, 33.

81. Rosenfeld Notebook no. 2, typed, 81–82.

82. Rosenfeld, "Halberline," Box 2.42, Rosenfeld Papers.

83. Mead Composition Notebook, Box 4.2, Rosenfeld Papers, 28.

84. Rosenfeld, "Halberline," Box 2.42, Rosenfeld Papers, 9.

85. Rosenfeld, "Gandhi: Self-Realization through Politics," in *An Age of Enormity,* 224–45.

86. Rosenfeld, "Gandhi: Self-Realization through Politics," 225.

87. Rosenfeld, "Gandhi: Self-Realization through Politics," 224–25.

88. Rosenfeld, "Gandhi: Self-Realization through Politics," 225.

89. Rosenfeld, "Gandhi: Self-Realization through Politics," 228–29.

90. Rosenfeld, "Gandhi: Self-Realization through Politics," 230.

91. Rosenfeld, "Gandhi: Self-Realization through Politics," 234.

92. Rosenfeld, "Gandhi: Self-Realization through Politics," 241.

93. Rosenfeld, "Gandhi: Self-Realization through Politics," 245.

Chapter Three. Paradise

Epigraph. Isaac Rosenfeld, "Adam and Eve on Delancey Street," in *An Age of Enormity: Life and Writing in the Forties and Fifties,* edited and introduced by Theodore Solotaroff, foreword by Saul Bellow (Cleveland, 1962), 183.

1. Diana Trilling, *The Beginning of the Journey: The Marriage of Diana and Lionel Trilling* (New York, 1993), 88–91.

2. William Phillips, *A Partisan View: Five Decades of the Literary Life* (New York, 1983), 21, 74; Norman Podhoretz, *Making It* (New York, 1967), 3.

3. Irving Howe, "The New York Intellectuals" and "Strangers," in *Selected Writings, 1950–1990* (San Diego, 1990), 241 and 329.

4. Isaac Rosenfeld letter of recommendation for James Arthur Baldwin, Box 39, Folder 2, James Baldwin Collection, Fisk University Archives. I thank Lawrence Jackson, Emory University, who provided me with this text.

5. Isaac Rosenfeld, *Passage from Home* (New York, 1946), 118.

6. Isaac Rosenfeld letter to Oscar Tarcov, undated, Oscar Tarcov Papers, private collection; Rosenfeld letter to his aunts, undated, probably 1947, Box 5.1, Isaac Rosenfeld Papers, Special Collections, Regenstein Library, University of Chicago; Rosenfeld, "The Situation of the Jewish Writer," in *An Age of Enormity,* 69.

7. Rosenfeld, "The Situation of the Jewish Writer," 67.

8. Rosenfeld, "The Situation of the Jewish Writer," 68–69.

9. Rosenfeld, "The Situation of the Jewish Writer," 69.

10. Rosenfeld, "Sholem Aleichem: The Humor of Exile," in *An Age of Enormity,* 72–74.

11. Rosenfeld, "Sholem Aleichem: The Humor of Exile," 74.

12. Isaac Rosenfeld, "Isaac Leib Peretz: The Prince of the Ghetto," in *Preserving the Hunger: An Isaac Rosenfeld Reader,* edited and introduced by Mark Shechner (Detroit, 1988), 136–38.

13. Rosenfeld, "Isaac Leib Peretz: The Prince of the Ghetto," 141–42.

14. Isaac Rosenfeld Notebook no. 1, typed, approximately 1948–50, private collection, 108–9.

15. Rosenfeld, "A Tailor," in *Preserving the Hunger,* 417.

16. Rosenfeld, "A Tailor," 417–18.

17. Rosenfeld, "David and Bath-Sheba," Box 1.2, and "King David," Box 2.22, Rosenfeld Papers.

18. Not until Philip Roth's *Goodbye, Columbus* would a piece of imaginative writing inspire as fierce and fractious a conflict in American Jewish life. And there are echoes in Roth of Rosenfeld's travails: In his novel *The Ghost Writer* (New York, 1979), Roth speaks of how the writings of his young protagonist Zuckerman inspire a Judge Wapter, greatly admired by his father, to send him a list of accusations. The last of these—by far the most provocative—asks, "Can you honestly say that there is anything in your short story that would not warm the heart of Julius Streicher or Joseph Goebbels?" (103–4). Whether Roth knew it or not—and as a graduate student at the University of Chicago he was quite close to several students, such as Ted Solotaroff, who followed Rosenfeld—this was almost the exact wording of the widely disseminated accusations against Rosenfeld circulated to the membership of the American Jewish Committee.

19. Bellow's foreword to *An Age of Enormity,* 11.

20. Rosenfeld, "Approaches to Kafka" and "For God in the Suburbs," in *An Age of Enormity,* 165 and 309; Sheila Stern letter to Joanne Joseph, August 1, 1956, Sheila Stern Aldendorff Papers, private collection; Bellow's foreword to *An Age of Enormity,* 13; Irving Howe, *A Margin of Hope: An Intellectual Autobiography* (San Diego, 1982), 133; Monroe Engel interview with the author, December 4, 2007.

21. Isaac Rosenfeld, "The Party," in *Alpha and Omega* (New York, 1966), 125.

22. Rosenfeld, "The Party," 143.

23. Rosenfeld, "Henry Miller in America," in *An Age of Enormity*, 117–18; Isaac Rosenfeld Notebook no. 2, typed, approximately 1948–50, private collection, 76; Rosenfeld Notebook no. 1, typed, 65; Phillips, *A Partisan View*, 216.

24. Saul Bellow, "Isaac Rosenfeld," *Partisan Review* 23, no. 4 (Fall 1956): 566.

25. Isaac Rosenfeld, "Kreplach," *Commentary* (November 1948): 487–88.

26. Rosenfeld Notebook no. 1, typed, 86.

27. Rosenfeld, "Adam and Eve on Delancey Street," 183.

28. Rosenfeld, "Adam and Eve on Delancey Street," 186.

29. Rosenfeld, "Adam and Eve on Delancey Street," 184–86.

30. Rosenfeld, "Adam and Eve on Delancey Street," 187.

31. Rosenfeld, "Adam and Eve on Delancey Street," 187.

32. M. L. Isaacs letter to Julius Slawson, November 13, 1949; Rabbi Samuel Kramer letter to Alan M. Stroock, November 10, 1949; *Yiddish News Digest*, October 31, 1949; *Hadoar*, October 21, 1949, in *Commentary* archive.

33. Simon Noveck, "Milton Steinberg," in *The "Other" New York Jewish Intellectuals*, edited by Carole S. Kessner (New York, 1994), 313–52; also see historian Jonathan Steinberg's article on his father, "Milton Steinberg, American Rabbi: Thoughts on His Centenary," in *Jewish Quarterly Review* 95, no. 3 (Summer 2005): 579–600.

34. "*Commentary* Magazine—Benefit or Detriment to American Judaism?" (lecture delivered by Rabbi Milton Steinberg before Park Avenue Synagogue, New York City, Friday evening, November 18, 1949), 1; confidential memorandum from Rabbi Milton Steinberg to *Commentary* editorial board and others at the American Jewish Committee (a sixteen-page excerpt of letters sent to Steinberg in support of his condemnation of *Commentary*); with an unsigned rebuttal written, probably, by Elliot Cohen, in the *Commentary* archive. Also see Steinberg's exchange of letters with Milton Weill, a member of his synagogue who was also on the Commentary Publication Committee: P-369, Folder 6, Milton Weill Collection, American Jewish Historical Society Archives, Center for Jewish History, New York.

35. Carl Alpert letter to American Jewish Committee membership, October 24, 1949, *Commentary* archive.

36. Philip Rahv letter to editors of *Commentary*, December 19, 1949, *Commentary* archive.

37. Elliot Cohen, editorial note, *Commentary* (November 1949): 501; Jacob Blaustein letter to editor of *Commentary* (December 1949): 594.

38. In the midst of the controversy, Bellow sent Tarcov a singularly self-pitying letter whose only references to Rosenfeld have to do with his negative feelings toward Bellow: "It's terribly disappointing. . . . But then Isaac is probably

not far from thinking the same things of me. I don't know how you stand with him these days. Better, I hope. I'm entirely in his dog-house, I feel." Bellow letter to Tarcov, December 5, 1949, Tarcov Papers.

39. Mary McCarthy letter to editor of *Commentary*, December 14, 1949, *Commentary* archive.

40. Irving Howe letter to editor of *Commentary*, December 18, 1949, *Commentary* archive.

41. Harvey Swados letter to editor of *Congress Weekly*, November 14, 1949, *Commentary* archive.

42. S. Niger, "The Spiritual Stocktaking of the American Jewish Intellectual," *Der Tog*, October 29, 1949, in *Yiddish News Digest*, October 31, 1949, 5, *Commentary* archive. On the attitudes of Yiddish writers in the United States toward American-born Jewish intellectuals like Rosenfeld, see the superb discussion in Anita Norich, *Discovering Exile: Yiddish and Jewish American Culture during the Holocaust* (Stanford, 2007), 17–41; the controversy over Rosenfeld's essay is also summarized in Nathan Abrams, *Commentary Magazine, 1945–1959: A Journal of Significant Thought and Opinion* (London, 2007), 81–84.

43. Isaac Rosenfeld letter to editor of *Commentary*, December 2, 1949, *Commentary* archive.

44. "An Act of Affirmation: Editorial Statement," *Commentary* (November 1945): 2.

45. Alexander Bloom, *Prodigal Sons: The New York Intellectuals and Their World* (New York, 1986), 161–66; Trilling, *The Beginning of the Journey*, 91–93.

46. Rosenfeld letter to his aunts, Box 5.1, Rosenfeld Papers.

47. Oscar Handlin letter to Herbert B. Ehrmann, December 16, 1949, *Commentary* archive.

48. Howe, *A Margin of Hope*, 252.

49. Podhoretz, *Making It*, 133–34.

50. Howe, "The New York Intellectuals," 241.

51. Phillips, *A Partisan View*, 67; Harold Rosenberg letter to editor of *Commentary*, December 14, 1949, *Commentary* archive.

52. Rosenberg letter to editor of *Commentary*, December 14, 1949.

53. Howe, *A Margin of Hope*, 259.

54. Harold Rosenberg, "Jewish Identity in a Free Society," in *Discovering the Present: Three Decades in Art, Culture, and Politics* (Chicago, 1973), 259–61.

55. Rosenberg, "Jewish Identity in a Free Society," 263.

56. Rosenberg, "Jewish Identity in a Free Society," 264–65.

57. Rosenberg, "Jewish Identity in a Free Society," 269.

58. Carl Alpert, "Obscenity and Insult," *Cross-Section U.S.A.* 2, no. 5 (August 3, 1950): 1, *Commentary* archive; Bloom, *Prodigal Sons*, 146–49.

59. Sidney Passin interview with author, October 28, 1997.

60. Rosenfeld, "David Levinsky: The Jew as American Millionaire," in *An Age of Enormity*, 273–74.

61. Rosenfeld, "David Levinsky: The Jew as American Millionaire," 276.

62. Rosenfeld, "David Levinsky: The Jew as American Millionaire," 276.

63. Rosenfeld, "David Levinsky: The Jew as American Millionaire," 278–80.

64. Rosenfeld letter to Tarcov, April 3, 1951, Tarcov Papers; Monroe Engel interview with author, December 4, 2007.

65. James Atlas, *Bellow: A Biography* (New York, 2000), 119–60; Rosenfeld letter to Tarcov, undated, probably 1950, Tarcov Papers; Rosenfeld, "Journals: Selected Entries," in *Preserving the Hunger,* 443.

66. Rosenfeld letter to Tarcov, undated, probably 1952, Tarcov Papers; Doris Taft Hedlund, "Call Me Isaac," *Minnesota Ivory Tower,* October 22, 1956, copy found in Box 5.18, Rosenfeld Papers.

67. Written by Joanne Joseph, private collection.

68. Written by Joanne Joseph, private collection.

69. Rosenfeld letter to Tarcov, undated, probably 1953, Tarcov Papers; Vasiliki (Sarant) White interview with author, February 2, 1996.

70. Mitzi McCloskey interview with author, January 18, 2006.

71. Rosenfeld letters to his aunts, Box 5.1, Rosenfeld Papers; Rosenfeld letter to Tarcov, probably 1948, Tarcov Papers; Bellow letter to Tarcov, March 26, 1953, Tarcov Papers.

72. Rosenfeld, "A Hot Time in the Old Town: The Great Chicago Fire, 1871," Box 2.36, Rosenfeld Papers; Vasiliki (Sarant) White interview with author, February 2, 1996; Rosenfeld letter to Tarcov, April 21, 1953, Tarcov Papers; Lewis M. Dabney, *Edmund Wilson: A Life in Literature* (New York, 2005), 378; Edmund Wilson and Leon Edel, *The Fifties: From Notebooks and Diaries of the Period* (New York, 1986), 168.

73. Monroe Engel interview with author, December 4, 2007; Rosenfeld letter to Tarcov, October 1955, Tarcov Papers; Wallace Markfield interview with author, October 30, 1997.

74. Hyman Slate interview with author, March 20, 1996; Journal, Box 4.6, Rosenfeld Papers.

75. Sheila Stern letters to Joanne Joseph, April 22 and August 1, 1955, Stern Aldendorff Papers.

76. Stern letter to Joseph, November 23, 1955, Stern Aldendorff Papers.

77. Stern letter to Joseph, February 21, 1956, Stern Aldendorff Papers.

78. Journal, Box 4.6, Rosenfeld Papers; Rosenfeld letter to Tarcov, summer 1955, Tarcov Papers.

79. Rosenfeld, "Life in Chicago," in *An Age of Enormity*, 328, 347.

80. Atlas, *Bellow*, 234; Daniel Rosenfeld interview with author, March 19, 1996; Arthur Geffen interview with author, April 20, 2008.

81. Journal, Box 4.6, Rosenfeld Papers, 1–2.

82. Journal, Box 4.6, Rosenfeld Papers, 5, 9–10.

83. Journal, Box 4.6, Rosenfeld Papers, 11–12.

84. Journal, Box 4.6, Rosenfeld Papers, 32.

85. Journal, Box 4.6, Rosenfeld Papers; Freda (Davis) Segel interview with author, March 19, 1998; Rosenfeld, "Ruth," Box 1.5, Rosenfeld Papers; Wallace Markfield interview with author, October 30, 1997; Hyman Slate interview with author, March 2, 1996; David Ray, "Isaac Again, for Barbara," unpublished poem, photocopy in author's possession.

86. Untitled fragment, Box 1.22, Rosenfeld Papers, 1.

87. Rosenfeld, "The World of the Ceiling," in *Preserving the Hunger*, 367.

88. Rosenfeld, "The World of the Ceiling," 367–68.

89. Rosenfeld, "The World of the Ceiling," 370.

90. Rosenfeld, "The World of the Ceiling," 370–72.

91. Rosenfeld, "The World of the Ceiling," 372.

92. Rosenfeld, "Wolfie," in *Alpha and Omega*, 239–40, 262.

93. Rosenfeld, "Wolfie," 262, 260; Oscar George email to author, April 20, 2008.

94. Ruth Denney letter to author, postmarked March 1, 1998, private collection.

95. Isaac Rosenfeld, "On the Role of the Writer and the Little Magazine," *Chicago Review* 11, no. 2 (Summer 1957): 5.

96. Rosenfeld, "On the Role of the Writer and the Little Magazine," 5.

97. Rosenfeld, "On the Role of the Writer and the Little Magazine," 13.

98. Rosenfeld, "On the Role of the Writer and the Little Magazine," 9.

99. Rosenfeld, "On the Role of the Writer and the Little Magazine," 14.

100. Rosenfeld, "On the Role of the Writer and the Little Magazine," 16.

101. Atlas, *Bellow*, 193.

102. Rosenfeld, "King Solomon," in *Alpha and Omega*, 263.

103. Rosenfeld, "King Solomon," 263.

104. Rosenfeld, "King Solomon," 266.

105. Rosenfeld, "King Solomon," 267.

106. Rosenfeld, "King Solomon," 270.

107. Rosenfeld, "King Solomon," 273.

108. Rosenfeld, "King Solomon," 276.

109. Rosenfeld, "King Solomon," 278–79.

Postscript

Epigraph. Isaac Rosenfeld, "The Misfortune of the Flapjacks," in *Alpha and Omega* (New York, 1966), 98.

1. Rosenfeld, "The Misfortune of the Flapjacks," 98.

2. Freda (Davis) Segel interview with author, March 19, 1998; Wallace Markfield interview with author, October 30, 1997; Sheila Stern letter to Joanna Joseph, August 1, 1956, Sheila Stern Aldendorff Papers, private collection.

3. Wallace Markfield, *To an Early Grave* (New York, 1964), 13.

4. Bernard Malamud, *Talking Horse: Bernard Malamud on Life and Work,* edited by Alan Cheuse and Nicholas Delbanco (New York, 1996), 136; Wallace Markfield interview with author, October 30, 1997.

5. For a text of "The Liars," see Box 1.37, Rosenfeld Papers, Special Collections, Regenstein Library, University of Chicago; a revised version appeared as "The Boys," in *Midstream* 4, no. 2 (Spring 1958).

6. Theodore Solotaroff's introduction to *An Age of Enormity: Life and Writing in the Forties and Fifties,* by Isaac Rosenfeld, edited and introduced by Theodore Solotaroff, foreword by Saul Bellow (Cleveland, 1962), 17–18.

7. Rosenfeld, "Gandhi: Self-Realization through Politics," in *An Age of Enormity,* 241.

8. Isaac Rosenfeld letter to Oscar Tarcov, undated, probably 1943 or 1944, Oscar Tarcov Papers, private collection.

9. Saul Bellow, "Isaac Rosenfeld," *Partisan Review* 23, no. 4 (Fall 1956): 565.

10. David Peltz interview with author, March 4, 1998; Marilyn Mann interview with author, February 17, 1998.

11. Marilyn Mann interview with author, February 17, 1998; Saul Bellow letter to Tarcov, June 6, 1950, Saul Bellow Papers, Special Collections, Regenstein Library, University of Chicago.

12. Bellow letter to Morgan Blum, December 12, 1956, private collection; I thank Philip Seigelman for providing me with a copy. See also Bellow's foreword to *An Age of Enormity,* 12.

13. Saul Bellow, *Seize the Day, with Three Short Stories and a One-Act Play* (New York, 1956), 114.

14. Daniel and Pearl Bell interview with author, February 13, 1998; James Atlas, *Bellow: A Biography* (New York, 2000), 239; Saul Bellow, *Henderson the Rain King* (New York, 1959), 193, 236, 274, 314. Daniel Fuchs, *Saul Bellow: Vision and Revision* (Durham, N.C., 1984), discusses Rosenfeld's impact on *Henderson the Rain King* on page 115. Based on his study of the manuscripts of *Humboldt's Gift*, he writes: "All these instances show that at one point in the composition Bellow thought of a character who would be a composite of himself and Isaac Rosenfeld" (335).

15. Saul Bellow, "Zetland: By a Character Witness," in *Collected Stories*, edited by Saul Bellow and Janis Freedman Bellow, introduction by James Wood (New York, 2001), 243. See Wood's discussion of the ways in which in Bellow "bodies are their confessions, their moral camouflage faulty and peeling" (xv).

16. Atlas, *Bellow*, 390–91; Monroe Engel interview with author, December 4, 2007.

17. Saul Bellow interviews with author, January 5, 1996, and February 12, 1998; Herbert and Sidney Passin interview with author, February 14, 1998.

18. Atlas, *Bellow*, 243; Marilyn Mann interview with author, February 17, 1998.

19. Bellow, "Isaac Rosenfeld," 567.

20. Alfred Kazin, *New York Jew* (New York, 1978), 52.

21. Saul Bellow, *The Victim* (New York, 1947), 16.

22. Morgan Blum, "Isaac Rosenfeld: For a Friend Who Died Alone," *The New Republic*, September 3, 1956.

23. John Berryman, "Of Isaac Rosenfeld," Box 5.18, Rosenfeld Papers.

24. Markfield, *To an Early Grave*, 101; James Atlas, "Isaac Rosenfeld Thinks about His Life," *Poetry* (July 1971): 213–15.

25. Kazin, *New York Jew*, 51.

26. Kazin, *New York Jew*, 59–60.

27. Kazin, *New York Jew*, 51.

28. Richard M. Cook, *Alfred Kazin: A Biography* (New Haven, 2007), 88.

29. Brian Morton, *Starting Out in the Evening* (New York, 1998), 61.

30. Rosenfeld letter to Freda (Davis) Segel, undated, Freda Davis Papers, private collection; Sheila Stern letter to Joanna Joseph, August 1, 1956, Stern Aldendorff Papers; Freda (Davis) Segel interview with author, March 19, 1998; Erica Aronson interview with author, October 20, 1996.

31. Freda (Davis) Segel interview with author, March 19, 1998.

32. Eleni Rosenfeld interview with author, February 26, 1996; Philip Seigelman interview with author, February 17, 1996.

33. Vasiliki (Sarant) White interview with author, February 26, 1996; Ann

Birstein, *What I Saw at the Fair* (New York, 2003); Mitzi McCloskey interview with author, January 18, 2006; Philip Seigelman interview with author, February 17, 1996; Elizabeth Pollet, ed., *Portrait of Delmore: Journals and Notes of Delmore Schwartz, 1939–1959* (New York, 1986), 610; David Britt White interview with author, January 5, 2008.

34. Bellow's foreword to *An Age of Enormity,* 12; Victor Gourevitch interview with author, September 17, 2006; Philip Seigelman interview with author, February 17, 1996; Herbert Gold interview with author, September 24, 1997.

35. Freda (Davis) Segel interview with author, March 19, 1998; Victor Gourevitch interview with author, September 17, 2006; "Eulogy to Isaac Rosenfeld, delivered on July 17, 1956 by Victor Gourevitch," Box 5.18, Rosenfeld Papers. While the dead writer described in *To an Early Grave* is modeled, as Markfield acknowledged, on Rosenfeld—as is the portrait of his wife—the novel's actual funeral scene might well have been drawn from elsewhere. Sidney Passin described to me the funeral of the composer Edith Lieber, and how Rosenfeld accompanied him there with the Poster brothers in Sidney's Model-T Ford. As depicted in the novel, they knew only that the funeral was somewhere in Brooklyn and got lost searching for it. Once they arrived, the officiating rabbi was vacuous (he compared life to a phone book), and Rosenfeld and his friends fell into a laughing fit much as Markfield depicts in his book. Sidney Passin interview with author, October 28, 1997.

36. Sidney Passin interview with author, October 28, 1997.

Bibliography

Manuscripts

Saul Bellow Papers, Special Collections, Regenstein Library, University of Chicago.

Commentary archive.

Freda Davis Papers, private collection.

Isaac Rosenfeld Notebooks nos. 1 and 2, typed, approximately 1948–50, private collection.

Isaac Rosenfeld Papers, Special Collections, Regenstein Library, University of Chicago.

Sheila Stern Aldendorff Papers, private collection.

Oscar Tarcov Papers, private collection.

Milton Weill Collection, American Jewish Historical Society Archives, Center for Jewish History, New York.

Periodicals

The Beacon

Commentary

Contemporary Jewish Record

The Hudson Review

Jewish Frontier

Midstream

The Nation

The New Leader

The New Republic

Partisan Review

Poetry

Der Tog

Tsukunft

Tuley Review

Books by Isaac Rosenfeld, Including Posthumous

Collections of His Work

An Age of Enormity: Life and Writing in the Forties and Fifties. Edited and introduced by Theodore Solotaroff. Foreword by Saul Bellow. Cleveland, 1962.

Alpha and Omega. New York, 1966.

Passage from Home. New York, 1946.

Preserving the Hunger: An Isaac Rosenfeld Reader. Edited and introduced by Mark Shechner. Detroit, 1988.

Other Works Cited in the Footnotes

Abrams, Nathan. *Commentary Magazine, 1945–1959: A Journal of Significant Thought and Opinion.* London, 2007.

Atlas, James. *Bellow: A Biography.* New York, 2000.

Atlas, James. "Golden Boy." *New York Review of Books,* June 29, 1989.

Atlas, James. "Isaac Rosenfeld Thinks about His Life." *Poetry* (July 1971): 213–15.

Atlas, James. "Starting Out in Chicago." *Granta* 41 (1992): 40.

Baldwin, James. "The New Lost Generation." In *Collected Essays,* edited by Toni Morrison. New York, 1998. Original essay published in *Esquire* (July 1961).

Barrett, William. *The Truants: Adventures among the Intellectuals.* Garden City, N.Y., 1982.

Bazelon, David T. *Nothing But a Fine Tooth Comb: Essays in Social Criticism, 1944–1969.* New York, 1970.

Bell, Daniel. "A Parable of Alienation." *Jewish Frontier* 13, no. 11 (November 1946): 12–19. Republished in *Jewish Frontier Anthology, 1945–1967.* New York, 1967.

Bellow, Saul. *Dangling Man.* New York, 1944.

Bellow, Saul. Foreword to *An Age of Enormity: Life and Writing in the Forties and Fifties,* by Isaac Rosenfeld, edited and introduced by Theodore Solotaroff, 11–14. Cleveland, 1962.

Bellow, Saul. *Henderson the Rain King*. New York, 1959.

Bellow, Saul. *Humboldt's Gift*. New York, 1975.

Bellow, Saul. "Isaac Rosenfeld." *Partisan Review* 23, no. 4 (Fall 1956): 565–67.

Bellow, Saul. "Isaac Rosenfeld." In *It All Adds Up*, 263–66. New York, 1994.

Bellow, Saul. *Seize the Day, with Three Short Stories and a One-Act Play*. New York, 1956.

Bellow, Saul. *The Victim*. New York, 1947.

Bellow, Saul. "Zetland: By a Character Witness." In *Collected Stories*, 240–54. New York, 2001.

Bellow, Saul, and Janis Freedman Bellow, eds. *Collected Stories*. Introduction by James Wood. New York, 2001.

Birstein, Ann. *What I Saw at the Fair*. New York, 2003.

Bloom, Alexander. *Prodigal Sons: The New York Intellectuals and Their World*. New York, 1986.

Blum, Morgan. "Isaac Rosenfeld: For a Friend Who Died Alone." *The New Republic*, September 3, 1956.

Byatt, A. S. *A Biographer's Tale*. London, 2000.

Clines, Francis X. "Laureate's Mission Is to Give Voice to a Nation of Poets." *New York Times*, March 17, 1998, National News section.

Cook, Richard M. *Alfred Kazin: A Biography*. New Haven, 2007.

Dabney, Lewis M. *Edmund Wilson: A Life in Literature*. New York, 2005.

Delbanco, Andrew. *Melville: His World and Work*. New York, 2005.

Dennison, George. "Artist in His Skin." *Commentary* (November 1966): 102.

Fuchs, Daniel. *Saul Bellow: Vision and Revision*. Durham, N.C., 1984.

Hook, Sidney. "The New Failure of Nerve." *Partisan Review* 10, no. 1 (January–February 1943): 3–23.

Howe, Irving. "The Lost Young Intellectual." *Commentary* (October 1946): 361–67.

Howe, Irving. *A Margin of Hope: An Intellectual Autobiography.* San Diego, 1982.

Howe, Irving. "Of Fathers and Sons." *Commentary* (August 1946): 190–92.

Howe, Irving. *Selected Writings, 1950–1990.* San Diego, 1990.

Howe, Irving, and Eliezer Greenberg, eds. *A Treasury of Yiddish Stories.* New York, 1954.

Kazin, Alfred. *New York Jew.* New York, 1978.

Kessner, Carole S., ed. *The "Other" New York Jewish Intellectuals.* Reappraisals in Jewish Social and Intellectual History. New York, 1994.

Lee, Hermione. *Virginia Woolf.* London, 1996.

Malamud, Bernard. *Talking Horse: Bernard Malamud on Life and Work.* Edited by Alan Cheuse and Nicholas Delbanco. New York, 1996.

Markfield, Wallace. *To an Early Grave.* New York, 1964.

McCarthy, Mary. *The Oasis.* New York, 1949.

Morton, Brian. *Starting Out in the Evening.* New York, 1998.

Norich, Anita. *Discovering Exile: Yiddish and Jewish American Culture during the Holocaust.* Stanford, 2007.

Ozick, Cynthia. *The Din in the Head: Essays.* Boston, 2006.

Phillips, William. *A Partisan View: Five Decades of the Literary Life.* New York, 1983.

Podhoretz, Norman. *Making It.* New York, 1967.

Pollet, Elizabeth, ed. *Portrait of Delmore: Journals and Notes of Delmore Schwartz, 1939–1959.* New York, 1986.

Richards, Janet. *Common Soldiers: A Self-Portrait and Other Portraits.* San Francisco, 1970.

Rosenberg, Harold. "Jewish Identity in a Free Society." In *Discovering the Present: Three Decades in Art, Culture, and Politics,* 259–69. Chicago, 1973.

Rosenfeld, Isaac. "The Boys." *Midstream* 4, no. 2 (Spring 1958): 41–60.

Rosenfeld, Isaac. "It Is Hard to Be a Jew" (reviews of Ben Hecht, *A Guide for the Bedeviled,* and Ludwig Lewisohn, *Breathe Upon These*). *The New Republic,* April 10, 1944.

Rosenfeld, Isaac. "Kreplach." *Commentary* (November 1948): 487–88.

Rosenfeld, Isaac. "On the Role of the Writer and the Little Magazine." *Chicago Review* 11, no. 2 (Summer 1957): 3–16.

Roth, Philip. *The Ghost Writer*. New York, 1979.

Shefner, Evelyn. "Monday Morning." *Hudson Review* 7, no. 4 (Winter 1955): 557–69.

Silber, Joan. *Ideas of Heaven: A Ring of Stories*. New York, 2004.

Solotaroff, Ted. *First Loves: A Memoir*. New York, 2003.

Solotaroff, Ted. "The Spirit of Isaac Rosenfeld." In *The Red Hot Vacuum*, 3–21.

Steinberg, Jonathan. "Milton Steinberg, American Rabbi: Thoughts on His Centenary." *Jewish Quarterly Review* 95, no. 3 (Summer 2005): 579–600.

Trilling, Diana. *The Beginning of the Journey: The Marriage of Diana and Lionel Trilling*. New York, 1993.

Trilling, Diana. *Reviewing the Forties*. New York, 1978.

Wald, Alan M. *The New York Intellectuals: The Rise and Decline of the Anti-Stalinist Left from the 1930s to the 1980s*. Chapel Hill, 1987.

Wilson, Edmund, and Leon Edel. *The Fifties: From Notebooks and Diaries of the Period*. New York, 1986.

Wisse, Ruth. "Language as Fate: Reflections on Jewish Literature in America." *Studies in Contemporary Jewry* 12 (1996): 129–47.

Wisse, Ruth. *The Modern Jewish Canon*. New York, 2000.

Zaretsky, Eli. *Secrets of the Soul: A Social and Cultural History of Psychoanalysis*. New York, 2004.

Zipperstein, Steven J. "The First Loves of Isaac Rosenfeld." *Jewish Social Studies* 5, nos. 1–2 (Fall 1998–Winter 1999): 3–24.

Zipperstein, Steven J. *Imagining Russian Jewry: Memory, History, Identity*. Seattle, 1999.

Zipperstein, Steven J. "Isaac Rosenfeld's Dybbuk and Rethinking Literary Biography." *Partisan Review* 69, no. 1 (Winter 2002): 102–17.

Index